T0394010

CAPSULES

This book investigates the architectural, product design, and urban typology of the capsule which, beginning in the 1960s, broadened the concept of the basic building blocks of architecture to include a minimal living unit, called the "capsule." Here it is presented with regard to the continuity of the development of the Modern Movement, its revisionist criticism, pioneering examples, as well as contemporary examples and uses. The typology of the capsule allows us to consider this theme in terms of the architecture of resistance, with the potential to search for an "other" architecture that is embedded in our contemporaneity (manifested in small dwellings, composite structures, and container units; shelters and mobile homes in nature and the urban environment; technology transfer in high-tech designs; devices, additions, and extensions, etc.). The concept of the capsule as a building element of architecture, as well as a spatial element, can therefore be regarded as having a generative potential for an architecture of personal space for the individual, forcing us to reflect on our existing living and dwelling conditions.

Peter Šenk is Assistant Professor of Architecture and Spatial Planning at the Department of Architecture, Faculty of Civil Engineering, Transportation Engineering and Architecture at the University of Maribor, Slovenia. He is a researcher and writer in the field of architecture, urban planning, and visual culture, an architect (co-founder of Studio Stratum), and a curator (at the House of Architecture, Maribor).

CAPSULES

Typology of Other Architecture

Peter Šenk

Routledge
Taylor & Francis Group

LONDON AND NEW YORK

First published in English 2018
by Routledge
2 Park Square, Milton Park, Abingdon, Oxon OX14 4RN

and by Routledge
711 Third Avenue, New York, NY 10017

Routledge is an imprint of the Taylor & Francis Group, an informa business

Translated from Slovenian by Laura Cuder Turk.

Published in Slovenian by Založba ZRC, ZRC SAZU 2015

British Library Cataloguing-in-Publication Data
A catalogue record for this book is available from the British Library

Library of Congress Cataloging-in-Publication Data
Names: Senk, Peter, author. | Translation of: Senk, Peter. Kapsula.
Title: Capsules: typology of other architecture/Peter Senk.
Other titles: Kapsula. English
Description: New York: Routledge, 2017. | Includes bibliographical references and index.
Identifiers: LCCN 2017022438| ISBN 9781138280342 (hb: alk. paper) | ISBN 9781138280359 (pb : alk. paper) | ISBN 9781315272177 (ebook)
Subjects: LCSH: Buildings, Prefabricated–Design and construction. | Architecture, Modern–20th century–Designs and plans. | Architecture, Modern–21st century–Designs and plans.
Classification: LCC NA8480.S4613 2017 | DDC 724/.6–dc23
LC record available at https://lccn.loc.gov/2017022438

ISBN: 978-1-138-28034-2 (hbk)
ISBN: 978-1-138-28035-9 (pbk)
ISBN: 978-1-315-27217-7 (ebk)

Typeset in Bembo
by Sunrise Setting Ltd, Brixham, UK

To my sons Matija and Martin

CONTENTS

FIGURES

ILLUSTRATION CREDITS

The author and the publisher would like to thank the following individuals and institutions for giving permission to reproduce the illustrations. Every effort has been made to trace copyright holders and to obtain their permission for the use of copyright material. The publisher apologizes for any errors or omissions and would be grateful if notified of any corrections that should be incorporated in future reprints or editions of this book.

Courtesy of The Estate of R. Buckminster Fuller: 2.1, 2.2

Courtesy of the Frances Loeb Library. Harvard University Graduate School of Design: 2.3, 2.4, 2.5

© Richard Hamilton, All Rights Reserved, DACS 2017. Photo: Robert Freeman, DACS 2017: 2.6

Archigram Archives © 2017: 2.7, 2.8, 2.9, 2.12, 2.13

NASA/National Aeronautics and Space Administration: 2.10, 2.11

© 1965 François Dallegret: 2.14

Cedric Price fonds, Collection Centre Canadien d'Architecture/Canadian Centre for Architecture, Montréal: 2.15, 2.16

Kikutake Architects: 2.17, 2.18, 2.19, 2.20

GK Design Group Inc.: 2.21, 2.22, 2.23, 2.24, 2.25, 2.26

Peter Šenk: 2.27, 2.30, 2.46, 2.47, 2.48, 2.49, 3.1

© Kisho Kurokawa Architect and Associates: 2.31, 2.32, 2.33, 2.34, 2.35, 2.36, 2.39, 2.40, 3.33

© Kisho Kurokawa Architect and Associates, photo: Tomio Ohashi: 2.28, 2.29, 2.37, 2.38, 2.41, 2.42, 3.34

JA: The Japan Architect, 127 January–February 1967, 44–45: 2.43, 2.44, 2.45

PREFACE

Although recently the term *capsule* has not been the word of the day, the spatial concept it provides in architecture has become ever more a part of architectural and urbanistic endeavors, real estate, and political decisions, and an alternative for sustainable lifestyles. Modular minimum living units and micro-apartments are again becoming popular and a reasonable solution as we rethink our housing needs and consider a possible future of contemporary compact urban living all over the globe. Meanwhile, the technology offers possibilities for their fabrication with a diversity of methods. With the development of 3D printing, the production of pods is not a technical issue anymore—neither for little off-grid refuges, nor for plug-in components in the urban environment. Nevertheless, the symbolic vibe the *capsules* carry seems to have quietened down since their inception. There have been some highly informative writing and exhibitions on or around the topic recently, but this book-length study takes the opportunity to present the concept of the capsule in its wider variety of contexts and manifestations. Therefore, this book is neither a complete catalog of architectural conceptualizations nor architectural objects called capsules. It rather exposes the idea of the capsule as a living or monofunctional unit, examines its concept, breaks it open, and tracks its implications in architectural, as well as in general, discourse, reconstructing it as a typology and opening up ways and points for further exploration.

This book is a revised English edition of the book *Kapsula: tipologija druge arhitekture*, which was published in Slovenian in 2015 by the ZRC Publishing House.

The initial Slovenian edition of the book would not have been put together in this scope without the enthusiastic encouragement of Petra Čeferin, who proposed that it should be published as the second book of the Theoretical Practice of Architecture series, and provided many guiding insights. I also thank other editorial board members: Rado Riha, for reading and pointing out terminology-related dilemmas, and Tadej Glažar during presentation of the edition, as well as Aljoša Kolenc for design issues, and Aleš Pogačnik for support in publishing.

It all started with a project on capsular environments called *FWC—First World Camp*, back in 2003. My first thanks go to my *co-campist*, Emil Hrvatin, *aka* Janez Janša, and everyone who collaborated on, or contributed to, the project. Its manifestations in the form of numerous exhibitions, lectures, and workshops since then pointed to the need for comprehensive research on the theme of the capsules.

Writing is a capsular endeavor. Although I have not acquired a capsule for myself (yet), I was lucky enough to acquire different quiet, introverted locations in which to pursue my intention. But it has not been, by any means, a completely lonesome project, and it is impossible to mention everybody involved, although my gratitude goes out to all.

In the first phase, the broader topic of *capsularity* has been extensively researched beyond the framework presented in this book, in my dissertation under the supervision of Professor Stane Bernik, and with the direction of Professor Aleš Erjavec at the University of Primorska. I thank them both for their generous support. With his indirect initiation of the topic, I owe much gratitude to Lieven De Cauter—for his support, generous advice, and comments.

Special thanks go to Hiroshi Kohno, who enabled me to sneak a view of Japanese culture, and without whom the section on Japanese capsule architecture would not have been possible. He helped with access to many printed sources and buildings, acted as a guide in Japan, as a translator and organizer of interviews with Kiyonori Kikutake, Fumihiko Maki, Hajime Yatsuka, and Kaneko Yasuke, to whom I am very thankful, as I am to Yasushi Zenno and Junko Tamura, for their comments, guidance, interpretations, information, and sources.

Special thanks go also to Hajime Yatsuka, for offering his private unpublished material, carefully reading the manuscript on Japanese capsules, and valuable suggestions and comments.

I am especially grateful to both enthusiastic translators from Japanese—Urška Capuder and Hiroshi Kohno, who also offered deep interpretations and communication interventions during our numerous discussions and correspondences throughout the years.

Many colleagues and friends have contributed to the project as readers: My thanks go to Uroš Lobnik and Kaja Pogačar from the Department of Architecture, Faculty for Civil Engineering, Transportation Engineering and Architecture, University of Maribor; to Polona Filipič and Marko Pretnar from the Studio Stratum office; to Mojca Krevel, Virginia Vrecl, Blaž Križnik, and Marko Peljhan, for their help, comments, and advice.

I would like to thank all the individuals, companies, and institutions who provided permissions and the graphic material for this book.

For precise translation and patience, I want to thank my translation team, Laura Cuder Turk and Noah Charney, who also provided enthusiastic and generous support, skillful guidance, and rigorous editing. I have been privileged to work with Routledge. I would like to thank Fran Ford for commissioning the book, Trudy Varcianna and Kelly Cracknell for all the help and support, and Jessica Stock and Patricia Baxter for consistent work and patience.

Last but not least, I would like to thank my parents, Marjeta and Marko Šenk, for their cordial support from the very beginning, without whom this project would not have been possible; my sister Marjana and her family; and, all the way through the research and writing endeavors, my wife, Vladka, and my sons, Matija and Martin, who have wondered why I needed to get "capsularized" in my little study so often, and to whom this book is dedicated.

Ljubljana, April 2017

1
FRAME(WORK)

No one can be close to others, without also having frequent opportunities to be alone.

Christopher Alexander, A Pattern Language[1]

The capsule is cyborg architecture. Man, machine and space build a new organic body which transcends confrontation.

Kisho Kurokawa, Capsule Declaration[2]

The creation of a style or a set of imitable mannerisms is one thing, but the creation of typologies is altogether more intriguing.

Peter Cook, Capsules, Pods and Skins[3]

At the end of the experimental 1960s, Peter Cook from Archigram emphasized that the 20th century provided "several occasions when science, technology and human emancipation have coincided in a way that caused architecture to explode."[4] In the first half of the 1950s, New Brutalism produced "a new belated explosion" in architectural theory. With its attitude to the use of materials, the direction of Alison and Peter Smithson, which implied the revival of the original morals of the Modern Movement, sought to establish a connection between buildings and their occupants. Architecture was supposed to be the direct result of a way of life.[5] Several active contemporaries expressed their disagreement with the socio-economic system in terms of the spatial and urban relationships it produced. New visions of time and space emerged in conceptualized experimental cities and architectures, heralding the rise of a mobile civilization in which architecture would be a medium for experimenting with ways to improve the lives of those who engage with the buildings. But twenty years later, the criticism of existing cities, and increasingly more frequent radical criticism of modern functionalism, together with the heralds of the new era of postmodernism, symbolically culminated in the destruction of the *Pruitt-Igoe* housing complex, the failure of which was a disappointment to many.[6] In the meantime, prior to the destructive detonations in St. Louis, architectural activities were marked by a number of explosions, producing a potential role model for the possibilities of a different, alternative mindset and actions in architecture.

The visions and conceptualizations of new spatial and social relationships for the new spatial and social conditions addressed in this book in many ways enhanced urban futures pledged to indecisiveness and experimentation, discredited and held a mirror up to the triviality of the situation at that time, and were a forecast of other architecture of the future.

The topical issues of contemporary architecture are reflected in the detailed analysis of protagonists' activities for whom architecture was (still) a public rather than a private affair,[7] of concepts of a (proto-) sustainable architecture of replaceable and potentially renewable parts of buildings, and of the attitude toward the environment in general, as well as of those who pointed out the opportunities for more democratic, fuller and livelier common urban futures through complete individualization and its reflection in architecture. Attempts to return to the original ideals of functionalism, attempts to seek new identity by maintaining tradition and modernity, and new architectural opportunities within technology and lifestyle indicated the emergence of an architecture that would respond to the actual needs of society, help transform it, and show hope for a brighter future of life in cities and for the development of individuals within them. The proposals discussed were by no means without shortcomings, even within the context and conditions of the time of their occurrence. So we do not assume that we can simply transfer the presented concepts, programs, aesthetic schemes, and the like into contemporaneity. Such a direct transfer would be extremely anachronistic. However, if we extract their potentials and take their shortcomings into account, we may expect an upgrade of the project from when it was launched in contemporaneity. Therefore, through the development perspective, we will attempt to show the projects; their use, transformations and deviations, as well as the emancipatory potential of the aspirations, desires, and efforts expressed in them which, in contemporaneity, may serve as a support and a role model in working toward changes in society, institutions, space, and in architecture of the future.

The protagonists addressed differ in their pursuit of a different architectural approach and expression. On the one hand, it includes completely radical proposals, breaking with tradition in the manner of the historical avant-garde. Some proposals are an upgrade of traditional concepts in a completely new manner, for example the so-called invisible tradition, while others seek a third way by surpassing conflicts and facilitating the cohabitation of diversity. The issue of otherness is split among diverse approaches with a common aspiration for what is other, what is different from the prevailing, for an otherness that would facilitate the surpassing of the status quo. A common feature of various approaches to a search for other architecture as we understand it is active involvement in the given moment of social, technological, and architectural reality. Stemming from realistic conditions, activities include a critical, and sometimes even a utopian dimension. The emphasized disagreement with the state of affairs expresses the demand for change. By discussing in detail the concept and typology of the capsule, we will attempt to show those characteristics of other architecture that disclose their relevance and potential subversiveness also in contemporaneity.

We will highlight the relevant topics that refer to the issue of technology and of suitable architectural expression, the issue of home, the individuals' dwellings, and communal space, the relation between architecture and land and its attachment to a place, the idea of withdrawal, and the autonomy of an individual and architecture in an individualized local world, and put them into context, with the help of selected pioneering and contemporary examples. We will attempt to disclose the differences between them, and show the path of their changes in the development of the concept and typology. The aforementioned topics aimed at examining the state of affairs in social, technological, and architectural reality call for alternative concepts, approaches, and typologies that track other architecture.

Quirky when they emerged, and nowadays still interesting concepts and approaches, such as an un-house, a realistic machine for living in, cyborg architecture, pop architecture, the use of materials as found, plug-in, clip-on, etc. launched the capsule into the orbit of architectural typologies in the 1960s. In its development, the typology of the capsule has unveiled its gene-alogy as proto-capsularity through the universalistic technocracy of Buckminster Fuller, and the American manifestation of resistance through the counterculture of "crash-pads." Through the avant-garde positions between ethics and aesthetics, through existentialism, pop, and New Brutalism, it followed Reyner Banham's radical *une architecture autre*, and manifested itself in provocative images of mechanization, and in techno-pop lifestyle or regional metabolic futurism. The typology of the capsule, which has always been committed to providing different, more suitable living conditions responding to necessary changes in society, is defined by its characteristics as one of those architectural concepts and typologies that may be attributed to the potential for seeking and manifesting other architecture.

The architectural typology called the capsule has been used in contemporary architecture since the 1960s, beginning mainly with the most notable now-legendary projects of Archigram and of the Japanese Metabolists. Since the 1920s, and particularly in the late 1950s and early 1960s, certain other architects and groups have been using technological, science fiction aesthetics with an obvious zest for the possibilities offered by super-technology, or even used the terms "capsulation" and "capsule."[8]

The term "capsule" was first used for independent, mobile, and technologically equipped living and monofunctional units especially by English contemporaries Archigram and Cedric Price, and members of the Japanese group of Metabolists. Warren Chalk from Archigram began using the term capsule in 1964, for prefabricated mass-produced living units called *Capsule Homes*. That same year, Cedric Price used capsules for the project of a regional educational environment called *Potteries Thinkbelt*, while in the Japanese group of Metabolists, the geneal-ogy of the Metabolist concept of the capsule which, with various names, has been present as such since 1959, was published by Kisho Kurokawa in *Capsule Declaration* (1969).[9] Members of Archigram were well aware of the fact that the idea of mass-produced housing units with replaceable elements was not new. Therefore a member of the group, Warren Chalk, presented reference examples in his "Housing as a Consumer Product" from 1966: Cooperation of Le Corbusier with Jean Prouvé, individual Prouvé projects; living and mobile experiments designated *Dymaxion* with a bathroom for Phelps Dodge by Buckminster Fuller; *House of the Future* by Alison and Peter Smithson; prefabricated hotel units by Ionel Schein; *Monsanto Plastic House* in Disneyland; works of Japanese Metabolists, and of Arthur Quarmby in England;[10] all these examples are attempts to find technological other architecture in the period of the desta-bilization of Heroic Modernism and the International Style. Characteristic of the aforemen-tioned reference examples of Archigram is their excitement over the opportunities facilitated by new technology, the use of new materials and structural solutions, and by mass production, wishing to offer individuals, society, cities, and the profession something brand new. In the new and different, Archigram recognized the potential to create new and lively lifestyles. The con-scious coupling of architectural expression with everyday life, in connection with popular culture, which was completely unacceptable for high modernism, was supported by the inter-nationalization and globalization of a consumer culture that was fully established and prevailing from as far back as the 1960s. Despite the criticism of American models constantly popping up, the post-war impetus was in full swing in the early 1960s. In many cases, issues of justification and the suitability of technological progress, consumerism, and scientific development were concealed by enthusiasm for the opportunities to create a better world.

The word capsule derives from the Latin word *capsula*, which means "a small case or box," and is the diminutive of *capsa*, which has a broader meaning: "a container, case, box (also a small box)," and is a derivative of *capere* meaning "seize, grab, take, capture." The term capsule is used for the literal, physical description of an item or structure and, figuratively, as a metaphor. We encounter the concept of the capsule particularly in the field of engineering and natural sciences, namely in pharmacology, anatomy, and medicine in general, in microbiology, botany, and biology, in space engineering, and also in architecture and space.[11]

Only in a handful of dictionaries and encyclopedias is the term capsule stated under headwords connected to the trend of megastructures and utopian radical architectural experiments, particularly of Archigram, the group of Metabolists, and Metabolism in general. They describe capsules as, for example, individual units that may be clipped on, or plugged in, a structural frame, which are mobile and expendable, and react to human desires.[12] Capsules are presented as prefabricated housing units that may be stacked into tower-like structures, or used in megastructures as extra-sophisticated units, or rather as products of industrial design that make cities more responsive to swift changes.[13] They are included in conceptual architecture, and are a product of praising popular taste and the potential of new technology. They are prefabricated, made with advanced technology in mass-production processes and as small housing units employ state-of-the-art technology.[14] Encyclopedias of architecture and historical overviews under the heading "capsule" most frequently mention projects and structures of Archigram, *Nakagin Capsule Tower* in Tokyo by Kisho Kurokawa, capsules at Expo '70 in Osaka and, naturally, capsule hotels, particularly in Japan.

We will follow the definitions of a capsule unit or capsule in architecture through the development of typology by reviewing the activity of its predecessors and main protagonists. As a starting point, let us use a corresponding and illustrative definition made by a contemporary of the capsule architecture pioneers, Günther Feuerstein, who defined a capsule as "the smallest, still moveable, and autonomous environment, well-equipped with communications."[15]

In pioneering examples of living unit designs from the mid-20th century, the concept of the capsule was related to the idea of facilitating a new lifestyle of intensive urbanity, or personal and social transformation on the basis of free will, independence, mobility, and even transcendence. In architecture, the concept of the capsule is usually presented in relation to the trend of megastructures and utopian radical architectural experiments, with uncritical faith in technological and scientific progress. A repeatedly mentioned practical derivation of the concept is the implementation of the typology of capsule hotels, which, however, has no direct connection with the original idea.

In the 1960s and 1970s, calling a spatial unit a capsule was limited to smaller, particularly individual monofunctional or living units intended for individuals, childless couples, and in certain cases in Japan, also for individual family members, whose individual capsules formed a "family" group. At the end of the 20th century, the capsule as a spatial concept was also used in literature for larger, extensive bordered, secured, and/or controlled spaces. In his articles, which have been published in specialized presses since 1998, and are collected in the book entitled *Capsular Civilization: On the City in the Age of Fear*, in which the concept of the capsule got its extended meaning, Lieven De Cauter referred to the concept of "capsular civilization" used by René Boomkens when describing the characteristics of experimental artificial biospheres in American deserts. In the aforementioned texts, the term capsule refers not necessarily to mere compact functional or living units, but rather to bordered and controlled spaces in contemporary urban environments, such as gated communities, transport hubs, such as airports, shopping centers, and amusement parks, as well as to microenvironments of "virtual capsules" facilitated by devices, for example, Walkmans, television screens, mobile phone screens, and the like.[16]

Despite the questionable terminological suitability of referring to technological prosthetics of electronic devices, compact personal living units, and extensive spatial envelopes and controlled territories with a common term capsule, such naming leads us to the rich metaphorical message conveyed by the term, and to its mobilization potential. However, although the definition of a capsule as a spatial unit is defined and used by pioneers and protagonists of capsule architecture, the term does not comply with the contemporary metaphorical use of the term for extensive environments. To surpass the terminological inconsistency, we propose a more general term, "capsularity," which encompasses both capsules—compact living or monofunctional units, and extensive areas of territorial capsularity as well as capsular structures, thus not losing the metaphorical potential of the term.

In architecture, a capsule is defined on the basis of the characteristics of the aforementioned pioneering proposals that were named as such with five characteristics:

1. relative impermeability of the envelope;
2. physical or simulated comfort of the introverted interior enabled by connection to the network;
3. structural, functional, and visual integrity;
4. temporal conditionality or interchangeability;
5. smallness enabling movability or mobility.

Only an item with all five characteristics may be called a capsule.[17]

Therefore, the term capsule defines a spatial structure that is compact and physically delimited, and is part of a network system, at least one of information flow, which ensures its connection with the outside world and/or internal atmosphere/ambience. It acts as a (partially) autonomous, and spatially, structurally, programmatically, and visually homogeneous whole which is never completely autonomous due to its integration to a network system. It is temporarily set or inset in a broader spatial context. It is minimal, movable, perhaps self-movable, transferable, either as a whole or in parts, a unit that can be reassembled or assembled/dismantled at another location. The characteristics that define the concept of the capsule are the actual physical characteristics of an item or architectural object with minimum connection to the micro-location itself but, at the same time, integrated into a broader spatial and network context. The concept of the capsule thus corresponds to the spatial scale of architecture or industrial design or, more precisely, to the scale of one spatial cell that may be an independent architectural whole or part of a complex architectural composition.

In respect to its structure, function, and representation,[18] a capsule is defined as a complex and homogenous whole that clearly differs from other housing units, and provides a framework for a special typology of living or monofunctional units.[19] In contemporary design and architecture, as well as in artistic practices, the typology of the capsule is frequently used either as such, or as the basis for various versions of mobile, particularly prefabricated, living units.

The ergonomics, anthropomorphic dimensions, and the legacy of the existential minimum undoubtedly represent a not-always-binding and explicitly used reference framework for both pioneering and contemporary examples. The legacy of existentialist avant-garde circles of the 1950s, and the ecology of fear of traumatic post-war years and of the Cold War, combined with consumerism and individualism, have created the foundation for the development of such introverted typologies with a fallout shelter as their model, whose security feature is metaphorically and explicitly present in many environments of territorial capsularity.

In the history of architecture, naming sealed independent housing units as "capsules" was not an isolated case. However, capsule projects, with their characteristic demands significantly differ from most similar concepts of living cells, living units, move-net units, gaskets, pods, monads, parasites, containers, and the like. Despite certain projects named after one of these concepts being recognized as capsules, their original concepts, considering our derived definition, are not completely equivalent to the latter, since they differ in, or incompletely determine, at least one of the basic characteristics and features. Therefore, they need to be addressed separately, on a case-by-case basis.

When the capsule projects of Archigram, Cedric Price, Reyner Banham, and the Japanese Metabolists speak in the language of an un-house, anti-architecture, or in the language of *une architecture autre*, individual spaces of territorial capsularity, for example gated communities, shopping centers, amusement parks, and similar, are designated as Marc Augé's "non-place," Michel Foucault's "other space" or "heterotopia," Edward Soja's "third space," or Zygmunt Bauman's "voluntary ghetto." Like the concept of capsularity, these terms denote similar phenomena of the contemporary situation in space, defined by concepts like Manuel Castells's "space of flows," Michael Sorkin's "antigeographical space," "ageographic city," and "generic urbanism," Peter Sloterdijk's "foam city," or Rem Koolhaas's "generic city."

The concept of the capsule and of territorial capsularity was most often a side product of modern nomadism and enthusiastic megastructuralism. On the one hand, modern nomadism in postindustrial society stems from the consequences of increased demands and mobility options facilitated by ever more perfect and available personal means of transport, and infrastructure, and from a suitable response to the situation in cities and socio-economic realities of the capitalist part of the world, which was clearly expressed by the countercultural movement in the USA in the 1960s. In the 1960s, many proposals, from Buckminster Fuller's experiments to Archigram's and Japanese Metabolists' proposals, were placed in the international company of publications of projects based on tents or canopies, trailers, and inflatable and other lightweight, collapsible, movable or transportable structures of the American counterculture. We may as well point out the experiments of spatial urbanists with Yona Friedman, Constant's utopian materializations of Situationists' "unitary urbanism," inflatable environments, and megastructures of the Austrian avant-garde and, last but not least, ironic and post-urban proposals of their "radical" Italian colleagues.

We need to distinguish between voluntary mobility and nomadism, in relation to analyses of existing lifestyles and the production of new ones, and forced nomadism of victims of natural disasters, wars, or of unbearable economic situations. Although at first glance the attention of proposals for housing units for modern nomads has been devoted to the satisfaction of needs of voluntary nomads since the second half of the 1950s, it is difficult to agree that the distinction between the two is completely clear, as seemingly voluntary nomads frequently do not have any other options than to play the game more or less subtly enforced upon them by the socio-economic system or the political situation.

Between the two world wars, mobility became the topic of the future. It has been a hot topic in architecture and urbanism at least since the Athens Charter (CIAM) from 1933, which emphasized transport, in addition to housing, production, and recreation, as one of the basic urban functions. Alison and Peter Smithson, who studied traffic arrangements in the 1950s, were aware of the multilayered-ness of mobility that became a characteristic of the period and, in their opinion, was both socially and organizationally crucial for urban planning, for "mobility is not only concerned with roads, but with the whole concept of a mobile, fragmented, community."[20] By recognizing that "roads are also places,"[21] the topic of mobility was transferred from a strictly technical discourse of engineers to the design of a living environment.

Another important starting point for the development of the concept and typology of the capsule refers to the experimental practices in architecture. In the 1970s, at the decline of the period, after Peter Cook's praise of the topic in *Experimental Architecture,* many proposals were comprised under the title *Urban Structures for the Future* by Justus Dahinden, a partner and contemporary of the "Megastructures International" or "the dinosaurs of the modern movement," as labeled by Reyner Banham a few years later, in a comprehensive review entitled, *Megastructure: Urban Futures of the Recent Past.*[22]

A look into the future, which included concepts of the capsule, was the product of techno-logical and scientific revolution, awareness of the urban environment as an artificial formation, and of the confrontation with the inevitability of open opportunities to be free of restraints of existing social structures, as well as of the concern for the future and for potential threats brought into society by the still-unfathomable, particularly technological, progress. The contemporaneity of euphoria and concern, awareness that the progress of technology in the media as an extension of man was, despite its unpredictability, too important to be rejected, and that it was crucial to critically understand their operation, to avoid unpredictable conse-quences of overexcitement, was established through the discussions of Marshall McLuhan in the early 1960s. In this way, McLuhan spread this responsibility across all of society, in which an individual was involved in mass culture production by being included in creative processes. Through the inclusion of individuals enabled by new technologies, McLuhan particularly pointed out the significance of the artist, and emphasized artists' responsibility: When the artist moves "from the ivory tower to the control tower of society," since the words of Wyndham Lewis that "the artist is always engaged in writing a detailed history of the future, because he is the only person aware of the nature of the present," as quoted by McLuhan, had already been generally accepted.[23]

The period since the late 1950s markedly favored experimental work of individuals who presented proposals for society and housing of the future, offering answers to the actual situation in social, economic, environmental and spatial, and artistic reality. In his review of proposals for urban structures for the future, Dahinden asked himself prophetically, "whether towns, conceived as specific concentrations and containers of human activities . . . if we consider that in our society the importance of physical contact is being diminished by the electronic media"[24] have a future at all, and even before reviewing proposals, outlines the urban crisis of the post-war period in the western world. Just like the countercultural hippie movement enabled the rise of new urban and social forms, to which temporary, minimal, and inflatable structures corresponded much more than traditionally built and existent structures, by creatively including an individual in spatial arrangement in its resistance against the existing social situation, the mobile urban forms that appeared critically pointed to the obsolescence and, in terms of contemporary spatial and social reality, inappropriateness of the traditional static city, as it had been defined by conventional bourgeois characteristics. However, in his justification of radical technological environments, Dahinden did not neglect the significance of the public sphere and community, which were supposed to be ensured by urban structures of the future, despite the potentially radical redefinition of social structures. To ensure the complexity of urban life, urban concentrations, which are manifested in experiments with urban structures of the future in the McLuhanian "global village," in the form of local macrostructures, spatial cities, and clusters, where the duality of artificial and natural environments must be preserved.[25]

Which then are the key characteristics of spatial elements that are to build the technological and liberated urban future? Temporariness, flexibility, movability or mobility, and expendability are characteristic of future-oriented structures which, however, were accepted in society with a feeling of discomfort or even reluctance. Dahinden comments that the paradoxical situation in which organized consumer society, which emphasizes its desire for variety and integral expendability, remains restrained when using such assumptions regarding the built environment, favors the uniformity, durability, and stability of houses. Dahinden attributes society's negative attitude toward utopian possibilities of the future to a fear of letting go of established and trustworthy institutions, and to the need for many radical changes that would include plenty of unpredictable risks. Just like the issue of the transfer of consumer characteristics into the built environment is present nowadays, in terms of ecology and the architectural object/product's life cycle assessment, the issue of risk is also characteristic of the present risk society, whereby risk nowadays is reality without any alternatives, as it already seemed to be during the period of the decline of megastructures. Despite criticism, megastructures were for many an opportunity to reintegrate social and urban structures worth taking the risk, and to integrate various social groups and activities. Unlike dispersed car-infused suburbs, they provided compact organized wholes. Through the idea of achieving urban concentrations of the past, they enabled free micro-organization of modernity and facilitated an unpredictable future.

Many positive characteristics of proposals for megastructures brought along unpredictable problems that seemed a lot more convincing to their critics. At the end of the 1960s, the excitement over megastructures was completely shaken. Many architects themselves recognized megastructures as politically problematic. Others, like Dahinden, persisted in their enthusiastic views, even at the beginning of the 1970s. Of course, investments in state-of-the-art technology were connected with capital, and would indirectly support the existing socio-economic system, boosted by multinational corporations. As pointed out by Reyner Banham, for many, megastructures were "an almost perfect symbol of liberal-capitalist oppression."[26] They were quickly incriminated, and only rarely were they brought to life.

Is the thoughtful and liberating potential of the concept and typology of the capsule just as problematic in its basis, since we know that capsule units are not necessarily connected to megastructure framework, but are also defined through the "problematic" characteristics of temporariness, flexibility, and expendability? The initially mentioned examples from Archigram's repertoire do not constitute the final list of references. Therefore, before we turn our attention to a further and more detailed discussion about individual representatives and their contemporaries with operative, radical, utopian, and revolutionary proposals for capsule architecture, and engagement following the lead of other architecture, we will expand the horizon by outlining events in the social, political, architectural, design, and theoretical arena until the beginning of the explosive 1960s.

Notes

1 Christopher Alexander et al., *A Pattern Language: Towns, Buildings, Construction* (New York: Oxford University Press, 1977), 669. By Permission of Oxford University Press © 1977 by Christopher Alexander.

2 Kisho Kurokawa, *Metabolism in Architecture* (London: Studio Vista, 1977), 75.

3 Peter Cook, "Capsules, Pods and Skins," in *Concerning Archigram*, ed. Dennis Crompton (London: Archigram Archives, 2002), 80. © Peter Cook, Archigram Archives.

4 Cook, *Experimental Architecture* (New York: Universe Books, 1970), 11.

5 "The New Brutalism," *Architectural Design* (January 1955).

6 See Charles Jencks, *The Language of Postmodern Architecture* (New York: Rizzoli, 1977).

7 See Rem Koolhaas and Hans-Ulrich Obrist, eds., *Project Japan: Metabolism Talks* (Köln: Taschen, 2011).

8 Bruno Taut, for example, in his book, *Die Auflosung der Städte oder die Erde eine gute Wohnung* (1920) describes the housing of the future as flexible, with easily movable walls, and one in which each member of the household easily encapsulates within a bigger capsule. /Ger. einkapseln/. Taut, *Die Auflösung der Städte oder die Erde eine gute Wohnung* (Folkwang-Verlag, 1920) in *Die Neue Wohnung: Die Frau als Schöpferin,* ed. Bruno Taut (Leipzig: Verlag Klinkhardt & Biermann, 1928), 92.

9 Cook, ed., *Archigram* (New York: Princeton Architectural Press, 1999), 44; Cedric Price, *Cedric Price: Works II, Architectural Association* (London: Architectural Association, 1984), 25; Kurokawa, "Capsule Declaration," in *Metabolism in Architecture,* ed. Kurokawa (London: Studio Vista, 1977), 75–85. Declaration was first published as a shorter version: Kurokawa, "Oh! The Code of Cyborgs" (Kurokawa, Oh! Saibogu no Okite), *SD – Space Design* (03, 1969): 50–53. Translation from Japanese Urška Capuder, Hiroshi Kohno, author's archive.

10 Cook, ed., *Archigram*, 17.

11 Dictionaries and encyclopedia define the capsule by areas. In pharmacology, a capsule is a medication in gelatine or starch shell; in microbiology and medicine, an envelope; in botany, a boll or pod, i.e. a closed structure, with seeds or spores, which opens when mature. In space engineering, a capsule is usually a small cone-like separable part of a spacecraft, without basic boosters and with a sealed cabin, which carries astronauts and instruments, and enables life during a spaceflight or flights at high altitudes. It is a sealed component or unit or, in general, an envelope, the function of which is to protect or isolate its contents. The characteristics of a capsule, in terms of design and material, define a capsule as a round, oval, or cylindrical receptacle, a small crate or container, particularly of metal.

12 R. Stephen Sennott, *Encyclopedia of 20th Century Architecture* (New York, London: Fitzroy Dearborn, 2004), headword "Archigram," 57.

13 Joseph A. Wilkes, ed., *Encyclopedia of Architecture: Design, Engineering & Construction* (New York: John Wiley & Sons, 1988–1990), headword "Archigram," 256; Tom Porter, *Archispeak: An Illustrated Guide to Architectural Terms* (London, New York: Spon Press, 2004), headword "Metabolism," 118.

14 Vittorio Magnago Lampugnani, ed., *The Thames and Hudson Encyclopedia of 20th Century Architecture* (London: Thames and Hudson, 1986), headword "Metabolism," 216; James Stevens Curl, *A Dictionary of Architecture* (Oxford: Oxford University Press, 2000), headword "Archigram," 9; headword "Kurokawa," 367; headword "Metabolism," 417.

15 Günther Feuerstein, "Der Mensch in der Kapsel," in *Wieviel Raum braucht der Mensch?: Wohnen für das Existenzminimum,* eds. Robert Haussmann and Karin Schulte (München: Aries, 1996), 61.

16 Lieven De Cauter, *The Capsular Civilization: On the City in the Age of Fear* (Rotterdam: NAi Publishers, 2004). The term *capsule* was used for "introverted worlds" in general, and for controlled and gated communities of the holiday parks used in the research *Euroscapes*, which analyzes the European landscape of the 21st century. Florian Boer and Christine Dijkstra, "Funscapes: The European Leisure Landscape," in *Euroscape,* eds. Robert Broesi, Pieter Jannink, Wouter Veldhuis and Ivan Nio (Amsterdam: Must Publishers, 2003), 167–214. Recent examples include the book and exhibition which present the "capsules" of different scales as a protecting media, enabling survival of humans in case of climate catastrophe. Friedrich von Borries, *Klimakapseln: Überlebens-bedingungen in der Katastrophe* (Berlin: Suhrkamp, 2010).

17 The definition is derived on the basis of pioneering British and Japanese examples substantiated with the aforementioned definition by their contemporary, Günther Feuerstein.

18 The triad *structure, function,* and *representation,* which will be used for a comprehensive analysis of concepts, typologies, and examples, and as a projection tool, is derived from the classical Vitruvian Triad, which defines good architecture: *Firmitas—strength, utilitas—use,* and *venustas—beauty.* In our

case, in the spirit of open contemporaneity, it is free from inherent value-related meanings of terms. It is also sensible to use modernized classical measures for the definition of *otherness*, since known criteria enable the establishment of *difference* from established (traditional) practices, concepts, and typologies.

19 In the concepts of capsules, pods, and skins, the creation of new typologies or mutations of old typologies was also pointed out by one of the protagonists of capsule architecture, Peter Cook. See Cook, "Capsules, Pods and Skins," 80–87.

20 Alison Smithson and Peter Smithson, "Mobility: Road Systems," *Architectural Design* (October 1958): 385.

21 Ibid., 385–388. Although the noble purpose helped to change the perception of the meaning of space in the planning of traffic surfaces, these surfaces outgrew the perceptive spatial dimensions, thus becoming modern *non-places*, with the expansion of mobility and requirements for the implementation of infrastructure on a scale that far exceeds the envisaged framework and measure of a man. *Cf.* Marc Augé, *Non-Places: Introduction to an Anthropology of Supermodernity* (London: Verso, 1995).

22 See Justus Dahinden, *Urban Structures for the Future* (New York: Praeger, 1972); Reyner Banham, *Megastructure: Urban Futures of the Recent Past* (London: Thames and Hudson, 1976).

23 Marshall McLuhan, *Understanding Media: The Extensions of Man* (Corte Madera: Gingko Press, 2003), 96, first published 1964.

24 Dahinden, *Urban Structures for the Future*, 8.

25 Ibid., 2–18. Thesis is corresponding to McLuhan's: the space capsule and the satellite have created a new environment for our planet, which has changed from "environment in time" into a "probe in space." It means that the planet has become an anti-environment, an art form, which generates a new perception of the new man-made environment; nature became obsolete, ecology is born. See McLuhan, "The Emperor's Old Clothes," in *The Man-Made Object,* ed. Gyorgy Kepes (New York: George Braziller, 1966), 90–95; and McLuhan, "The Rise and Fall of Nature," *Journal of Communication* (27.4, 1977): 80–81, quoted in *McLuhan in Space: A Cultural Geography,* ed. Richard Cavell (Toronto, ONT: University of Toronto, 2002), 176. As Fuller before him, McLuhan also acknowledges the potential of the concept of the space capsule living unit, in which the mimicry or simulation of the planetary environment is facilitated by technology.

26 Banham, *Megastructure*, 209.

2

DEVELOPMENT

Pioneers and contemporaries

Subsistence minimum (*Existenzminimum*), CIAM, and the new generation

In the legacy of the functionalism of the Modern Movement and the Congrès Internationaux d'Architecture Moderne (CIAM) congresses, subsistence minimum[1], together with and in relation to the subject of prefabrication, should be highlighted as one of the key topics, being an important basis for the formation of radical minimal environments and the development of the typology of the capsule. The minimum dwelling, or a rhetorical question of how much space a person really needs to live, could be discussed from various aspects: From anthropological, biological, sociological, cultural, economic, to technological and architectural angles. Our discussion will focus on the latter.

Subsistence minimum (*Existenzminimum*) was the main topic of the second CIAM Congress in Frankfurt in 1929, at a time when the experimental field for new housing typologies, which should suit the needs and abilities of the then working class, was established in Frankfurt, under the leadership of Ernst May.[2] In the 1920s, Margarete Schütte Lihotzky also designed the famous Frankfurt kitchen, which was installed in most housing projects designed by May and his group.[3] The ergonomically determined "laboratory kitchen" was a rational functional unit of housing, maximizing the use of space by minimizing work energy consumption, and could be denoted as a predecessor of compact monofunctional service units. In the expanded program context, this was also an indispensable model for the interior design of subsequent capsule dwellings.

The issue of minimum required housing for the working class had been topical even before the congress, certainly since the 19th century, in France and England.[4] The size of a living unit was not only limited to a one-bedroom unit, like a studio, as in the case of the capsule, but to various configurations of multi-room housing for social units of different sizes, from individuals to families, as well as collective dwellings with shared common spaces. Social changes which dictated improvements in the structure of dwellings, and attempts at collective social systems, following the example of Soviet communal houses (*dom-kommuna*) addressed the changed character of a family by emphasizing the individual, the economic independence of women, and increased mobility.[5] That same year, Sigfried Giedion, one of the key personalities and secretary-general of CIAM, published a book entitled *Befreites Wohnen (Libertated Living),* in which he connected the openness, lightness, and flexibility of *modern architecture/New Building*[6] with rationality, functionality, industry, and the subsistence minimum, in addition to defining a house as a useful asset which is amortized, and may be written off after a certain period. This should enable liberation from the burden of tradition and of high rents, which was one of the key initiatives for minimum dwellings. In his statement, Giedion discusses subsistence minimum, which is one of the most important tasks of New Building, as the basis for the development of new culture of everyday life, and directly connects new architecture to social emancipation.[7] Also important is an interesting fact that, in his seminar at the congress, Walter Gropius upgraded the maxim of biological conditions of a minimum dwelling—the basic minimal space, air, light, and heat, where residents may fully develop their vital functions, demanding that "every adult shall have his own room, small though it may be!"[8]

Standardization, industrialization, and Taylorization, sociological findings, economic requirements, requirements to ensure basic natural elements, and the biological nature of living were the topics discussed at lectures at the congress, or the basis of projects for a comparative exhibition of layouts of 207 minimum dwellings from twenty-six European and US cities, the sizes of which ranged from 29.5 to 76.5 m^2 for single-family houses, 24.7 to 52.7 m^2 for individual units in two-family houses, 23 to 91.2 m^2 for multi-family houses. It also included the plans for a 7.4 m^2 ship's cabin and a minimal hotel room.[9] In comparison with the technocratic program of the *Socialist City (Sotsgorod),* published by a Bolshevik activist and urban planner, Nikolai Aleksandrovich Miliutin in the Soviet Union, the suggestions of CIAM are still rather traditional. Miliutin suggested an apartment building with certain collective functions and independent living units of 8.4 m^2 in size and 21.84 m^3 in volume, which should suffice for minimum comfort, comprising a sleeping room, a work desk, and space for storing bedding, clothes, medicines, and other personal belongings.[10]

Miliutin's expressly functional urban suggestion was, like the work of the protagonists of *New Building,* aimed at aesthetic goals, which should be expressed in an environment of simple, functional, and economic buildings. At the beginning, the project of subsistence minimum housing was more than an instrumental response to the social housing problem, since *New Building* architects, in addition to ensuring a housing program for underprivileged social classes, saw in it an opportunity to realize the ascetic ideal, honesty in the use of materials, and truth, instead of representation[11]—construction which would be reduced to its essence, responding to the minimum spatial and sanitary requirements of new society. It would also be authentic. However, the economic crisis directed it toward the rationality and functionality of cost efficiency.[12]

The Czech avant-garde artist, writer, and critic, Karel Teige, who presented his views in the publication of the next CIAM congress, could not agree with such a technicist reduction of a working-class dwelling. In the book entitled *Nejmenší byt (The Minimum Dwelling),* published in 1932, he points out that "the term 'minimum dwelling' is not to be understood as a tiny dwelling for a little man!" Therefore, such a dwelling should not merely be a smaller form of bourgeois housing, modified rented shacks at a higher level. Instead, it requires a holistic approach and answers to the modern lifestyle of the whole population, in which women are also included in the production processes and in public life.[13] The problem Teige pointed out is that the definition of subsistence minimum alone excludes dwelling, in its conventional sense. In comparison with the functional diversity of ruling-class dwellings, he did not attribute dwelling in rented apartments or shacks of the proletariat and the poor as living in the real sense, but merely as shelter. Teige, who did not link the subsistence minimum with the smallness of housing, emphasized the requirement for housing of unique quality, which should be designed to really suit the social lifestyle and cultural needs of its residents, pointed out a solution in apartment buildings with common functions, and placed the whole problem in the context of necessary radical changes in housing and land policies, and changes in the political system, moving toward socialism. Teige was incredibly critical of the most prominent representatives of the Modern Movement who, by constructing villas, mainly served the system, or as he put it: "A machine for living? No, a machine for representation and splendor, for the idle, lazy life of the bosses playing golf and their ladies, bored in their boudoirs."[14] This was unacceptable to him, because he believed in the power of architecture as a discipline which actively participated in the fight for a brighter and socially more equal future. Contrary to the traditional scheme of a dwelling arrangement based on the concept of a family, Teige presented the minimum dwelling in a common building as a complex of individual living units—one room for each adult, with common facilities in the building—and pointed out attempts in this direction from the Soviet Union. He believed that the result of the understanding of the minimum dwelling is a change from quantity to quality, as an individual living unit no longer included a dining-room, a parlor, and a children's room, but is merely a place for enjoying private intellectual and emotional life, a place for sleep, rest, and study.

From achieving the aforementioned dimensions, as proposed by Miliutin, some proposals for other experiments were even more drastic, as they included the area of a living unit not larger than 3–9 m^2, with 5 m^2 per person being more than the norm in a worker's dwelling at that time.[15] In his enthusiasm, Teige predicted a bright future for Soviet experiments, and showed the concept of a living unit as liberating. Residents will no longer have to take care of vast housing, and perfect comfort will be provided in common facilities. A living unit is a strictly standardized and mass-produced living environment, where no one will be a slave to his or her home. Moreover, Teige also emphasized the political point of view, as

> the standardized aspects of the living cell, for an individual, help subvert such notions as "home," "native land," and "family," and prepare the conditions for the emergence of a new psychological type of human … the living cell for one person becomes our modern barrel of Diogenes.[16]

Separate individual functions, which were part of traditional housing, are now positioned throughout the collective houses, which fully anticipated the systems of megastructures that peaked thirty years later.[17] At the same time, designs of modernist minimum living units for individuals could be deemed proto-capsule units, in comparison with which the capsules of the 1960s are a technological upgrade, and the fulfillment of the typical obsession of the post-war period: The condition of mobility.

The topic of the minimum standard also became a field of criticism of capsule dwellings of the 1960s. Determining subsistence minimum, as emphasized by Teige before this time, was the subject of scientific discussions which, however, were criticized by many as being overly technocratic. The technocratic approach may also be attributed to Teige and Soviet revolutionaries who, by designing dwellings, pursued the idea of complete social reform, although Teige himself emphasized the social role of architecture, the starting point of which is a man, not a building or a material structure. Marxist revolutionaries were aware of the significance of machinery, and the fact that they helped determine the working class but, with contempt for Fordist principles, they believed in the revolutionary change in this relationship and potential liberation. At the same time, they tried to find a means of representation beyond the unacceptable form of traditional dwellings, which was based on the dualism of machine technology and art. According to Teige, architecture could be transformed into a new science, connecting technological, sociological, and psychological factors of life.

In the pre-war period, it seemed that modernism, with functionalist rhetoric, would remain on the edge of social acceptability. But in the post-war period, it was completely established as the norm in the New Building programs through an emphasis on efficiency, the use of state-of-the-art techniques, and slightly more flexible and less orthodox architectural language. The period after World War II in Europe was marked with the urgency of the reconstruction of demolished cities, the provision of dwellings, and social assistance. In addition to the fulfillment of basic living conditions, better standards of living not only for individuals, but society as a whole, soon became one of the main topics. Many architects and designers who underwent schooling in functionalist principles of modernism saw an opportunity to use their skills for the welfare of society, in the reconstruction of a demolished Europe. The morphological form of the post-war situation in architecture, with the reconstruction of buildings as "a key sociopolitical task of the period, realized on the basis of the living functionalist tradition and the simultaneously open CIAM discourse," was called by Stane Bernik "extended functionalism,"[18] and is also suitable for many more radical proposals in the wider global context.

The post-war period was marked with the revisionist criticism of CIAM with the diversity of ideas flowing from New Brutalism, Structuralism, to Metabolism, with many leading protagonists originating in Team 10. In the process of modernization, members of Team 10 sought concepts and strategies to facilitate and develop space with individual and collective identity, and involve users in the adjustment of living environments, according to their own wants and needs.[19] Denying the strict universal functionalist doctrine, deeming it unsuitable for the human environment, members of Team 10 were interested in historical and social dimensions of architecture and urbanism, emphasizing regional qualities, and the significance of context and the specificity of each project. Projects and discussions, which express the speculative dimension, mirror the criticism of consumer society, the topic of the participation of residents in decision making, and urban renewal. With the built environment and context-related composition of buildings, they wanted to create conditions for the self-realization of society and places "where a man can realize what he wishes to be."[20] This also emphasized the relationship between the individual component and the collective structure, which was later the subject of the open design of megastructures, in which the relation between individual capsule units and the common megastructure framework was established, at the beginning of the 1960s.

Technological development for the needs of products also contributed to the development of prefabricated dwellings and the use of new materials. Obsession with dwelling production following the model of car production was already present among the pioneers of modernism. In 1923, Walter Gropius and Le Corbusier both realized that the history of the off-site fabrication of buildings and the history of an architectural culture of prefabrication were different.[21] On the one hand, we follow the history of architecture, from transported structural and sculptural elements for the erection of Roman temples in North-African colonies, to churches made of wrought iron, wooden and metal houses for the colonial world, Japanese systems of traditional wooden modular construction, and similar Scandinavian examples. On the other hand, the modern aspiration to combine architecture and industrial production means a change in relations between the architect, the client, and the construction itself, as well as a change in the conception of a house, a dwelling, as traditionally rooted at a specific location brought new meanings of beauty with a factory-produced house delivered to the location. Efforts and attempts by Le Corbusier, Gropius, Wachsmann, Prouvé, and others before and during World War II, provided a relevant answer in the post-war period, as a quick and effective solution to the lack of apartments in the USA, Europe, and Japan, especially in the form of panel systems. While modular prefabricated elements, which composed larger architectural compositions, were the continuation of the traditional construction procedures, with the added industrial approach, the emerging concept of a modular living unit, as a prefabricated whole, was revolutionary.[22]

In 1943, Marcel Breuer developed a prototype of a house called *Plas-2-Point*, which was one of the first projects in which the external membrane also had a structural function, and was the predecessor of experiments with a uniform load-bearing "shell," the so-called *monocoque* construction, which were put into force with the development of the plastics industry at the end of the 1950s.[23] In general, the research and projects in the field of prefabricated dwellings can be divided into frame structures—designs of vertical, horizontal, and diagonal supports between which space is formed with prefabricated partitions, ceilings, floors, as well as spatial elements, etc., and self-supporting, usually single-volume, *monocoque* constructions.[24]

Certain achievements in the arms industry were used immediately after World War II as consumer goods. The American company Monsanto was aware of the opportunity to use new plastic materials, developed for the needs of devices in military aircraft as early as the interwar period. The opening of the *Monsanto House of the Future*, made of fiberglass, in Disneyland in 1957, and other similar products that affected the dimensions of buildings, confirmed the general belief that development for the needs of war contributed to the transformation of products to be used in times of peace. Due to the lengthy period of tension and competition during the Cold War, the duality of development for the needs of war and peace was completely blurred—progress for the needs of the arms industry directly affected everyday life, because militarism and consumerism were developing at the same time. A key role was also played by architects and designers who got involved in the Cold War competition, through numerous controversial situations.[25] The use of Buckminster Fuller's domes, serving the establishment, army, and counterculture, may be mentioned as one of the most explicit examples.

Many starting points and issues regarding a dwelling appropriate for modern man, subsistence minimum, the relationship between technology and art, representation and attitudes to social reality, gained new interpretations, answers, and redefinitions throughout the development of the Modern Movement and avant-garde currents. Meanwhile, they also achieved characteristic materializations through countercultural movements, radical and utopian architectural and design projects in the 1950s and at the beginning of the 1960s, which was the key period for the concept of the capsule. Pre-war modernism introduced normative methods through the functionalist operation of CIAM and, in its desire to achieve a social balance, strove to ensure at least an acceptable minimum standard of housing for the whole population. In a similar fashion, post-war modernism, characterized by a softer tone in considering the basic needs of the people, represented the basic operational field for the development of the concept and typology of the capsule. While the internal organization of the capsule is based on the technocratic escalation of the issue of the minimum standard of living and the tradition of subsistence minimum, a dwelling as a mobile unit rejects the rationalist logic of total planning, and leaves composition of architectural and urban form to the impulses and desires of residents. Modernism, which evades definition, always meant the introduction of the new into the existing system, its upgrade or a complete break with it, and paved the way for experiments. The heterogeneity of modernism, and the open understanding of modernity as "contemporariness and progress" which, in pursuit of "the new" in the spirit of the time, always succumbed to the fashionable, is the experimental field which facilitated the development of the concept of the capsule. It was not always the case that it came at the cost of a complete denial of the past, but always as a complex and critical response to it. Although experiments in science and technology have a different connotation than in art, they are virtually inevitable and necessary, in order to critically verify the existing and the past, which is not necessarily absolute and suitable.[26] This hypothesis with activities in the architectural laboratory of the 20th century is confirmed for architecture, as well.

To what extent may the concept of the capsule be understood as the product of explosions in architecture, and how may it be defined and evaluated in the context of design, architectural and spatial practices, and their economic, social, and political dimensions? The review of rebellious, radical, and utopian practices and projects will be introduced by the diversity of the works of Buckminster Fuller, a key figure who, in the conditions of the Modern Movement, and by criticizing the International Style with his innovative derivations, influenced the realization of the real fusion of technology and construction, with a prophetic technological component. With his enthusiasm, he also influenced the development of certain individualized and self-sufficient spatial formations of the countercultural movement in the USA, and he strongly influenced radical and utopian design, architectural and urban practices of the 1950s and, especially, of the 1960s, worldwide.

From Buckminster Fuller to counterculture 1960

Machine for living in versus machine aesthetics

When Reyner Banham's book, *Theory and Design in the First Machine Age,* was first published in 1960, the prospects of the tradition of explosion continuing, both in theory and in the practice of architecture, supported by the development of technology, foretold the search for new ways for new conditions.[27] In the supplemented second edition twenty years later, Banham explains the situation at that time with a distance:

> Most of the beliefs on which the Modern Movement had been based were still standing and in good order, and what appeared to be a Second Machine Age, as glorious as the first, beckoned us into the "Fabulous Sixties"–miniaturization, transistorization, jet and rocket, wonder-drugs and new domestic chemistries, television and the computer seemed to offer more of the same, only better.[28]

Buckminster Fuller, who was a contemporary of the First Machine Age, of pioneers and masters of the Modern Movement, was actually a representative of a Second Machine Age within the first one, and an early herald of the transformation of the First Machine Age into the second. He was one of those people who criticized the accepted modern "machine aesthetics" with their work, and advocated complete connection of industry and construction processes to meet people's needs and provide the freedom that pertains to people. Fuller's definition of *industry* was very precise: "By industry, I meant in 1927, and as yet mean the following: '*The integrated, teleological objectivity of the full gamut of the exact sciences,*' no more–no less."[29] In the 1950s, Banham and other revisionists strove to proceed with the project as it had been started, by openly criticizing functionalism, arguing that it did not manage to utilize all the technological options and empower architecture to keep the promises of the Machine Age, and fulfill the social mission to use machines as a means for the liberation of people from past servitude and exploitation. This was actually the project in which modern buildings were meant to persist in connecting technology, serving advanced ideals and dreams of a better world in which Fuller had been active as early as the late 1920s.[30] Fuller thus reverberated Le Corbusier's call to merge industry and construction.[31] However, he went one step further, as he really, *literally*, wanted to build a house-machine, with a critical approach to the main apologists of the International Style and its main representatives, claiming that they used industrial lines as a cosmetic cover on handmade buildings, and only assumed the aesthetics of machine production, instead of utilizing the real industrialization of the construction industry.

World architecture

In the introduction to the monograph about Richard Buckminster Fuller, John McHale, a member of the British Independent Group, emphasized an important context of his work in the early 1960s—*world architecture,* which was then a rather new phenomenon as an independent term.

Increased communication speeds enabled architects or engineers in the 20th century to work in remote locations with different climate and social conditions, and their works could be known all over the world with the flow of ideas, as they worked in a world context.[32]

In addition to the information omnipresence of man all around the world, changes were also taking place in the opposite direction. On the one hand, man was changing the world around himself with technology, which in turn enabled him to exercise inner changes as the consequence of reforming his lifestyle. Faith in the improvement of living conditions by directly using science in industrial technology opened up an experimental field—the discovery of new living patterns in view of new needs.

With his *4D Timelock* project, in 1928, Fuller developed a system which corresponded to global requirements. A multistory house was designed to be transported by Zeppelin anywhere in the world, and erected all in one day. Michael John Gorman believes that this was the most innovative element of Fuller's proposal which, however, was not realized until 1954, when the U.S. Marines' Sikorski helicopter lifted and flew with the geodesic dome; on this occasion, Fuller wrote on the back of a photo: "First airlift of man-usable shelter in history."[33] Using the technologies of the shipping and aeronautical industries, Fuller clearly expresses the opinion that global accommodation issues can no longer be resolved with outdated craft-based forms of construction, because they do not meet the requirements to fulfill needs immediately. Therefore, he sees the solution in the complete utilization of science and industrial technology for the needs of construction, following the example of the automotive industry, which leads to the redefinition of the meaning of "home." Fuller's student and subsequent coworker, J. Baldwin, remembers Bucky's words: "Homes should be thought of as service equipment, not as monuments."[34] The making of a home as *service equipment* has clear role models in the making of *mobile equipment* in the automotive industry, which served as a reference industry for Fuller. McHale reminds us that, in 1925, five million cars and only half a million single-family houses were made, but the automotive industry did not achieve maximum performance per pound of material invested, which was one of Fuller's main principles.[35] So we can understand the extended field of Fuller's work with a wide range of various projects, innovations, and inventions as a response to the state of technological solutions for everyday needs which, in his opinion, did not comply with the opportunities provided by modern science and technology. With this, Bucky wanted to realize the idea of global, omnipresent, and affordable architectures—shelters which, at the global level, are part of the science-supported use of global resources for the needs of the whole of humanity.[36]

Dymaxion *individualization machine*

Fuller's *Dymaxion House*[37] is the result of the study *4D Timelock*, and was perceived as a radical criticism of the International Style, as it managed to carry out everything the early Modernists promised, but did not realize. When the International Style crystallized into the prescribed forms which should symbolize the Machine Age, Fuller really used the state-of-the-art technological solutions of the time in his *Dymaxion House*. The *Dymaxion House* was named in 1929, and was subject to Fuller's research and improvements between 1927 and 1946, when it emerged reformed in an industrial version as the *Wichita House*.

In the *Shelter* magazine (November 1932),[38] Fuller honestly, in the context of the American building, shows role models for the design and concept of the *Dymaxion House*, which directly reflect the technocratic spirit and faith in the technological engagement with the environment. The hexagonal lighthouse *Love Point Light* in Maryland defies the conditions in the middle of the sea, and seems like a design and metaphorical prototype of the *Dymaxion House*; it represents self-sufficiency in difficult living conditions, and gives light and orientation—a genuine metaphor for an intellectually independent modern man. The hexagonal fort and the octagonal house are presented as examples which reduce wind resistance, and facilitate orientation in several directions. The octagonal house is an echo of the popular typology in America in the mid-19th century, which was described by its main herald, Orson Fowler, as an example of spacious, light, economical, and cheaper construction. The design determines the individualistic character of octagonal buildings, which did not form dense urban fabric and defied the orthogonal order of the neighborhood. The sixth example is a hexagonal pig incubator. The structure with the main core, which contains heating and ventilation devices, and where piglets can keep warm, is a house-machine, which protects pigs on the coldest days. Alongside the references presented, the photo of the model of the *Dymaxion House* seems like a real scientific upgrade—a home for an individualized man of the scientific and technological age which, according to Fuller's definition, should be, just like a person, as independent as possible, with its own character, dignity, beauty, and harmony.[39]

Despite standardized mass production and formal similarity, Bucky's houses should express the owner's individuality, since they should facilitate and promote contemplation and innovation. Due to the non-traditional layout and shape of rooms and living arrangements in such dwellings, residents are put in a position where they need to discover and develop different, individualized living patterns. The *Dymaxion House* contains yet another program innovation—the so-called "go ahead with life" room. In the plan, it is marked as a library, but it is more than that. In addition to mobile bookshelves, this "personal (proto)multimedia center" also contains a world globe, maps, a radio, a television, a typewriter, a drawing board. In this room, which was the most important for Fuller, children can learn on the basis of choice, not on the basis of formulas imposed on them. Such learning was of the utmost importance for Fuller, since it should enable children to develop into independent persons. The house also contains built-in devices, which were extremely sophisticated for that time.[40] In addition to the household being automated, Fuller's was also guided to inventions by his desire to produce a self-sufficient dwelling, which consumes as little energy and natural resources for its functioning and comfortable life as possible. The autonomy facilitated and promoted by the house aimed to satisfy basic human needs, including a spontaneous intellectual development.[41]

Who was such a house intended for? For everyone. Its mass production would make it available to the broadest possible range of consumers, and it could be paid off in a few years, just like cars. The house is intended for individualized modern people with faith in science, and its achievements supported by economic logic, which was always part of Fuller's designs. The entire structure of the new dwelling is a completely logical and minutely rationalized machine for living in, intended for residents who are not emotionally attached to traditional ways of living and established patterns of built space. Has the resident of the *Dymaxion House* already been liberated from attachment to society and land, which is shown in a dwelling, which is lifted off the ground, self-sufficient, and without connections to public infrastructure? Perhaps we can find a hint in an interesting, ambiguous, ironically real definition of a man provided by Fuller, in his book *Nine Chains to the Moon,* from 1938, where he describes a man as a mechanism equipped with a phantom commander, who is a metaphor for a human spirit, and enables a man to be a "uniquely 'individual' man."[42] If people are mechanisms, they need devices which are most adapted to their functions to satisfy their needs. With the *Dymaxion House*, Fuller managed to do just that: Design a dwelling as technological prosthetics, which changes, developed with residents and the requirements of their spirit, and functions as an organism.

Inventions in the houses were intended for their residents. Nevertheless, Fuller's goal was to improve the living conditions for mankind. Fuller believed philosophy was effective only if applied mechanically, explaining that the "[m]entality must be balanced with mechanics."[43] In accordance with his transcendental philosophical background, he established a relationship between the mind, which is manifested in individual development and the use of intuition, and the matter—the body as an invention warehouse, a mechanism where natural processes, which need to be discovered to understand the integrity of living, take place. These processes may be used to develop new tools or house-machines adapted to the body, which facilitate the rebalancing of important functions with mental development, in an endless dynamic process. The shape of tools must, therefore, fit their purpose. Louis Sullivan's maxim "form follows function," which he inherited from Horatio Greenough, an American sculptor, who advocated the establishment of a functional relationship between architecture and decoration, in his essays under the influence of the naturalist philosophy of Ralph Waldo Emerson, gained momentum with transcendental background, again with Fuller's literal use in some kind of a feedback loop. Fuller perceived shelter as designed, but not for the purpose of aesthetics. He perceived it as a mute instrument, which is tuned by a resident at a functional and aesthetic level, for their own needs. Fuller facilitated the development of human inner content with living equipment and fulfilled material conditions, which are realized in the awareness and experience of the abstract, and in the tradition of American transcendentalism facilitate the realization of the truth through individual intuition in nature. The *Dymaxion House* was designed as a house-machine, which should eliminate hard work, selfishness, exploitation, politics, and centralized control, making time for education, entertainment, and progress.[44] Despite economic calculations made by Fuller, or due to excessive and too risky initial input in real terms, his machine for living in was unrealizable in the given situation. For the early 1930s, the *Dymaxion House* was especially financially too demanding to be realized in mass production.[45]

Fuller managed to realize the concept in imperfect and limited versions, with single and double versions of the *Dymaxion Deployment Unit,* in 1940 and 1941, which were meant to be used during the war, and were significantly less sophisticated than the basic *Dymaxion House.* The units were used as radar stations, hospitals, dormitories, etc. at various locations in completely different climatic conditions.

The *Dymaxion* house-machine, or the *Wichita House* from 1946, ended the period of Fuller's research designated *Dymaxion,* and it finally looked like he would reach the target production sector. The house was designed with the use of tools and a conveyor belt from the Beech Aircraft in Wichita in Kansas, and was an attempt to use the latest technological achievements, not for military purposes, but to improve living conditions. Unlike the *Dymaxion House,* the ground plan of the *Wichita House* was circular, while structural solutions were improved for accessibility and the use of new materials. The living quarters were lifted from the ground, while the garage was beneath it. A unit of the *Wichita House* was intended for the greatest mobility possible. Its structure, the design of the membrane, and the choice of materials made it completely resistant to the external influences of fire, tornadoes, hurricanes, and earthquakes.[46] The flirtation between the design of the house and mobile dwellings of nomadic tribes is obvious, which conveys Fuller's respect for traditional knowledge and faith in human resourcefulness and which he "translated" into a modern variation of dwellings, improved with technological development and a scientific approach.

From the first ideas and designs of the *4D Timelock* through the *Dymaxion House* and to the *Wichita House*, the machine aspects of a dwelling for an individualized modern man with a new lifestyle of physical, intellectual, and social autonomy were emphasized throughout, which is, undoubtedly, a political act gaining utopian dimensions with the concept of "individual units for the entire world," to paraphrase Fuller. Banham marks the pragmatic concept of the *Dymaxion House* as totally radical, since its structure does not stem from a classical compositional approach or elemental aesthetics to materiality, which would be elevated to the level of a symbol for a *machine*, but from the adjustment of the method of using lightweight metals in the manufacture of planes of that time.[47] In addition to fascination with the explicit use of the machine expression in architecture, faith in the possibility of complete control of the environment is clearly expressed, too. McHale explains, in heroic manner: "This was not simply an aesthetic 'machine to live in,' but a machine like the auto or airplane, designed to extend the potential of living—either in or out!"[48]

Remember that 1927 was the year when an international exhibition of housing architecture opened in Stuttgart, under the auspices of German Werkbund with *Weissenhofsiedlung* (*Weissenhof Estate*)[49] as an early manifesto of the International Style, which saw the participation of the pioneers of the Modern Movement. In spite of the use of prefabricated building elements and technical improvements to construction, which facilitated the making of twenty-one buildings, with 63 apartments, in a mere twenty-one weeks, it seems that examples of buildings have not reached the rhetorical promises of *New Building*.

The science behind the space house

In his lecture, "World Design Initiative," in Mexico City in October 1963, Fuller pointed out the relationship between architecture, dwelling construction, and science, with obvious excitement about the space house. He was fascinated by the fact that a shift in the scientific treatment of human needs and the scientific design of dwellings happened—in the interest of life in space, although it took place due to the Cold War competition and the conquering of space. He was aware of the fact that, for this purpose, the processes of the human zone, and the volume for the transformation of energy, must be reduced to a minimum and all human material and psychological needs must be scientifically anticipated and met.

> In order to be able to do that, we are in effect, building a little house, a little space house. We had been used to the word "capsule" which has hidden from man the fact that what science is really working on is a little house; not much room to move around in, no garden of roses outside, but nonetheless, a little house with a six billion dollar mortgage.[50]

Fuller also warned the predominantly architectural public:

> . . . what the space scientists are working on is in fact the design of a house: That is architecture—the scientists are in your business competing with you in the solution of all the problems that a house for regenerative man involves.[51]

In the projects of Archigram, Fuller's prophetic connection of the space capsule and a small house was first manifested a year later, in the form of living *capsules* which, as opposed to many previous and modern similar experiments, were also called living capsules.

Fuller's early experiments with autonomous dwellings for autonomous individuals, the *Dymaxion* projects, established the cultural and theoretical basis for the development of the typology of the capsule in the 1960s. Therefore, Fuller's scientific approach, with technological solutions and proposals to redefine habitation of both individuals and society is, at the same time, also a paradigmatic example, albeit of the unconscious dealing with the concept of capsularity, and all its not-yet-imagined, thought-out, and unimaginable consequences, which were churned by the flow of time from the optimistic faith in the bright future to its opposite.

Garden of Eden

Ever since his *4D Timelock* and *Dymaxion* projects, Fuller's anti-urban visions, in which cities are corrupt, dirty, unhealthy, and unsuitable for life and work, included projects intended for individualized individuals or families that were able to emigrate to "healthy natural" suburban environments, by way of structures supported with technological progress.

Buckminster Fuller is also deemed the inventor of the geodesic dome, which is only partially true. Even though he developed it on his own, and patented several of them, the triangular composition of the geodesic dome had been discovered about thirty years before him, by engineer Walter Bauersfeld, when he was seeking a solution for the structure of the dome of the Zeiss Planetarium in Jena, in which the sky is projected onto an icosahedral structure.[52] Bucky dubbed the first useful outdoor dome with a transparent envelope, under which residents could control weather conditions, the "Garden of Eden."[53] While his previous structures, *Dymaxion* and *Wichita* houses, offered a 360-degree horizontal view, the view of the residents in the transparent geodesic dome shifted upwards toward the sky. Parallel to the research of the structural geometric characteristics of geodesic domes, desiring to design a product that would provide the greatest possible autonomy, this was followed by the

Autonomous Living Package project in 1949, which complemented the dome project, and comprised equipment and appliances for a six-member family, and was not connected to municipal public infrastructure. To be transported, the whole package could be folded into a container and, together with the dome, constitutes a movable living environment.

A similar machine package, in a significantly smaller volume, was designed by Fuller as early as 1940, when he combined the projects of the *Dymaxion Bathroom* (for Phelps Dodge) (see Figure 2.1) sanitary unit with the chemical processing of waste, and kitchen, laundry room with a sink, cooker, and a fridge, all into a mobile trailer. The latter was equipped with a central diesel engine as an energy unit for an air compressor and an electric generator. The movable machine–architectural combination foretold another radical redefinition of dwelling, with a hint of a romantic return to nature, enriched with the capacity of new technologies.[54] Fuller's Garden of Eden seems like an image of biblical paintings transmitted

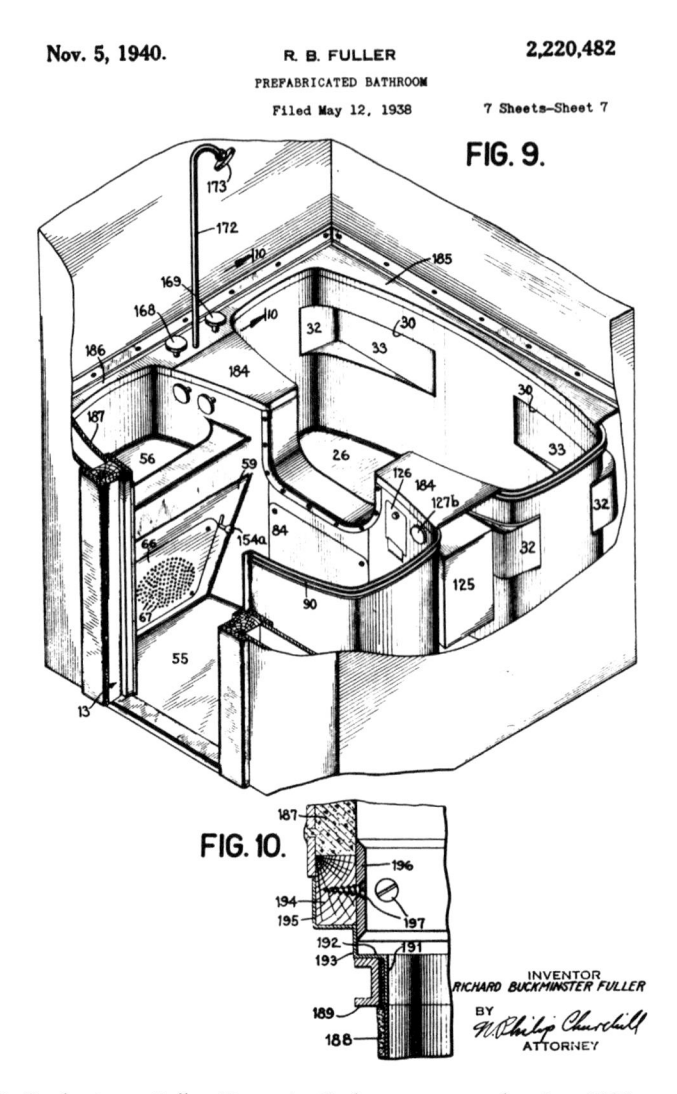

FIGURE 2.1   R. Buckminster Fuller, *Dymaxion* Bathroom, patent drawing, 1938

FIGURE 2.2 R. Buckminster Fuller, geodesic dome model—a climatic envelope for the Standard
of Living Package

into reality, but devoid of theological and symbolic disposition, which perhaps appeared even
more inspiring and open for interpretation in the American alternative counterculture of the
1960s, which claimed, with much approval, the dome to form its own living space.

As a social and cultural achievement, geodesic domes follow Fuller's philosophy of a
connection between mass industrial production, air delivery, and intellectual and physical
autonomy, which are also alternatives to perpendicular architecture. Mass use enables structures
to adapt Fuller's heterogeneous "philosophical moment" to individual purposes and/or world
view or practical framework—as a top technical invention, they were intended for military
purposes, as a roof over large complexes of thematic and exhibition programs engaged at the
symbolic level, as a sophisticated envelope for state-of-the-art technical consumer goods at
the level of state propaganda, and as a realization of dreams about life free from limitations and
control, in counterculture.

Fuller developed the concept of the geodesic dome in the late 1940s, and patented it for
the first time in 1954. His geodesic dome worked as a technological apotheosis of mobility
and technical craftiness, which passed the test of exceeding geopolitical boundaries and the
limitations of discipline at trade fairs all around the world, and appeared, without contradictions, in both mainstream and alternative (countercultural) media. How can we understand
the substantive flexibility of the virtually technocratic concept which, in the early 1950s,
seemed anything but appropriate for the construction of new politically opposing communes
in the second half of the 1960s?

The answer should also be sought in Fuller's understanding of the built environment, and
his wider world view, influenced by the didactic, utopian, and individualistic transcendentalism, with an addition of faith in science, human resourcefulness, and the need to return to
nature. By 1959, over 1,000 versions of the geodesic dome had been built worldwide, on the
basis of Fuller's patent.[55] As he was established in the academic sphere, a political noncon-
formist, and a skillful, renowned speaker, Fuller literally mobilized American youth eager for
novelties and changes, and inspired them to build geodesic domes. His fans, students, and

coworkers borrowed and adapted his concepts to the needs of self-built communes, which grew in the surroundings of American cities. In addition to Fuller's pragmatism, drop-outs, constructors and popularizers, and self-builders, who adopted Fuller's mindset and his concepts of spatial units saw, in the differences of geodesic domes and similar structures, a spatial form that symbolizes rebellion against all norms and repressive institutions.

Radical environments of the psychedelic sixties

"Crash pads" and "replicators"

The 1960s in the USA were marked with the Cold War, the space program, liberal reforms, race riots, anti-war demonstrations, and counterculture, which responded rebelliously to the state of society. The paradigmatic fact is that researches in outer space by the American space agency, NASA, and of human inner space by the likes of psychedelic guru, Timothy Leary, both got plenty of media attention, and took place at the same time. In social reality, the inward–outward force spans the new generation of hippies, which inherited its countercultural stance from the older generation of beatniks, and enhanced it with psychedelic rock music, the sexual revolution, and the consumption of hallucinogens to achieve other states of consciousness. Changes in society affected the establishment of a new attitude to space, which emphasized the freedom of movement, without hurdles and spatial boundaries. The transformation of everyday dwellings, and planned and formed spaces expressed the aforementioned main characteristics of the "liberated and liberating" space with a revolutionary disposition—with a type of a special spatial ambient, so-called "crash pads," in urban environments, with so-called "acid retreats" in rural environments, and at other mobile events and environments—literally.[56]

New environments can be divided up on the basis of purpose into two key co-dependent types, the spatial realizations of which, in accordance with the non-limiting logic, were not used unambiguously. On the one hand, there were environments for experimenting with psychological states which, due to special feelings of traveling to other spheres of consciousness and returning back to everyday life, required a suitable ambience. On the other, there were environments which trigger or replicate similar psychological states without drug consumption. The second type is closely related to the use of technological devices which enabled the creation of "the art of dislocation." The bombarding of the senses produced the feeling of breaking with the traditional parameters of space and time, which facilitated the experience of an endless fluid space, where air, color, and form interlace. Characteristic of rebellious environments was also the redefinition of their content, which should represent a blend of art, life, and politics.

As a spatial type, the predecessors of "crash pads" were found in bohemian artists' basements and attics, and in hideouts for getting high on opium, used by the beatnik generation. For American youth, they were the first step toward independence and a symbol of breaking with the institutions of family and school. In new environments intended to overcome selfishness and possessiveness, as illustrated by Alastair Gordon, the traditional concepts of a room, a home, a family, and a community were completely transformed in the review of the radical environment of the psychedelic Sixties:

> Everyone wanted to sit, squat, kneel on the floor, join hands in a circle, assume the lotus position, sleep, or make love on the floor. This was a major shift, one of the first actions taken in the transformation toward Aquarian living. It signaled a return to primitive

origins, to Mother Earth and the beginnings of environmental consciousness as well as a more tribal mindset that would shape so many environments of the sixties.[57]

Timothy Leary, a professor at Harvard and a psychedelic generation guru, experimented with a suitable environment for LSD sessions, which was supposed to be an enclosure with soft corners—like a submarine or a common spaceship, with rounded walls which contribute to "hive consciousness."[58] A suitable form of space should be the form of a womb, which is supposed to represent primary protection and a return to physical origin. In an underground guide to crash-pad decor, Thad Ashby speaks about the meaning of softness in the "womb room."[59] In Leary's community of Castalia in Milbrook, the interiors of bedrooms were transformed into womb rooms.[60] The effect of hallucinogenic substances caused an organism to interlace with space. Gordon begins the description of the psychedelic radical environments of the Sixties by saying: "Edges softened. Corners vanished. Boundaries dissolved, along with simultaneous dissolution of ego."[61]

The internal psychological transformation of an individual is presented in direct relation to the change in perception of the physical environment. Therefore, the physical environment is reshaped for the needs of experimenting with psychological states. Soft forms without edges, single-space arrangements where the floor acts like a continuation of the landscape, intensive light and audio impulses, and fragrances redefined the Cartesian coordinates of traditional space. The experience of a soft embrace of the endless fluid space affected individual experiences of intranauts.[62] Travelers around the vastness of the interior of the psyche were part of the paradigm of the research of indoor and outdoor space, the internal and external universe of the 1960s. Buckminster Fuller's famous statement: "We are all astronauts,"[63] inspired generations to consider the world as a whole, without political boundaries, especially after the first photo of earth was taken from space by Apollo 4, on November 9, 1967. The perception of space as a free and unlimited continuum, on the basis of psychedelic research, got a visual material reference on a macroscale, as well. The visual matter and the concepts of experience of intranauts, and the technology of astronauts, merged in many spatial designs of the radical environments of the 1960s, which wanted to replicate the experience of hallucinogens, but without drug consumption.[64]

If "crash pads" reminded one of transitional "basic shelters" for psychedelic experiments, various derivatives of the latter were defined in much more detail, in terms of space and content. Young rebellious designers translated their inner experience to the spatial forms of the psychedelic flow. They wanted to create scenarios in which interiors, or even whole buildings, would become *cellular entities,* independent from traditional engineering, floating, almost non-existent.[65] They wanted to change everyday architecture into a spectacle, free themselves from the tyranny of rectangular space, and establish a new child-like attitude to floor surface, which changed into a landscape suitable for crawling and rolling. "Change your surroundings and change yourself," were the words of architect and activist Sim van der Ryn, recalling Fuller's famous statement.[66] Certain places had special anti-noise protection, and meditation areas were equipped with acoustic absorption materials. If there was furniture, it was built in, hidden, or acclimated into multipurpose islands or devices that could be disassembled. Conventional seating was replaced by soft amorphous bubbles, which adapted to the human body. Paradigmatic facilities were presented at the exhibition, *Contemplation Environment* at the Museum of Contemporary Crafts in Manhattan, in the winter of 1970. As published in *Time Magazine*, the facilities "provide a peaceful corner in the bustle of city life, where any and all might stop for a moment to think, muse, daydream or simply enjoy a quiet interlude."[67] The purpose of the exhibition was to explore and display fresh solutions for residents' needs for solitude, in the midst of overcrowded city places.

Similar environments emerged in the second half of the 1960s, as expressions of rebellious hedonism. Lying around in Verner Panton's cushioned environments which consisted of flowing stripes of psychedelic colors attempted to recreate the feeling of happiness before birth. Tom Luckey designed the *Rotating Barrel Room*, which is similar to the spatial transmutation of LSD.[68] In a similar way, tightened fabrics were used to create Aleksandra Kasuba's environments, Lester Walker's multi-color kinetic sculpture *Super Cube* from 1967, and Gamal El Zoghby's *Multi-Level Living Environment* from 1969, where the ceiling, the walls, and the floor become one, and expressive fascinations with micro-ambients were created inside conventional space. Many ambients from the mid-1960s remind us of Frederick Kiesler's *Endless House,* or even use it as a reference. Unlike Kiesler, whose architecture was comprehensive, attempts by psychedelic environments seem, many times, created at the level of ambient, backdrop, or, in the case of multimedia ambients, even non-material space, which depends on time.

Rural communes

Combining art, life, and politics into a homogeneous experiential state was most convincing in so-called rural communes, which swept the American Southwest from the mid-1960s. Some runaways were chased from cities by violence; others were lured to the natural environment by the possibility of experimenting with hallucinogenic substances, to blend with the basic elements, and to feel the pulsating rhythms of planets, away from the artificial urban environment. Others saw the potential to create a new art of life, life as art, in the wilderness. "Drop-outs" inspired by Thoreau were ready for a simple life and even poverty, and complete mutual trust.[69] Although estimates vary, there were supposed to have been many thousands of rural communes worldwide by the end of the 1960s, 8,000 in North America alone.[70] Runaways from cities lived in tents, temporary dwellings, converted cars and trucks, and in domes, which became the media hallmark for the dropped-out/outlaw generation.

A paradigmatic and vivid example of a drop-out community is *Drop City,* one of the first self-sufficient communes, which combined dissidence, zeal for information technology, revolutionary interest, the new art of life, and the focus of energy on the construction of new institutions, becoming the media icon of the dropped-out/outlaw generation. The community was established by three art students at the University of Kansas, who attended Buckminster Fuller's lecture at the University of Colorado in Boulder in April 1965. They became fans of his mindset overnight, and decided to build domes. They wanted to build a completely open, anarchistic society—a space for personal reinvention on an empty 2.4-hectare goat pasture in southern Colorado.[71] Under the influence of multimedia events of the avant-garde of artistic centers such as New York, the *Drop City* project was devised as an artwork in progress. They called it "Drop Art," which rhymed with two main trends of the art scene at the time: "Op Art" and "Pop Art." They organized multimedia, dance, and other public events, attended by several hundred people. However, the most important contribution of the revolutionary synergy was manifested in the building of domes, which established *Drop City*, through media response, as the first capital of the outlaw nation. Steve Baer suggested using sheet metal from car tops as material for the external cladding of domes, which was completely consistent with the principles of the use of "free waste," developed by "Droppers" as a parallel economic system.[72] In 1967, when ten domes had already been built, a few of which were geodesic, while others were polyhedrons of a different type, *Drop City* received Buckminster Fuller's *Dymaxion* Award, for innovative and economic construction of dwellings.

While smaller individual domes were erected in *Drop City* and other places, a different type of a dwelling, in terms of its program, was built in the *Red Rockers* community, which realized Marshall McLuhan's turn from individualism to collective tribalism—a large dome, a uniform, inclusive primal group shelter for several people, as Thoreau had dreamed, though only through the metaphor of life in the Golden Age. Radical leftist hippies, *Red Rockers,* wanted to build a structure which would not remind them of anything they knew, and the design of which would include a negative attitude to individuality—everything would be open and visible in the dome.[73] In the case of *Red Rockers*, the acceptance and transformation of the concept of the dome, which arose from Fuller's individual-oriented conception, into its complete non-individualized opposite, confirm its openness for appropriation. The dome was a structural reality and the symbol of the connection between equal elements, which seemed a metaphor for the connection between lives in the community or in the dome itself.

In some places, the dome was perceived as an extension of meditation, as an architectural form of yoga, where structural elements are visually merged into mandalas. In other places, the dome was symbolically erected as a spiritual center of a complex.[74] Building domes was also part of the restructuring of an institution. In the second half of the 1960s, Pacific High School on the West Coast, not far from San Francisco, replaced the curriculum with a set of unstructured practical and expressive activities, among which the building of domes with Lloyd Kahn, a co-editor of certain editions of the *Whole Earth Catalog,* and an expert on self-building, was extremely popular.

Also the editor of the famous publication *Shelter,* from 1973, which returns to the abundance of options for traditional human dwellings, vernacular architecture of the world, and anticipates the nowadays popular environmentally conscious construction, Lloyd Kahn included also the third part of the *Domebook* series. A year after the publication of *Domebook Two*, after many years spent in the dome, and the realization that domes as dwellings do not work, Lloyd Kahn self-critically assessed: "Metaphorically, our work on domes now appears to us to have been smart: mathematics, computers, new materials, plastics . . . We now realize that there will be no wondrous new solution to housing, that our work, though perhaps smart, was by no means wise."[75] Years of euphoric enthusiasm were followed by disillusionment. Domes did not prove to be a durable solution, let alone a sustainable one. Since the whole dome structure is actually a roof, unlike buildings with vertical walls it is fully exposed to all weather conditions. Domes had almost unsolvable problems with leakage, the fixing of elements, and the placement of furniture. In cases of domes as group dwellings, problems pointed out included the dome's single space, where everybody shares sounds, fragrances, and vibrations; if it was to be divided into several parts, it would lose its meaning, in terms of structure and perception. Such a problem turned out to exist even in the most idealistic communes, such as *Red Rockers*, where everybody lived under the roof of a single dome and, after many years of cohabitation, desired more privacy, crucial for personal growth and development.

Although domes were the most recognizable type of a dwelling in drop-out communes which caught media attention, experiments with forms of dwellings evolved in various directions. A range of inspirations, from Frederick Kiesler's *Endless House*,[76] organic structures from D'Arcy Thompson's book *On Growth and Form,* to free interpretations of traditional nomadic and permanent dwellings and the use of modern materials, gave experiments a variety of forms. Paolo Soleri's *Arcosanti* has been operating in the Arizona desert as a research urban laboratory of architecture fused with ecology. Charles Harker's amorphous sprayed polyurethane buildings experiment with sprayed concrete. *The House of the Century* of the progressive group, Ant Farm, could also be included, as could mobile units of converted trucks, houses, and houseboats, shacks, tents, wigwams, yurts, igloos, teahouses, treehouses, and inflatable and other derived structures. They all fused, or in their way responded to, the characteristics of the concept of the nomadic landscape of the countercultural movement. Although drop-out dwellings of anarchistic communes took various forms, most of them were characterized by single space, individual articulation of liberating forms, self-building without permission, and socially unacceptable lifestyle. Many communities felt the intolerance and physical violence of locals, had problems with the authorities, and were badgered by internal problems of mutual relationships, apathy, and life on the verge of existence. Only few such communes still exist today.[77]

In the early 1970s, geodesic domes seemed outdated and predictable: A hippie cliché. In view of the desire of total liberty of many anarchists, they were structurally too rigid and constraining. To achieve the anticipated effectiveness, they were technologically too demanding for self-builders, and marked as another urban construct of the technology of white people, which chased members of counterculture into the wilderness.

Certain parts of countercultural movements, which combined advanced technology, and the return to the origin and common ways of living with nature, were antipodes to radical urban projects of that time. While the American counterculture realized rebellion and the creation of *other* manners of living with the popular "DIY" approach, many radical practices with a similar formal expression and design elements elsewhere in the world resorted to utopian and rhetorical visions of urban futures.

British techno-utopia and experiments for the immediate future

Architecture of resistance—New Brutalism and une architecture autre

In the field of architectural theory and practice, the post-war period in Britain was anything but calm. We follow the emergence of a new generation which contradicted the dogmas of the patriarchs of Modernism and academism of institutions.[78] Within the London Institute of Contemporary Arts, an informal group called the Independent Group was formed, which was officially meeting between 1952 and 1955, and within which the basis for New Brutalism in architecture developed, in addition to the emergence of *pop* in the field of art in general.[79] The main representatives—artists Richard Hamilton, Eduardo Paolozzi, John McHale, William Turnbull, and Nigel Henderson, architects Alison and Peter Smithson, and critics Lawrence Alloway and Reyner Banham, who dealt with the research of modern culture *as found*—were often designated as the fathers of pop, although most important were their critical mindsets and creativity within the field of visual culture, the establishment of relationships between architecture and advertising, high art and mass culture, film and technology.

Through exhibitions, theoretical discussions, and architecture, the group offered provocative objections and alternative realities, aimed against the enthroned sweet national functionalism, and generally against "formal" and "machine" aesthetics of functionalism. With their projects and contributions in the second half of the 1950s, architects Alison and Peter Smithson, and critic Reyner Banham prepared a favorable ground for the proliferation of experimental architectures of the 1960s. By using various sources, from sci-fi magazines to modern architecture to Jackson Pollock's "high art," modern and popular technology, and Hollywood movies, to everyday life in the streets of London—modern culture *as found*—individuals in the Independent Group responded critically, and worked radically in the field of visual culture. The theories and practices of the Independent Group also had an important role: They focused on the erasing of the high/low cultural divide and, with their innovative approach, they reevaluated expendability, short duration or temporariness,[80] which turns out to be one of the key characteristics, both in production and in the use of the concept of the capsule which, however, was only developed in architecture by the next generation.

At their first meetings in the spring of 1952, sculptor Eduardo Paolozzi, with his projection of a collection of photos and advertisements from American popular magazines, hinted at the direction which pointed to the beginnings of "an other art"—which arose from the European avant-garde legacy, and was aimed against high art. The directness of Paolozzi's projection facilitated *imageability*[81] which, much like *un art autre*, had a special meaning for Reyner Banham, when devising his views following the concept of other architecture—*une architecture autre* as architecture suitable for the Second Machine Age.

The term *une architecture autre* was first used by Reyner Banham in the article "The New Brutalism" in 1955, which was considered to be a more relevant manifesto than the statement published by the Smithsons earlier that same year.[82] In this text, Banham links the New Brutalism with *le béton brut*, Le Corbusier's bare untreated concrete, and artist Jean Dubuffet's non-architectural *art brut*, certain aspects of the works of Jackson Pollock and Karel Appel, including Eduardo Paolozzi and Nigel Henderson from the Independent Group. The Smithsons set up the exhibition *Parallel of Art and Life* with the latter, which was for Banham a non-verbal theoretical framework of the emerging New Brutalism.[83] At the exhibition which was set up at the Institute of Contemporary Arts (ICA) in 1953, the aforementioned *avant la lettre* Brutalists presented a collection of 122 large, coarse-grained photos of machines, studies of slow motion, x-ray photos, non-western dwellings, tribal ceremonies, the anatomy of plants and other miscellaneous images which resist the conventional standards of design, beauty, and meaning, with the only image of "high art" a photo of Jackson Pollock at work in his studio. The selection criteria were imageability and emotional impact.[84] The Brutalist sensibility of the "rough poetry," which was developed, in its architectural sense, by Alison and Peter Smithson, through cooperation with Paolozzi, was an alternative to pop culture-related sophisticated stylization within Banham's critical field, and a completely authentic and valid response to the conditions of "mass production society."[85] The terms introduced by Banham to describe or evaluate the New Brutalism are the direct *brutality* of the expression of design, the integrity of the *image*, and radical *otherness*, which he reads in individual examples of architectural projects, and compares with their parallels in art.

The New Brutalism, which developed in Britain, does not denote an architectural style, but rather a program or an architectural demeanor which, according to the protagonists, is based on ethics, rather than aesthetics. The post-war generation of "Cathar" architects, within which the demeanor of the New Brutalism was formed, strove to reevaluate the origins of the Modern Movement, and to return to its ideals through the honesty that was, according to many contemporaries, expressed brutally, in the selection and use of building materials in the industrial, non-craft, manner, which should establish a connection of attraction between buildings and humans, and facilitate architecture as a direct result of the way of life. In the Smithsons' personification, the New Brutalism competed against the achievements outside the national borders, which distanced it from the then-modern "Britishness," and realized Fuller's goal of *world architecture*. In the socially responsible program, New Brutalism strived to encompass the cultural objectivity of society, its needs and methods, and to face and straighten things out with mass-production society, and especially to be objective to reality.[86] Of course, we cannot go past a comment that Banham recognized the decisive visual component by establishing memorability as an image in the rough poetry of the whole. He found this also in the Smithsons' New Brutalist school in Hunstanton, which had been designed even before the term was established among professionals, through the definition of three virtues— memorability as an image, clear exhibition of structure, and valuation of materials "as found."[87] Banham defined the image as something that is visually important, but not necessarily by the standards of classical aesthetics. By comparing to Thomas Aquinas's understanding of beauty as something pleasurable, the New Brutalist image would subsume pleasure caused by beauty and its negative pole—anti-beauty. In this situation, which transcends the "either-or" principle, affecting the emotions by practicing "anti-art" is emphasized. Banham concludes with an existentialist tone: "What pleased St. Thomas was an abstract quality, beauty—what moves a New Brutalist is the thing itself, in its totality, and with all its overtones of human association."[88] Although, according to Banham, the concept of image was common to all aspects of New Brutalism in England, he provided a more accurate explanation as an example of its use in architecture which, naturally, exceeds the field of classical aesthetics. In order to define the concept of image, he relates the visual and its physical, tactile properties of a building form. Visually perceived form is supposed to be confirmed by its physical experience in use. Banham emphasizes the importance of choice of materials, as well: "Further, that this form should be entirely proper to the functions and the materials of the building, in their entirety."[89] Slightly surprising is Banham's "classical" conception of a good building which, according to adjusted Vitruvian principles, determines the relationship between structure, function, and form. However, Banham then defines the difference between a *good building* and *important architecture* by means of the image, which must be immediately apprehensible and memorable.

The Smithsons who, in addition to the tradition of modern architecture, included their interest in older traditions of classicism and Japanese architecture in the reference field of New Brutalism, which enthralled the pioneers of modern architecture from the beginning of the 20th century, justified the use of materials and the informality of design with architecture as a direct consequence of the way of life, as in the original country life, beyond the interest in any of historical architectural styles, traditional canons, or aesthetic rules. But in their project at the University of Sheffield, Banham recognized another characteristic which points to the possibility of other architecture—a search for *une architecture autre*. He compared the use of *topology* instead of *geometry* as a composition tool, in this project with the replacement of Thomistic *beauty* with Brutalist *image,* and designated it as the only building or plan which completely corresponds to the threats and promises of the exhibition *Parallel of Art and Life*.[90]

When designing the concept of other architecture—*une architecture autre*—Banham leaned on Tapié's concept of *un art autre*, whereby the former should mean something similarly radical:

> An architecture whose vehemence transcended the norms of architectural expression as violently as the paintings of Dubuffet transcended the norms of pictorial art; an

architecture whose concepts of order were as far removed from those of "architectural composition" as those of Pollock were removed from the routines of painterly composition; an architecture as uninhibited in its response to the nature of materials "as found," as were the composers of "musique concrète" in their response to natural sounds "as recorded." Thus the final and absolute abandonment by "musique concrète" of any traditional kind of scale or even the twelve-tone series, and with it the abandonment of any kind of harmony or melody (in the sense accepted in the theory of music as taught in the "conservatoires") gave a measure of the extent to which "une architecture autre" could be expected to abandon the concepts of composition, symmetry, order, module, proportion, "literacy in plan, construction and appearance," in the sense accepted in the theory of architecture, as taught in the Écoles des Beaux-Arts, and piously preserved in the Modern Architecture of the International Style, and its post-war successors. By this token, "une architecture autre" ought also to have abandoned even the idea of structure and space – or rather, it ought to abandon the dominance of the idea that the prime function of an architect is to employ structure to make spaces.[91]

Banham's calls for *intangible* architecture, as an example of which he summarized Fuller's attempts to enable the conditions in the environment, with construction being a mere by-product, completely correspond to his positions stated in the essay "A Home Is Not a House," a year before the publication of the review entitled *The New Brutalism: Ethic or Aesthetic?*

For Banham, the concept of *une architecture autre* is a subversive proposal which would change the conception of architecture in its traditional sense. Therefore, Banham expressed his positive attitude toward Alison and Peter Smithson's project, *House of the Future* (see Figures 2.3 and 2.4), and his explicitly negative attitude toward other seemingly more traditional projects, such as *Patio and Pavilion*, with which the Smithsons and their supporters turned away from *une architecture autre* and, in his view, above all *vers une architecture*. When pursuing his ideals, Banham was relentless and, according to Whiteley, his championship of *une architecture autre* was radical. But, for the description of the value of certain New Brutalist projects in another way, comparable with Kenneth Frampton's concept of architecture of resistance, Banham relied on an architect in whose hands it can be "dumb insolent" and rebellious progressive architecture.[92] According to Banham, the architecture of resistance affirms itself in the Smithsons' New Brutalism through the execution of requirements to be objective about reality exposed in their definition, and advocacy of the ethical dimension of architecture, in spite of a slight and gradual withdrawal from *une architecture autre* by including diversity of formal expressions used in their projects in the 1950s.

Typologies of tomorrow—experimental practice of Alison and Peter Smithson

In 1956, two important exhibitions took place within the circle of the Independent Group. For one of them, Richard Hamilton designed the famous advertisement poster, entitled *Just What Is It That Makes Today's Homes So Different, So Appealing?* This was a collage from American mass media sources for the *This is Tomorrow* exhibition, which encouraged potential forms of cooperation between architecture and the fine arts.[93] Several groups, consisting of a sculptor, a painter, and an architect participated in this exhibition. By presenting the relevance of pop culture and Brutalism, it significantly influenced the generation of the 1950s and

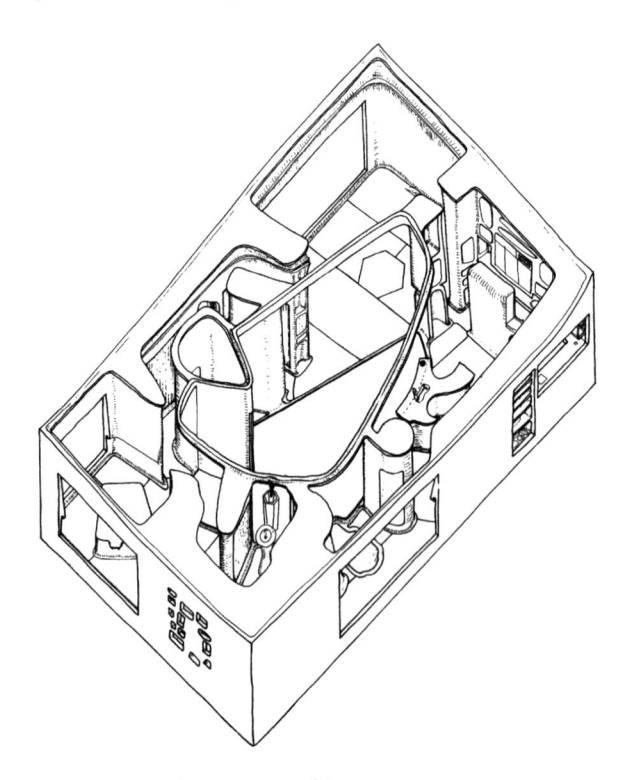

FIGURE 2.3 Alison and Peter Smithson, *House of the Future*, 1956. Axonometric

1960s. In cooperation with Paolozzi and Henderson, Alison and Peter Smithson erected the metaphorical shack with a backyard *Patio and Pavilion*, which was designated by Kenneth Frampton as an ironic interpretation of Laugier's *Primitive Hut* from the 18th century, adjusted to the conditions of suburban reality.[94]

In the context of the Cold War, the setting at the Whitechapel Gallery hinted at landscape which could derive from the ancient past or from the future after the holocaust.[95] Four months before the opening of this exhibition, the Smithsons presented the *House of the Future* at the exhibition *Jubilee Ideal Home Exhibition,* under the auspices of the *Daily Mail*, which is seemingly a contrasting vision of the *Primitive Hut*. It seems that the *House of the Future*, in the context of the Independent Group activities, indicated the ideal *different* dwelling suitable for Hamilton's muscleman, and his charming partner from the collage on the poster for the *This is Tomorrow* exhibition, and is merely a transfer of pop rhetoric to architecture, which was also mentioned by Frampton, with a negative attitude toward such experiments. A more comprehensive discussion of the British avant-garde of the 1950s puts such an instant image into a complicated context, since the similarity between the two is greater than seems at first sight. Although it seems that the pavilion projects are completely different, the authors and many critics insisted on their connection and continuity, as they both address numerous similar and popular topics, and conflicting social issues, and are aimed at the search for *different* patterns of living and the articulation of architecture.[96] The *Patio and Pavilion* and the *House of the Future* contained essential necessities for a human dwelling. They both encompass ambiguity and the intellectual response to the modern reality of the Cold War, technology, and consumer

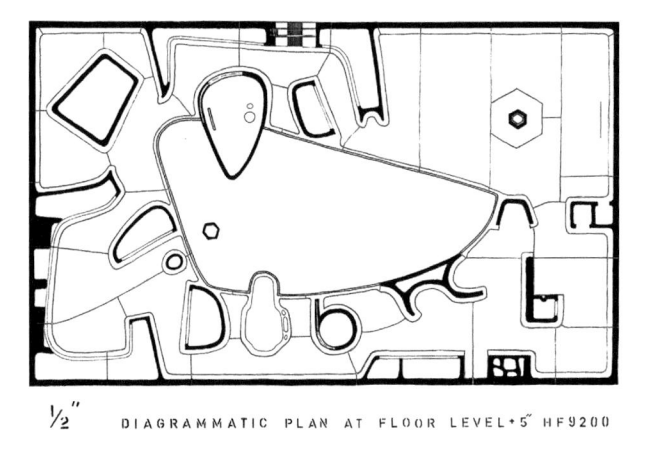

½" DIAGRAMMATIC PLAN AT FLOOR LEVEL+5" HF9200

FIGURE 2.4 Alison and Peter Smithson, *House of the Future*, 1956. Plan

society and, according to Alison Smithson, they represent continuity, as many ideas in the *Patio and Pavilion* had already been explored in the *House of the Future* in a different form: "The *Patio and Pavilion* was a pavilion in a patio. The *House of the Future* was a patio encapsulated by its pavilion."[97]

The paradigmatic projects of Alison and Peter Smithson, who were presented at both exhibitions in 1956 as life-size models, significantly influenced the experimental practices in the next decade. In the case of the *House of the Future*, the design, which seemed to many contemporaries a mere realization of pop architecture, was fully adjusted to the implementation in the anticipated material of the future: Plastics. Although Peter Smithson explained that the exhibition pavilion was actually made from plywood, as aircraft models used to be,[98] the forms fully utilized the characteristics of the anticipated material and mass production.

Plastics, which were invented in the 19th century, and were first patented and began to be more widely used in production only at the beginning of the 20th century, were used in the post-war period for car bodywork, bodies of vessels, and geodesic domes. The year 1956 saw a great breakthrough in the use of these new synthetic materials in living units, with the appearance of the first prototypes: Ionel Schein's completely plastic house, Schein and Coulon's mobile hotel units, prototypes of shelters for the extreme conditions of the Sahara and for the needs of the Swiss army, and, last but not least, the Smithsons' *House of the Future*, which was succeeded by the famous *Monsanto House of the Future* in Disneyland, with recognizable representatives also in Ceasare Pea's *Montecatini* and Rudolf Doernach's plastic houses at the end of the 1950s.[99] From the outside, the *House of the Future* was rectangular and without external openings, while on the inside, the composition of curved walls created an interior of ergonomically shaped ambients, and opened into an atrium made entirely of glass.[100] Most furniture and household appliances were anticipated to be of plastics and were built in. The flexibility of space was also improved, with an electronically controlled table and bed, which could be lowered to ground level when not in use. The interior was anticipated to be completely air-conditioned and heated. There was one entrance, which was well-controlled. The only contact with the outside world was a breath of "unbreathed air" in the patio, and a "part of the sky" which followed the *vertical tube of unbreathed private air* diagram in which the ultimate sense of privacy is represented by the only possible view from the patio—focused upwards, toward the sky.[101]

The projection of the *House of the Future* set in 1981 is also the result of predictions based on expert opinion: A period of twenty-five years in the second half of the 20th century was supposed to bring as many revolutionary changes as the last 100 years.[102] The curved "plastic" interior walls merely divided the homogeneous space, which was completely adjusted to industrial production, following the example of the automotive industry, which does not contain any repetitive elements as imagined for the prefabrication system by, for example, Konrad Wachsmann. With a reference to Frederick Kiesler's experiments from the 1930s, Fuller's sanitary unit, *Dymaxion*,[103] or even to "life in the womb,"[104] the house equipped with media devices—Captain Cousteau's underwater film was running on the TV—and food packed in plastic packaging, glamorous "spacesuits" of residents who simulated future living in far-away 1981, pictures of the exploration of the universe, etc., misled many contemporaries to have an unambiguous notion of the *House of the Future,* with emphasized characteristics of popular culture and mass technology, especially in connection with automobile aesthetics and consumerism.[105]

The Smithsons nurtured the idea of new consumer technology architecture in the form of experimental projects known collectively as *Appliance Houses,* all the way to the end of the 1950s, when demanding new projects and commissions significantly reduced their interest in experimental projects and conceptual thinking.[106] Their contributions, however, cannot be equated with excitement over consumer society, which provided the context for the creation of the concept of the capsule in Britain, although many topics of their endeavors were interpreted by members of the next generation of architects in a way suitable for them. Van den Heuvel pointed out that their endeavors for "architecture without rhetoric" were not aimed at welcoming, or even submitting to, consumer society, but to the connection between such society and architecture equipped with appliances.[107]

Although the *House of the Future* was not characterized by mobility, the Smithsons' aspiration for this ideal, despite the fact that such dwellings were in conflict with the environment, was clearly expressed in their fascination with a caravan, which got the closest to a mobile appliance house, a model of new freedom. Of course, the idea of a dwelling as a device is not new. Remember Le Corbusier's call to merge industry and construction, from the beginning of his book *Vers une architecture* (*Towards a New Architecture*) which, however, is slightly altered at the end of the book, in the chapter entitled "Mass-production Houses:"

> Eradicate from your mind any hard and fast conceptions in regard to the dwelling-house and look at the question from an objective and critical angle, and you will inevitably arrive at the "House-Tool," the mass-production house, available for everyone, incomparably healthier than the old kind (and morally so, too) and beautiful in the same sense that the working tools, familiar to us in our present existence, are beautiful.[108]

House-machine and *house-tool* are topics which constantly recur and interlace, and are later compactly combined in the apotheosis of the capsule architecture by its main protagonists.

As early as the end of the 1950s, Alison and Peter Smithson aspired to a mobile appliance house by relying on the caravan as its closest product on the market. They described the caravan as well-ordered equipment which has all the necessary components desired by the then contemporary user including miniature appliances, space heating, etc. In this sense the caravan relates to new forms of freedom and nomadism. The Smithsons also emphasize its symbolic potential for the "population in flux" and conclude: "as a form of dwelling … the caravan contains much greater potential as a possible pointer to a new basic 'parent' cell, embodying and implying a new way of life, than anything else in this country built since the war."[109]

The population in movement is also anticipated by the *House of the Future*, as it is designed in shapes that hint at movement—rooms flow smoothly one into another, as in a cave—and, in the conditions of a mobile society, it is intended for a young couple without children who will have to move eventually.[110]

In the *House of the Future*, architectural historian and theorist Beatriz Colomina sees, beyond pop aesthetics and excitement over the advantages of modern technology—particularly the architecture of paranoia—as a dwelling, the pavilion was completely closed but, like modern houses in reality shows, it was present not only in print media but also in television shows. Her comparison of the *House of the Future* with a bunker, a mechanism of withdrawal, represents the other pole which, a decade after the end of World War II and during the Cold War, established the typology of withdrawal from threats of the present, as well as a response influenced by still fresh memories of the war.[111]

At this point, a direct comparison is established with the explicit existentialist setup of the *Patio and Pavilion* which, according to its authors, was envisaged as a kind of symbolic "habitat" responding to basic human needs, including a piece of ground, a view of the sky, privacy, the presence of nature and animals, and symbols of the basic human urges, such as to extend and control, to move.[112] A wooden shack fenced on three sides and built on a sandy floor was covered with a corrugated clear plastic roof. Collages of photos, sculptures, and found items were placed in the pavilion, on the roof of the pavilion, and in the patio. But Peter Smithson also highlighted the other pole, and wrote on the setup as a painting of artistic flow, from the period of Samuel Beckett, Jean Dubuffet, Jackson Pollock, and Berthold Brecht with an existentialist tone. Although *Patio and Pavilion* was supposed to present a completeness, it exposed its unpredictable character of emptiness after it had been left by its inhabitants.[113] Openness for personal interpretation, getting accustomed and, also literally, self-reflection in the exhibited ambient, and expressed urgency and emptiness of space, led critics to seek meanings in the field of existentialism. In his negative attitude toward the *Patio and Pavilion* project, as if to say that such architecture comprises inherent fondness for tradition and the past, due to its fundamentalism, which was not in accordance with its orientation to the present of the Second Machine Age and the future based on it, Reyner Banham also recognized the dark side of its facing the past, which seems, in the exhibited work, as if it had been excavated after an atomic holocaust.[114]

Sarah Williams Goldhagen sees in both projects a complex criticism of early Modernism, and a response to the political, cultural, and social characteristics of Great Britain after the war, and stresses their existentialist tone. She believes that both the *House of the Future* and *Patio and Pavilion* encourage visitors of exhibitions to imagine inhabitation that would force them to radically evaluate themselves and their dwelling, as they represent a different vision of life which, with its aspirations for freedom and authenticity, questions socially accepted conventions.[115] One of the principles of the Independent Group was aimed at the authenticity of everyday life. Peter Smithson especially highlights the "content" of wealth and authenticity of the *Patio and Pavilion,* "loaded" with items made or found by Nigel Henderson and Eduardo Paolozzi, which cannot be imitated by any reproduction device, while vague images reflected on the patio's walls allow for a variety of interpretations.[116] The authenticity of the experience is supported with rough poetry of the Brutalist materiality of this "primitive hut," which emphasized haptics before the visual.

Materiality was one of the main topics of Modernism, and was particularly emphasized in the post-war period by many architects, from Le Corbusier's aesthetics of *béton brût* to Aldo Van Eyck's anthropological approach. In its definition, New Brutalism included an emphasis on the *truth to materials*, which is shown in both Smithsons's projects, discussed without deviation. If on the one hand the Smithsons wanted to create a spatial tool for the realization of freedom in the political and socio-economic sense with their architecture, they wanted at the same time to create a different, more personal, freedom based on a genuine contemplative manner of dwelling in their architecture. Williams Goldhagen adds that the Smithsons believed, or presumed, that such freedom, as summarized by Sartre's notion of authenticity, may be encouraged by the aggressive materiality of their architecture, in both the projects presented.[117] Therefore, a sensible solution to the issues of democratic freedom, expressed materiality and its relation to the notion of personal freedom, and continuity between the *House of the Future* and the *Patio and Pavilion* is contained in the concept of authenticity, which is the only thing that can connect, and give meaning to, these diverse phenomena.

Perhaps the answer to the question about the need to complete enclosure of dwellings is provided by the concept of authenticity which, in dialectic sense, extends between the outside world, sociopolitical–economic public space, and the enclosed space of privacy, which facilitates self-fulfillment, even literally, through the reflection of the outside world as self-reflection in its otherwise distant spatial context. The fact that the surface of the "glass walls" of the patio in the *House of the Future,* and the internal side of the enclosure in the *Patio and Pavilion,* clad in a reflexive envelope, acted as literal reflexive surfaces is not irrelevant. The awareness of oneself in the given space and time enables one to experience the fullness of life, which Henderson, Paolozzi, and the Smithsons wanted to present with the *Patio and Pavilion*, and in the form of a manifesto written in 1955 prior to the *This is Tomorrow* exhibition:

> The architect's work of providing a context for the individual to realize himself in, and the artist's work of giving signs and images to the stages of this realization, meet in a single act, full of inconsistencies and apparent irrelevances of every moment, but full of life.[118]

Although the existentialist search for authenticity, through the dark corners of confrontation with a disaster, is perhaps in contradiction to the presented *fullness of life*, both projects speak about a piece of sky, a vertical view of an individual in his or her dwelling, like in the diagram of the *vertical tube of unbreathed private air*. In addition to awareness of the authenticity of living, they both emphasize the peripheral protection of the habitat against external influences, and the verticality of the view based on it.

Buckminster Fuller's design of the *Garden of Eden*, a dwelling in the Arcadian landscape surrounded by a protective transparent dome, facilitated a view toward the sky, and defined a part of the sky as "your private sky." In the case of the *House of the Future*, similarity is also indicated by a painting which, in addition to the underground caves in Les Baux-de-Provence in southern France, enabled the Smithsons to realize the atmosphere in the house.[119] The *Garden of Paradise* by a German Master from the 15th century[120] depicts an enclosed garden with a fountain, full of tranquil life, birds, and greenery, and with a hexagonal table which got its mobile modern replica in the *House of the Future*.

Contemplation on pavilions and modern living conditions in general are presented by Alison Smithson in various articles in the 1980s and 1990s through an allegory about Saint Jerome,[121] with idyllic images from his life. On the one hand, she highlights the desert image, where Saint Jerome represents the human desire for freedom, and realizes it with ascetic withdrawal into a constantly reviving and, at the same time, unchanged natural environment of a cave in the desert.[122] On the other hand, the state of a complete ascetic surrender to the laws of pristine nature, and complete self-sufficiency beyond the socially dependent patterns, is balanced by an image of Saint Jerome in his study. The latter is the ideal space for the silence of internal peace in which a human who commits to a self-imposed task works. It is also an allegory of the desire to enjoy built order, the support by civilized services, the climate and weather control, and a perfected functional place of work.[123] Saint Jerome's *Study* is an idyllic civilized dwelling completely protected against external influences. Alison Smithson emphasized the urgency of such protected environments, which she compares with a *house-machine* from the texts from the heroic period of the Modern Movement, which also strove to enhance the meaning of this minimum *cell*: "Whether in an urban setting or in nature, all creative activity relies on being cocooned."[124] It seems that, particularly in the context of pavilions projects, she exposed a complexity which facilitates protection and even inviolability—the latter comprised of a functional space within a protected enclave.

In the *Patio and Pavilion,* a multilayered structure is uncovered: An "enclosed garden of (self)reflection" with a functional pavilion fully corresponds to the definition above, whereas in the *House of the Future*, enclosed functional space is also a hybrid peripheral protection structure, which facilitates a similar effect. However, the conceptually exposed vertical connection fits into the latter, which was designed as being completely separated from the surroundings, while it is manifested as the "weakest link" in the chain of protective mechanisms of the house. Pursuing a complete confinement of the *House of the Future* from external influences, Beatriz Colomina points out another detail which, in addition to the planned plastic cloud and artificial sun, was not carried out, only remaining a thought. The closing of the patio during the winter, with a mechanism similar to a camera shutter, was also a discussed possibility. If Le Corbusier's house, with a longitudinal window, is a camera focused on the landscape outside the house, the Smithsons' *House of the Future* replaces a horizontal view of the landscape with a vertical one.[125] Like a camera, it does so with a shutter lens, literally. Is the dialogue between the camera and verticality about a conscious play on the phenomenon of photography, the mechanism for the production of images of the pop everyday which, in any given case, "snaps" the dynamics of the infinity of the sky, about the fascination with the up-and-coming period of space exploration, or perhaps just about an existentialist or even paranoid response to the basic human need of a "view toward the sky?"

While the openness of the house toward the sky leaves questions unanswered, the duality between its designed interior and the generic impermeable circumference, which protects the living against any kind of communication with the outside world and, at the same time, completely denies the traditionally representative character of the envelope of the building, is completely unambiguous. This is also corroborated by a sketch of a potential urban setting of prefabricated *Houses of the Future* in mat cluster, cut up by the street network. *House of the Future* was not designed as a mere exhibition pavilion, but as a cell in the design of an urban "compact community."[126] Peter Smithson's drawing from 1997 (see Figure 2.5) highlights the characteristics of such an urban setting which, in an inverted sense, reminds one of drawings of the repetitive elements, perfect interior and endless cities, as ironically

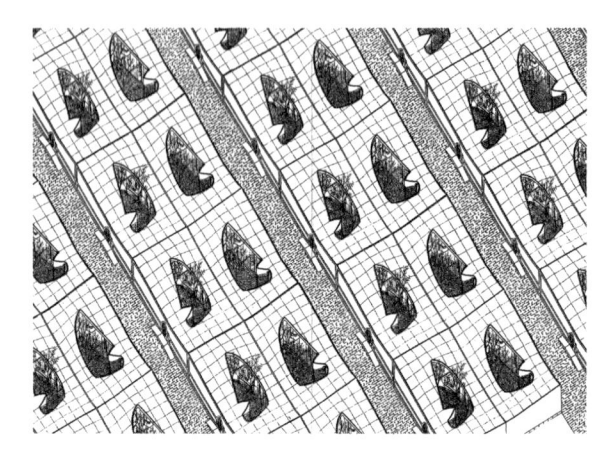

FIGURE 2.5   Peter Smithson, *House of the Future.* Axonometric from 1997

designed in the 1970s by the Italian (neo-)avant-garde, headed by the groups Archizoom and Superstudio.

Considering the openness, which was nurtured by members of the Independent Group by their rejection of the dualism of *either-or* and the favoring of *both-and*,[127] the *House of the Future* avoids the finality of interpretations with its own intentional or random ambiguities and comparisons with the *Patio and Pavilion*, and leaves them to the "fullness of life" flow. Due to the reserve of the Smithsons in the face of pop interpretation of their work, albeit the futuristic design of the interior and stylized space uniforms of "residents" of the pavilion, pop aesthetics noticed in contemporaries is only superficial. However, complexity enabled it to boost contemplation about a different, potentially other architecture. Reyner Banham briefly describes the *House of the Future* as a new point of view of the house built as a car, stemming from Le Corbusier's pun with Citroën and Citrohan, used in his first extensive discussion about prefabrication and mass production in *Vers une architecture,* from 1923. Banham also emphasizes a significant difference, since the Smithsons accept the technical obsolescence and material expendability which were rejected by Le Corbusier as non-architectural characteristics, as an inevitable part of the state of mass production, and use them in the typology of a house with a garden—one of the most classical architectural designs.[128] Despite fascination with the project, we must not overlook Reyner Banham's "ultimate" skepticism from the beginning of the 1960s, about the possibilities of genuine pop and other architecture—*une architecture autre,* both in the present and future, since buildings, in his opinion, are too durable to achieve the latter.[129] Therefore, Nigel Whiteley, despite a promising intention of product design to be transferred to the realm of architecture, which was implied by the *House of the Future*, and by emphasizing the fact that houses are not like consumables, as they are not portable, decides that this makes the Smithsons' *House of the Future* seem a deceptive promise of other architecture—*une architecture autre*.[130]

Did this indicate sufficiently explicit conditions, and a requirement for the realization of genuine pop, expendable, mobile, and technologically sensitive other architecture? The answer should be sought in the next, "fourth generation," which developed the *House of the Future* to completely new typologies with its obsession with industrially made, technological architecture, following the example of a car—namely, it is followed by the period of Archigram.

If Reyner Banham had reservations about the *Patio and Pavilion* project, which followed the *House of the Future*, Peter Cook from Archigram also wondered why the Smithsons terminated research projects like the *House of the Future*. These projects provided the next generation with starting points for the development of their own designs: "in the projects by my friends David Greene and Warren Chalk (the Pod and the Capsule respectively), homage is offered quite openly to them ... [while] I could dream of a mechanized *Cluster City* invaded by stacked-up *Houses of the Future*."[131]

The *House of the Future* hinted at the direction of potential realization of *une architecture autre*, which disappeared in the "traditional framework" of *vers une architecture* in next, explicitly Brutalist, projects. Therefore, we can conclude that Reyner Banham does not classify it in the recapitulation of the New Brutalism only to *brût,* but to *pop*, as a serious attempt of another approach to other architecture—pop architecture, even before *pop* was asserted in the form of *pop art* in the 1960s, and the Smithsons distinctly distance themselves from it.[132] Nevertheless, through an analysis of the New Brutalism between 1953 and 1956, Irénée Scalbert derives a statement that the *House of the Future* can be perceived as a Brutalist project *par excellence* by exposing materiality and formlessness.[133] According to the Smithsons "any discussion of Brutalism will miss the point if it does not take into account Brutalism's attempt to be objective about 'reality' – the cultural objectives of society, its urges, its techniques, and so on."[134] At least in the initial phase of the Smithsons, New Brutalism was not concerned with aesthetic traditional and classical notions of architecture, due to the exposed ethical dimension. We can corroborate Irénée Scalbert's statement with the logic of inclusion, which is characteristic of the Independent Group, as well as of New Brutalism,[135] and expand it, since of all New Brutalist projects, it was the *House of the Future* that laid the foundations for, and facilitated subsequent realization of, Banham's *une architecture autre*—particularly in the field of fusing modern technology and pop culture—genuinely other architecture, non-architecture, caused by consumerism and expendability, technology and mass production, which was brought by the Swinging Sixties, with the invention of new living patterns and the responding typology of the capsule.

The *House of the Future* comprises the physical closeness of the external envelope of the building with the supervision of the entrance and the technological surveillance of the interior with technological equipment connected to the infrastructure and facilitating contact with the outside world. It is fully made of one material and is suitable for mass production. Its informal configuration of the interior and distinct non-representative character of the envelope are emphasized, and functionally and ergonomically conditioned. As a whole, it indicates the characteristics of a consumer product, and provides the comfort of living in the perfect interior, "like in a womb." It does not meet the criteria of the concept of the capsule only in terms of mobility. Therefore, it can be unequivocally marked as proto-capsule architecture *par excellence*, which brings a wide range of architecturally articulated topics, questions, and responses into the discourse of *capsularity,* beyond the basic characteristics of the architectural object.

Reyner Banham's Second Machine Age—mechanical sensibility and democratization of the machine

By addressing technology in an emphasized manner, Reyner Banham, a member of the Independent Group, a promoter of the New Brutalism and pop, and an idealist pursuing *une architecture autre,* discussed the "mechanical" characteristics of design in the Modern Movement, in his articles from the second half of the 1950s. He did not link an adequate expression of modern architecture with style or engineering aesthetics. Instead, he was focused on architecture formulating its own aesthetics, which would be based on the technological reality and modernity of life in the 20th century. The revisionist criticism of the Modern Movement, which includes hints of suitable modern tendencies, was cultivated by Banham through the idealized *mechanical sensibility,*[136] which he clearly distinguished from the modern *machine aesthetics.*

Like Fuller before him, Banham saw, in machine aesthetics particularly, a dissonance between advanced slogans of the pioneers of the Modern Movement and their buildings, which merely simulated the effect of machines on construction with the simplicity of shapes and the smoothness of finishes, although the quality of final surfaces of the buildings most frequently depended on manual labor. Machine aesthetics clearly showed the incomprehension of the characteristics of engineering and machine production, and therefore Banham was in favor of accepting the machine *as it was.*[137] With his sharp, or rather genuine functionalist position, it was not hard for Banham to see a response to stylized Modernism in the emerging New Brutalism, which was similar to his own position. By engaging historiography, and with sincere optimism about the future, he provided theoretical and moral support to certain experimental practices in the 1950s, and particularly in the early 1960s.

With his extremely influential book, *Theory and Design in the First Machine Age,* which was published in 1960, Banham filled the void from 1914, when Nikolaus Pevsner concluded his *Pioneers of Modern Design.*[138] Desiring to resolve the problem in the remnants of academic culture, which obscured the understanding of the modernist vision of the future of the Machine Age, he included in his discussion those architects who, in his opinion, truly influenced the development of Modernism, with their sincere faith in the power of technology and science to support the development of architecture. With the rehabilitation of overlooked movements, such as Expressionism and Italian Futurism, which were discussed by historiographers before him only briefly, or were completely left out by them, in their reviews of modern architecture, due to inconsistencies with the image of a stable Modern Movement, Banham emphasized the technological factors of buildings, which influenced their shape, and eagerly marked Futurist Antonio Sant'Elia "a pioneer of the International Style."[139] Banham was particularly fascinated with the Futurists' radical idea of technology, which enables constant changes. In his manifesto of Futurist architecture, Sant'Elia highlighted changeability as a quality of the movement: "the fundamental characteristics of Futurist architecture will be its impermanence and transience. THINGS WILL ENDURE LESS THAN US. EVERY GENERATION MUST BUILD ITS OWN CITY.[*sic.*]"[140] This is a historically important position since, as Whiteley points out, obsolescence and transience have never been promoted as key characteristics,[141] but they were, together with liberating technology, particularly attractive for Banham's theoretical position and the search for other architecture— *une architecture autre.*

Faith in the liberating effects of technology, in the fields of society, politics, culture, and, last but not least, dwelling of each individual, is not characteristic of the post-war period. It merely followed from the period of Heroic Modernism, while most protagonists still viewed technology optimistically, but with a critical response to superficial derivations of the canon. Banham was a modernist in the real sense of the word, but with more complex positions regarding proverbially modernist disambiguations, and also highly optimistic about modern technology which, for him, did not have a political disposition. For him, technology was

FIGURE 2.6 Richard Hamilton, Self-Portrait, cover of *Living Arts,* 2, 1963. Photo: Robert Freeman. The cover image, set by technological consumer goods and pop lifestyle artifacts included the Mercury capsule. In the magazine, it was accompanied by Hamilton's saturated text Urbane Image with the glossary of the "expert" pop/technology terms, which portrays the affirmative culture of the early 1960s

"morally, socially, and politically neutral, though its exploitation may require adjustments of social and political structures, and its consequences may call moral attitudes in question. Technology is a commonwealth of techniques exploited to serve a disparity of human needs."[142] The optimistic view of technological progress and the bright future of the generation of enthusiast "experimentalists" in the early 1960s were as strong as Banham's, so that it took him quite a few years to admit his naivety.[143]

In the epilogue to *Theory and Design in the First Machine Age,* Reyner Banham doubts the suitability of modernist machine metaphors, as if to say "It may well be that what we have hitherto understood as architecture, and what we are beginning to understand as technology, are incompatible disciplines."[144] However, in his activity as a critic, he attempts to maintain the pace, which can be recognized in the book on the basis of the historical discussion and "mistakes of predecessors," and is described as:

> The architect who proposes to run with technology knows now that he will be in fast company, and that, in order to keep up, he may have to emulate the Futurists and discard his whole cultural load, including the professional garments by which he is recognized as an architect. If, on the other hand, he decides not to do this, he may find that a technological culture has decided to go on without him.[145]

Although Banham does not provide a definition of the Second Machine Age, the main difference from the first is indicated through the meaning of mass availability, and the use of domestic electronics, which enthrones a democratic period of an average man equipped with technology and mass culture. Despite losing hope that *pop architecture* and *une architecture autre* would be realized at the end of the 1950s, an impulse occurs for Banham on the experimental architectural scene at the beginning of the 1960s, which gave him new zeal and the possibility to revise the refuted assumptions. This is about a new generation of architects which, in Swinging London, shook the traditional framework of the profession, and by pursuing the *new* and the *other* by carrying out experiments of the previous generation, devises also a new typology of the capsule.

Technology, pop, and consumerism—experimental typologies of Archigram

The avant-garde position with non-avant-garde tone—pop culture of mass media, consumerism, and free time of the Independent Group, the New Brutalism as a return to the roots of Heroic Modernism, with means adequate for the *Zeitgeist* of modern society, and Reyner Banham's commitment to mechanical sensibility and *une architecture autre*—paved a favorable way for carefree British experiments at the turn of the 1960s. The arrival of the new style, "the look," the democratization of avant-garde, and generally accepted consumerism, which contributed to the eruption of Swinging London in the mid-1960s with shopping, proclaimed Britain as the leading global power of pop culture.[146] One of the main reasons for the perfect success of the explosion of the "city of youth" in the early 1960s can be found in the connection which fused already generally accepted pop music and pop art with emerging pop fashion and pop design.[147] Aestheticized and humanized Contemporary Style of the *Festival of Britain* based on Modernism was considered the mainstream aesthetic orientation at the beginning of the 1960s, when it was rocked by "revolutions." "The look," however, meant a return of geometric correctness and modularity, which was demonstrated in product design and, in architecture, in the use of circles and cylinders, squares and rectangular solids, as well as balls, domes, and facilities based on a hexagon as constituents of characteristic compositions. In architecture, the attachment to geometric formality can be found particularly in the design of individual elements (living units) while, in accordance with the legacy of the avant-garde of the 1950s, compositions follow the a-formal principles, in which connections between elements enable or indicate vagueness or incompleteness of the whole composition.

While the Smithsons's desire was to reestablish, with the New Brutalism in the 1950s, the connection with the original principles of the Modern Movement, and give meaning to them in the post-war social, cultural, and economic reality of new technologies, consumerism, and popular culture, the emerging British neo-avant-garde of the 1960s was less academic, at least as far as the establishment of the modernist continuity is concerned. Like Buckminster Fuller in the late 1920s, and Brutalists and the influential Reyner Banham after him, Archigram from London, composed of Warren Chalk, Peter Cook, Dennis Crompton, David Greene, Ron Herron, and Mike Webb, whose experiments included the definition of a new typology of the capsule, first desired to clear things up once and for all with machine aesthetics. In the first issue of the *Archigram* magazine, in 1961, David Greene announced the orientation of the group: "A new generation of architecture must arise with forms and spaces which seems to reject the precepts of 'Modern' yet in fact retains these precepts. WE HAVE CHOSEN TO BY PASS THE DECAYING BAUHAUS IMAGE WHICH IS AN INSULT TO FUNCTIONALISM." [*sic.*][148] Post-war skepticism about the redeeming power of technology of Team 10, and certain representatives of the older generation, did not shake the open optimism and enthusiasm with the *new* for Banham and Archigram, but were still within the functionalist direction.

Although architectural drawings of Archigram seem unrealizable, because of their affection for the future, we cannot accuse them of being disconnected from reality: Since they draw from everyday life the actual reality of the modern world—from popular culture, mobility, advertising, and fashion to state-of-the-art technology, the use of materials, and achievements of space engineering. With distinct efforts to truly realize Le Corbusier's and the modernist maxim of *machine for living in*, mobile projects of Archigram, according to Simon Sadler, relativized the relationship between the *firmitas* of a building as an essential prerequisite of its *utilitas* and *venustas,* and destabilized a historically conditioned thesis of the architecture of the western world that the latter is static art.[149] The architecture of Archigram was clearly anchored in the Second Machine Age, and was emotionally and technologically connected with the "space age" of the 1960s. With its independent, portable, and completely equipped structures, it even shook Banham's skeptical stance on the possibility of pop architecture, which thus got a new dimension, and new hope for the realization of *other architecture—une architecture autre.*

The poetry of mass production found its successors in Le Corbusier and the Smithsons, and the *House of the Future* got its first reinterpretations on home turf. For student apartments, Peter Cook's project *Car Body/Pressed Metal Cabin* from 1961 proposed dwelling units mass-produced like cars, and stacked around the central service core. This project shows the duality between infrastructure/construction and living units, which peaked in his *Plug-in City* (see Figures 2.7 and 2.8), and best summarizes in the first half of the 1960s the endeavors of the group and the conceptual background of many individual projects of other members of the group. The definition of *Plug-in City* reads:

> The Plug-in City is set up by applying a large scale network-structure, containing access ways and essential services, to any terrain. Into this network are placed units which cater for all needs. These units are planned for obsolescence. The units are served and maneuvered by means of cranes operating from a railway at the apex of the structure. The interior contains several electronic and machine installations intended to replace present-day work operations. Typical permanence ratings would be:

Bathroom, kitchen, living room floor: 3-year obsolescence
Living rooms, bedrooms: 5–8-years obsolescence
Location of house unit: 15 years' duration
Immediate-use sales space in shop: 6 months

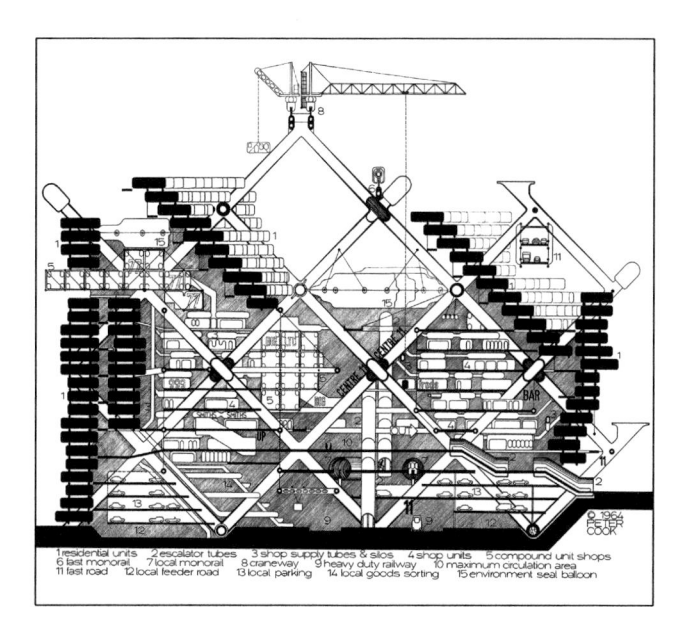

FIGURE 2.7   Peter Cook, Archigram, *Plug-In City*, Typical Section, 1964

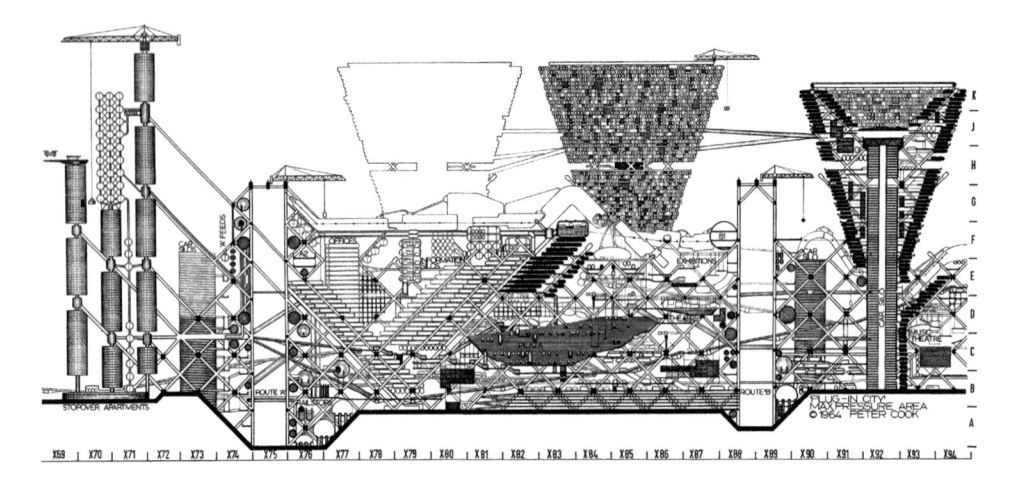

FIGURE 2.8   Peter Cook, Archigram, *Plug-In City*, Max Pressure Area, 1964

> Shopping location: 3–6 years
> Workplaces, computers, etc.: 4 years
> Car silos and roads: 20 years
> Main megastructure: 40 years.[150]

The proposal, however, was not completely unfounded. The idea of factory-made dwellings following the example of a car was not just a pop deviation, but was focused on solving the housing problem which, in the British Government's plans in the mid-1960s, comprised 400,000 new homes annually. According to Sadler, on the way to attain this goal, *Plug-in City* with *private* capsules, which are connected to *public* infrastructure, was perhaps the "third way" between public- and private-sector housing.[151]

From the second half of the 1950s, the interest of architects in mobile shelters for extreme conditions during Antarctic expeditions, with designs of circular shelters, under the leadership of Vladimir Bodiansky, the scientific and technological approach to space exploration and shelters on the moon, the conditions in underwater worlds, the technological prosthetics for humans, and for the symbiosis of technology and ecosystems was very much alive. In addition to the direct relation between the concept of the living capsule and the space capsule there was a field of inspiration for experimental projects.[152] When Warren Chalk began using the word *capsule* in 1964, Archigram also operated as part of *Taylor Woodrow Design Group* led by Theo Crosby, who supplied it with experimental projects.[153] The duality between infrastructure and living units was anticipated as the only limitation in the design of completely prefabricated apartments, which should be stacked in the structure of a tower. When designing the circular tower, employing plug-in prefabricated living units,[154] Chalk was inspired by the space capsule with a completely different concept and effectiveness from the traditional building, which is shown in *Capsule Homes* (see Figure 2.9) with "the ergonomy and the sophistication of a space capsule."[155] Peter Cook highlights the characteristics and the name of the capsule inspired by a space race, before its final form:

> That this particular piece of design was to do with production, expendability, extend-ability and consumer association cannot avoid the contention that to name it "capsule" at that point in time (1964) was highly evocative, even if the unit itself does not actually have to look like a capsule.[156]

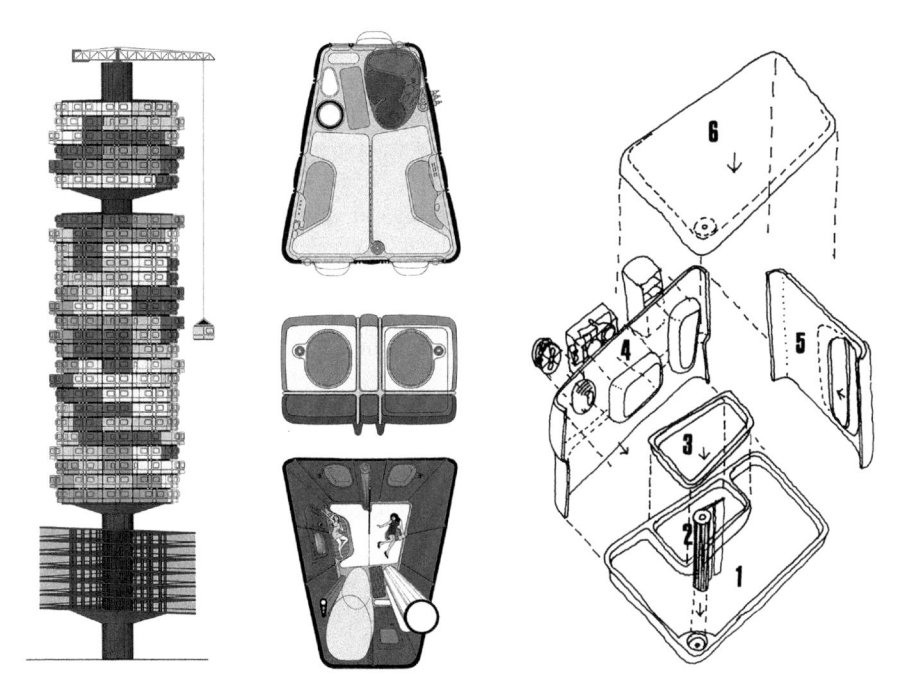

FIGURE 2.9 Warren Chalk, Archigram, *Capsule Homes*, 1964. Tower and Capsule elevations, plans, and details: (1) floor tray, (2) pull-out screen, (3) bed tray, (4) audio-visual component, (5) inner wall leaf, (6) ceiling tray

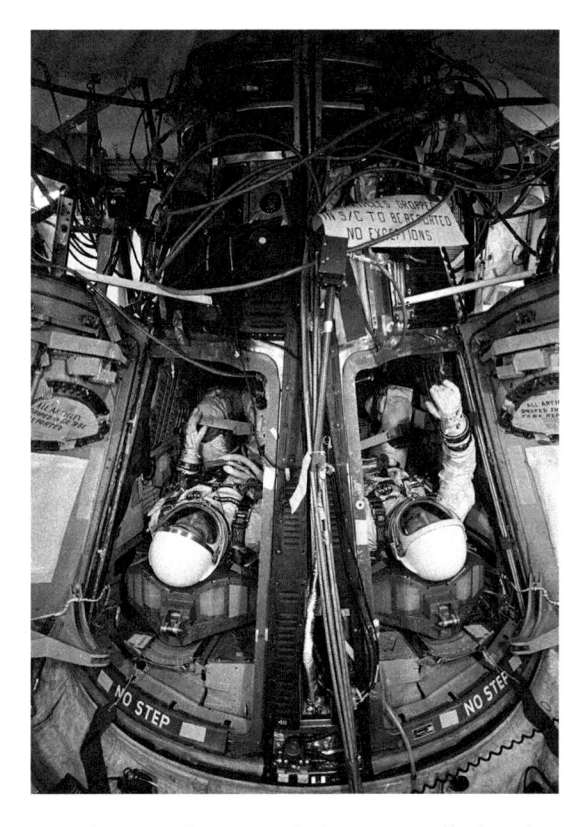

FIGURE 2.10 Astronauts Walter M. Schirra Jr. and Thomas P. Stafford in the *Gemini-6* capsule during a simulated test at Launch Complex 19, Cape Canaveral, Florida, 1965

Following the example of a car, the capsule was composed of individual parts which were completely replaceable, in view of the needs and development of technology.

> Conceptually, the "capsule" serves to describe an approach to housing by presenting a series of very sophisticated and highly *designed* elements locked together within a "box" which is itself highly tailored. It is an industrial design approach. It implies a deliberate—even a preferred—lifestyle. It suggests that the city might contain a defined conglomeration of such a lifestyle, rather like a hotel.[157]

At first, units were anticipated to be made of sheet metal or plastics but, later, the group was also interested in the use of paper as the basic material. As in Fuller's designs *4D Timelock* and *Dymaxion House*, the mast constitutes the central load-bearing infrastructure-equipped core, to which individual capsules are clipped. All parts could be opened up, detached from or attached back to the core. The manipulation of smaller elements and their clip-on to the load-bearing infrastructure was technically integrated into the design, while the manipulation of larger parts was anticipated to be carried out with a crane, which later became a recognizable emblem of *high-tech* architecture.

Warren Chalk's capsule has the basic characteristics of a single-space cell with a tight envelope, to be made of one material (sheet metal, plastics, or paper), complete furnishings with an ergonomically designed sanitary section, a wall to which various technological devices are clipped and on which individual parts may be replaced, a storage unit, and service connections.

A transportable and mobile *capsule home*—a living unit—also includes smaller monofunctional capsules. Despite minimum spatial conditions, partial flexibility, which implies the possibility of using the space of the living unit in various ways, is provided with a pull-out screen, which divides the capsule into two parts. The capsule, the design of which does not remind one of a space capsule, is wedge-shaped, brought on by the radial design of the tower and clipping units on the central core. But a direct comparison of Archigram's capsules with space capsules is interesting. Due to their position on the rocket, the latter were cone-shaped and, therefore, wedge-shaped in the ground plan or cross-section. If we disregard size, the shape of the partition in *Capsule Homes* from 1964 is very similar to the *Gemini* space capsule tested by NASA from April 1964 (see Figures 2.10 and 2.11), which took a crew to space several times in 1965. The capsule from the Ron Herron and Warren Chalk's *Gasket Homes* project from 1965 is also visually related to the characteristics of the sealed capsule, with the shape of its sealing edge.[158]

Rounded corners of the unit correspond to the method of mass production of individual components of the anticipated material, and to the design trends of the 1960s. Contact with the outside world is provided, in addition to the entrance, by two small "airplane" windows and, particularly, by the technological equipment, as part of the clip-on appliance wall with audio-visual components. Warren Chalk's capsule is a logical project for mass-produced living units as consumer products, which originate in, or result in, latent nomadism, and the restructuring of social relations.

The typology of the capsule is a compatible experiment also used in the whole composition of Peter Cook's *Plug-in City*, then and still today the most impressive product of Archigram.[159] *Plug-in City* was a combination of ideas from the period between 1962 and 1964, and is based on a massive megastructure with replaceable living units from the aforementioned projects

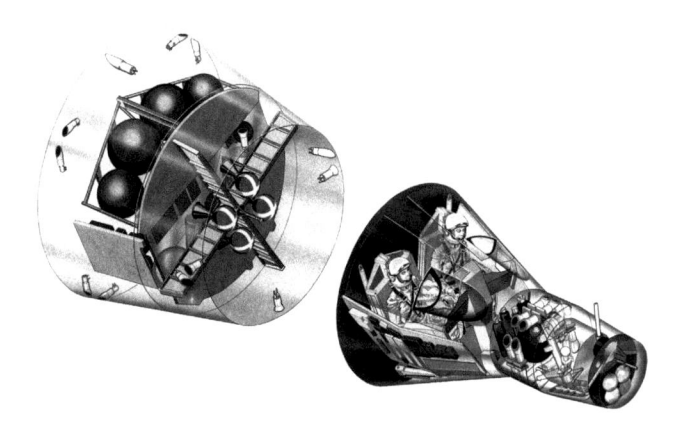

FIGURE 2.11 *Gemini* spacecraft with a Command Module for two astronauts

on student apartments. According to Banham, it radically changed the style and tone of megastructuralism throughout the decade.[160] At the scale of the whole city, the dynamic megastructure comprised all key elements of technological pop architecture for a pop lifestyle of constant changes and stimuli, excitement, action, fun, and expendability. The key to the possibility of constant incompleteness and indeterminacy of design or informality lies in the concept of a "plug-in," where the living cell/capsule is plugged into the infrastructural frame of the megastructure, like in a socket. The idea of the unlimited repetition of mass-produced modular elements pinned to one another—for example with the Consortium of Local Authorities Special Programme (CLASP) system, with which several schools were built in Great Britain in the post-war period—was designated by Reyner Banham as a predecessor of the new generation, which does not regard endlessness by assembling individual building elements, but as the assembly of parts which are units large enough to live in. The legacy of the New Brutalism, and contemplation about the design of endless and informal or even a-formal buildings, the parts of which are interchangeable and replaceable, led to architecture that is indeterminate in design. Architectural design was focused on *enabling,* not on *determining* a larger composition of a city, and on designing ergonomically fitting constituents of individual units. In search of the predecessors of plug-in and clip-on capsules of Archigram, Banham recognized the qualities of living cells, which were increasingly part of industrial design and less a part of architecture, in the Smithsons' *House of the Future* and in Schein and Coulon's mobile hotel units. According to Banham, the living capsules as completely furnished mobile and transportable independent units, were supposed to enable "the psychological and aesthetic break" which is necessary to liberate architecture from its traditional rootedness in the ground.[161]

Banham illustrates the clip-on concept with an outboard motor, with which any vessel may be equipped, and compares it to Fuller's *Mechanical Wing*, which may turn any living envelope into a dwelling fit for living. Originally, the clip-on concept was that of clipping a source of energy onto a living cell which, according to Banham, may also be used in the opposite direction of clipping the living cell onto an infrastructure, for which Archigram used the term "plug-in." Banham emphasized that the concepts were "technically often intimately confused in a single project," and underlines the point in aesthetics: "The aesthetic is still the Clip-on Aesthetic. But multiplied by a wild, swinging pop-art vision …," which differs greatly from the established intellectually rigorous prefabricated systems of pragmatic picturesque technology.[162] In the first half of the 1960s, the concept of the capsule unit was presented by Archigram as an element clipped onto the load-bearing and infrastructural frame, or the core, of a megastructure. The duality between a permanent megastructure, and temporarily clipped-on or plugged-in and expendable capsules fully corresponds to the functional model of consumer society, and mirrors the still present desire to at least regulate, if not design, architecture and the city.

Plug-in City is directly related to the *Living City* exhibition set up by Archigram at the ICA in London in 1963. As the first joint work of the group through structured situations, entitled "Man, Survival, Community, Communications, Movement, Place, and Situation," the installation established a framework *modus operandi,* which can be seen in the group's projects over the next years, and was fueled through the informal expression, temporariness, consumerism, fun, democracy, individuality, social, political, and economic liberalism, and through "belief in the city as a unique organism."[163] The aim of the exhibition was to depict a sense of living, which was the key quality for the new generation. Simon Sadler sums up that the exhibition, by its "assault on the senses" through image, text, sound, and light, was an attempt to convey the key characteristics of the constantly emerging city, and highlight the natural and cultural pluralism as an inevitable quality of urbanism. It proposed an "existential" approach to design, with the problem of being taking precedence over knowledge.[164] Although Archigram's projects may seem to be a radical break, without any continuity, the group wanted to show itself, in addition to perhaps the inexplicit British "existential" approach, which was also developed by the Smithsons, in the historical context.

The *Living City* exhibition was presented in the continuity of important exhibitions in Great Britain, from the presentation of modern architecture of the Mars group in 1938, which inspired post-war architecture, through the *Festival of Britain* exhibition, the influence of which degenerated into Victorian picturesqueness, to the aforementioned *This is Tomorrow* exhibition in the Whitechapel Gallery, where several works of various groups were exhibited, with the influences of the latest architectural culture of the New Brutalism, and American popular culture. The latter greatly influenced the generation that organized the *Living City* exhibition, while Archigram showed its respect for predecessors by including a picture of the mascot—Robby the robot of Group Two, composed of Richard Hamilton, John McHale, and John Voelcker, which established pop culture as a credible means of artists, designers, and intellectuals, without which the *Living City* exhibition would be hard to imagine.[165] Through the emphasized and also inherited existentialist demeanor of the exhibition, which led the visitor through displays of life in the city, individual thematic clusters conveyed a general impression of the functioning of a living, lively city, which is completely different from the strictly planned and regulated modernist cities criticized by Archigram. The emphasized individualism, and the awareness of the need to establish personalized relationships, may be understood in *Plug-in City* as a democratic gesture of a constantly emerging city, and a city shaped by as many forces as there are residents or, more accurately, individual users of individual units—like capsules. Although *Plug-in City,* with the *Living City* exhibition, was focused on the human, many critics made comments about proposals of Archigram as being inhumane.

Warren Chalk from Archigram believed that, in the technological society, more and more people will co-create their individual environment, for which architects create the conditions for liberation from limitations presented by the chaotic situations at home, at work, and throughout the entire built environment.[166] Care for people was present in the work of

Archigram, but not within the traditional framework. The *Living City* exhibition presented their interest in behavioral patterns and the ways of life of a modern man which, in their opinion, did not correspond to the conventional approach to architecture. Therefore, the impulse of the social situation, in connection to the implicit need to create opportunities for modern, emancipated life, caused the need to seek new solutions in the field of science, new materials, and science fiction, desiring cities to enable *situations*, events, to generate, reflect, and activate life and motion within an organized structure. That is why we cannot ignore the fact that *Plug-in City* indeed *looks like* a "plug-in city," which could, ironically, also mean a reflection of a modern metropolis as a concrete capitalist jungle, this time carried out by Archigram with a completely democratic indeterminate concept of design, at the threshold of anarchy. The inclusion of an individual in the design and consumption of the city should give it the necessary vitality.

The framework of the desired dynamic atmosphere of the city caused aspirations for a structured plug-in city filled with capsules with various functions, although, regarding life in a living unit—*Plug-in City* capsule—Archigram remained within the framework of pragmatic logic, and the idea of housing as a consumer product. There was no authors' in-depth theoretical explanation about the devising and actual functioning of such a city, although many critics of Archigram would want it, which is corroborated by Reyner Banham when he marks Archigram as "short on theory, long on draughtsmanship and craftsmanship."[167] *Plug-in City* does not pay much attention to the possibility of functioning of a megastructural city, as it deems its visualization more important for the progress of technological architecture. Banham substantiates this thesis with an operational turn, which established architecture as the leading discipline: "Archigram can't tell you for certain whether Plug-in City can be made to work, but it can tell you what it might look like."[168]

Potential for Banham was, above all, represented by the fact that aesthetics, especially the *image* of architecture, could be the trendsetter in the development of technology. Banham even designated Archigram's set of living cells and support structures as the first successor of the image of architecture of technology provided by Bucky Fuller's Geodesic domes in the 1950s.[169] He relies on the liveliness and directness of the city of plug-ins, which also looks as such, and observers tend to understand this constantly emerging and changing incomplete organism, because of this. In addition to the visually attractive *look*, the understanding of the structure and functioning was part of a mosaic of the image. But complex images of various projects were not an end in themselves and due to their utopian potential and slogans, which call for a different future, they could not be marked as one-dimensional illustrations for mass consumption. If anything, we could claim the opposite. Sadler points out that, with *Plug-in City*, we are on the outer edge of the avant-garde of the 1960s, an avant-garde which was, like early avant-gardes, motivated to change the world with architecture, and not to create architecture which functions better.[170] At the same time, according to Banham, we should not mistake in ideal megastructural cities "a piece of British graphic opportunism for an ideological program," since collages of colorful plans settled by young attractive residents of "the leisured postindustrial world of the New Utopians" signify "an empirical solution to the problem of finding someone – anyone! – to populate them as it is a theoretical proposal for who *should* populate them."[171] From today's perspective, changes of the world envisaged by Archigram seem full of contradictions. However, just like with Banham at the time, their infinite technological optimism prevailed over the possibility of critical reflection, which followed in the second half of the 1960s and means, for Archigram, a shift in interest from the *hardware* of megastructural compositions to the *software* of individualized and *ad hoc* interventions.

In the second half of the 1960s, Archigram's capsule units freed themselves from megastructures, and pursued the realization of a true nomadism, temporariness, and mobility, and the radical change in social relations with absolute individualization.

Desiring to make a prototype of the capsule, which sprang up during Peter Cook's lectures at Hornsey College of Art, the group distinguished themselves with a more pragmatic approach, and designed the *Hornsey Capsule* with standard elements, intended as pre-family dwellings.[172] The concept of the capsule stimulated many of the group's designs. The experiment of capsule dwellings, called *Gasket Homes* (see Figure 2.12) from 1965 by Ron Herron and Warren Chalk was made up of plastic, was more independent from infrastructure, and announced new designs of independent living cells, such as *Living Pod* (see Figure 2.13), *Cushicle*, and *Suitaloon* from the next years. Similarly, in the case of Ron Herron's *Capsule Pier* from the same year, capsules may hang from infrastructure, and form a mutually independent random composition, either in the air or in water. This explicitly indicates the direction of Archigram's deviation from the megastructure to the interest in autonomous living cells as flexible, adaptable, and non-monumental as they can be, independently of any other support system.[173]

In 1965, David Greene designed the "living envelope" *Living Pod,* which is an autonomous and independent capsule with pertaining monofunctional parts—smaller capsules—which may also be used outside it. The exterior of the *Living Pod* recalls an independent lunar module on metal legs with the design characteristics of Kiesler's *Endless House*, which is equipped with movable capsules for the here and now of the Second Machine Age. Greene flirts with nomadism facilitated by greater personal mobility and the development of technology by rejecting permanence and security, and their replacement by curiosity and a search related to requirements about the house, and concludes: "It is likely that, under the impact of the Second Machine Age, the need for a house (in the form of permanent static container) as

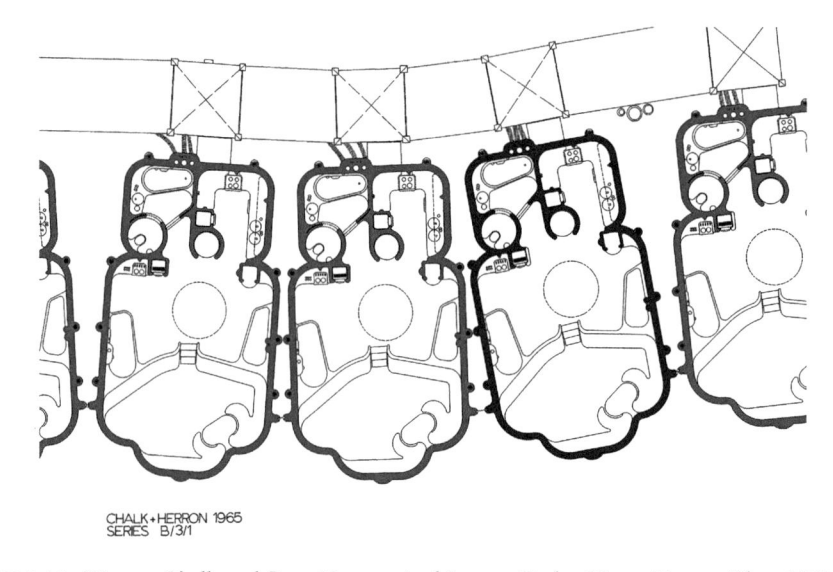

CHALK + HERRON 1965
SERIES B/3/1

FIGURE 2.12 Warren Chalk and Ron Herron, Archigram, *Gasket Homes,* Terrace Plan, 1965

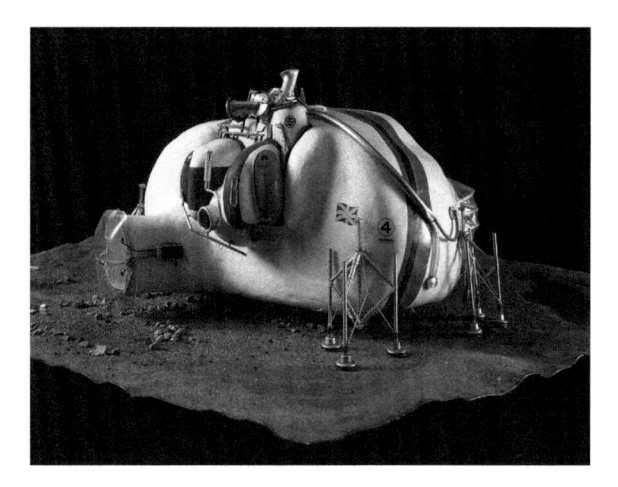

FIGURE 2.13 David Greene, Archigram, *Living Pod*, Model Photograph, 1965

part of man's psychological make-up will disappear."[174] The *Living Pod* was a hybrid unit, which could be erected independently, following the example of Fuller's *standard of living package,* or fixed to the infrastructural core or network. The *Living Pod* was Archigram's response to the Smithsons' call to "seek a positive message" in caravans from 1959, and helped realize Banham's call from 1960 which, by propagating mobility, showed the direction for radical proposals. For an established attitude of architects, a proposal that caravans were not standard apartments, but that, in many functions, apartments were substandard to caravans, was much more rebellious.[175] While the capsule is the realization of a machine for living in, and a house is an appliance for carrying with you, a city in Archigram's diction is a *machine for plugging into.*[176]

The 1960s also produced a phenomenon of a *bubble,* manifested in various ways, from the bubble fashion and economy, to the expressive temporariness of the bubble inflatable furniture and architecture. The design of inflatable space corresponded to the basic paradigms of the redefined perception of space of the Sixties: In the case of bubble architecture, a single space, roundedness, soft transitions between the ceiling, walls, and the floor, changeable shape, the changing of the light characteristics of the envelope, softness, mobility, and adjustment to consumerism were a very suitable consequence of the material being naturally given and of simple technical feasibility. Inflatable structures were constantly present in counterculture, at rock festivals and anti-war demonstrations, and established as consumer products in mainstream culture.

In 1965, Reyner Banham published his famous essay, "A Home Is Not a House," in *Art in America*, which encompassed telltale drawings by François Dallegret (see Figure 2.14) in which, following Fuller's *standard of living package*, he reduced a human dwelling to a technological services system, where the Modern Movement dream of total transparency and fluidity between indoors and outdoors could become an instant reality with a floating balloon—bubble *un-house*.[177] In the essay, Banham takes issue with the American dream of life in the suburbs, the question of controlling the environment, and the American way of spending money on mechanical services packed in an unnecessary monumental envelope, and enthusiastically proposes a more suitable form of a transparent balloon. Alastair Gordon

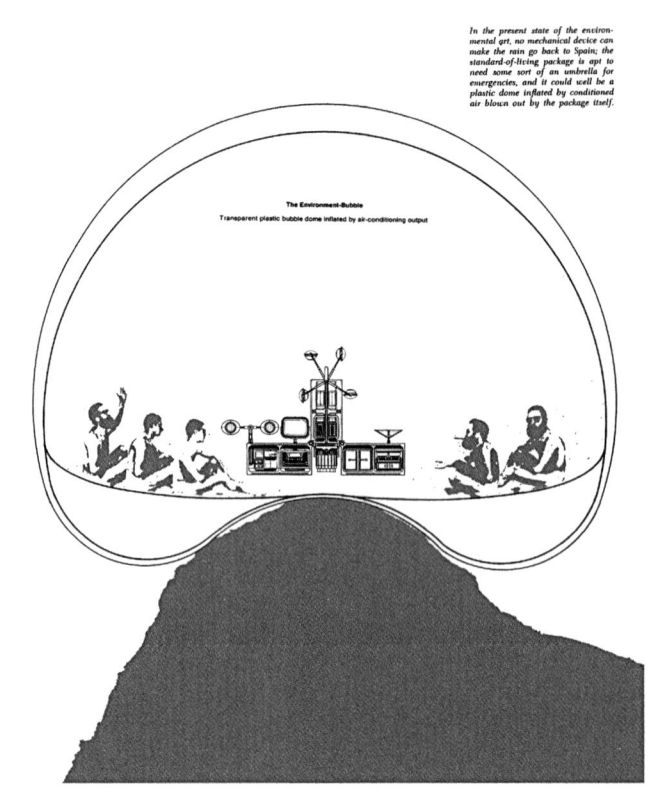

FIGURE 2.14 François Dallegret, "The Environment-Bubble Transparent plastic bubble dome inflated by air-conditioning output," showing architecture as a "fit environment for human activities;" from Reyner Banham, "A Home Is Not a House," *Art in America* (April 1965)

describes the situation in an utterly illustrative manner: "The astronaut sits across from the caveman, trading stories within the transparent igloo. In place of an open fire stands a high-tech service core for climate control and communication," and with a reference to Banham's essay, "Monumental Windbags," concludes that Banham's *Environment-Bubble* is an un-house artifact, where Fuller's theory of ephemeralization, of doing more with less, and McLuhan's retribalization cross-pollinated.[178] The connective media, in the form of the presented tools and equipment, reduced unnecessary material for a dwelling while encouraging communication and establishing new relations among its detribalized users.

In his essay, Banham explicitly rounds off the period of researching new living conditions in the Second Machine Age and responds, almost in a manner of correspondence, to Fuller's statement/question that "With the ever-increasing scientific development, the environment will be completely controlled and the concept of the house will be eliminated—we are working toward the invisible house—what will you do with architecture then?" with the concept of "un-house"—an environment-bubble or a *fit environment for human activities*.[179] It seems that Banham's focused essay, "A Home Is Not a House," is the final confrontation with the machine aesthetics and the monumentality of architecture in general, since he highlights the house-machine "as found." Banham wonders: "When it [your house] contains so many services that the hardware could stand up by itself, without any assistance from the house, why have a house to hold it up?"[180] Fuller's concept of *standard of living package* or *autonomous living package* thus gains a successor, which is attached to infrastructure, reducing its independence.

The development of Archigram toward dematerialization of the envelope was also the result of the perception of parts of a home as hybrids, which are comprised of different components with various mutually connected characteristics. Hybrid structures between a part of a building and furniture, a robot and a device, a device and a room, etc. led to solutions which made, with a tight envelope, users integral parts of the house-machine—cyborgs.[181] Michael Webb's *Cushicle* and *Suitaloon,* from the second half of the 1960s, are completely adjusted to nomadic life, and following Banham's example of an un-house, present an extremely dynamic execution of the concept of the capsule, with a clear definition: "Clothing for living in – or if it wasn't for my Suitaloon, I would have to buy a house."[182] The concept of the inflatable equipped space suit includes all the necessary supply for the minimum dwelling, and is the source of motion of the larger envelope provided by clothing, and of power. But Webb does not ignore the possibility of social interaction, since individuals' envelopes may be fused together, plugged to one another, and thus they enable individuals to enter and exit the envelope, and may mutually be bound together to form larger spaces. The aforementioned transportable dwellings combine the understanding of clothing and housing as one thing, which McLuhan still distinguishes as communication media and mechanisms for heat control—but potentially, as one medium, they bring the immediate design and structuring of human relationships and *ad hoc* communities, by propagating nomadism.

In the second half of the 1960s, the concept called capsule was more and more used for monofunctional constituent units of dwellings. In Archigram, we can follow projects focused on random and flexible space formation adjusted to individual events, which require parts to be assembled from the smallest monofunctional units. In the *Control and Choice* project, the concept of the capsule was reduced to an individual "personal capsule," where an individual may withdraw if they want to be alone,[183] whereas in the winning competition project for an underground flexible cultural and entertainment space, in Monte Carlo in 1970, the capsule was used to name individual mobile sanitary units and control kiosks.

In a retrospective on the creation of new typologies, Peter Cook marked the "capsule" as a "convenient term with which to discuss the perfected, industrially designed prototype home—with the space capsule somewhere in the background, creating the necessary rhetoric but also calling to mind the concept of totally interrelated parts and appliances."[184] Peter Cook mentions Buckminster Fuller as the godfather of the concept, the obvious reference to space capsules which provided necessary inspiration, as well as the "competitor" in the field, Japanese Metabolist architect Kisho Kurokawa, whose capsules were "the ones to beat." Nevertheless, Archigram was not alone in Great Britain in the field of capsule architecture. The new typology of the capsule emerged as the result of the changing social and technological reality, and preoccupation with the future, the information framework of which was being defined by certain professional magazines. If the leading magazines provided information on the progress of materials and methods of construction, and facilitated theoretical responses to "radical" projects, student and alternative magazines from the mid-1960s, according to Whiteley, fused "radical technology" and "pop technology," which formed the *autre* or the genuine *other* of the concept of architecture, which could be realized by Banham's *fit environments for human activities*.[185] On the other hand, Anthony Vidler pointed to the theoretical shift since, in certain projects, the use of the New Brutalist image together with technological innovations and pop rhetoric in pursuit of *une architecture autre* and Banham's exposed importance of aesthetics, which include the observer as well as their experience, showed the possibility of transcending the modernist duality between form and function, and enabled a comprehensive view on the environmental conditions, technology and design inventions.[186]

Technology and social transformation—Cedric Price and scientific technocracy

In British experimental architecture and design, the way was paved by architects from the Independent Group circle: Alison and Peter Smithson's and Reyner Banham's theoretical positions, as well as those of James Stirling and James Gowan. Cedric Price was an extremely active architect in the 1960s, along with Archigram, with similar interests but with a much more prudent, almost technocratic, iconoclastic, and practical approach—an architecture without the representative rhetoric. Desiring to facilitate a better life, and expand human potential in accordance with social changes, Price's projects and work proposed radical new concepts of architecture and the architectural profession.

His most notorious project, the *Fun Palace* (see Figure 2.15), was created in several versions between 1961 and 1966. It signified the establishment of a connection between technological flexibility and public participation, improvisation and play as an alternative to the outdated system of education and traditional spending of free time. Meanwhile, the project *Potteries Thinkbelt* from 1964 (see Figure 2.16) with the early use of the typology of the capsule, used the cybernetic structure at the regional level to revitalize deserted industrial areas, and to merge them into a regional educational center, a think tank.

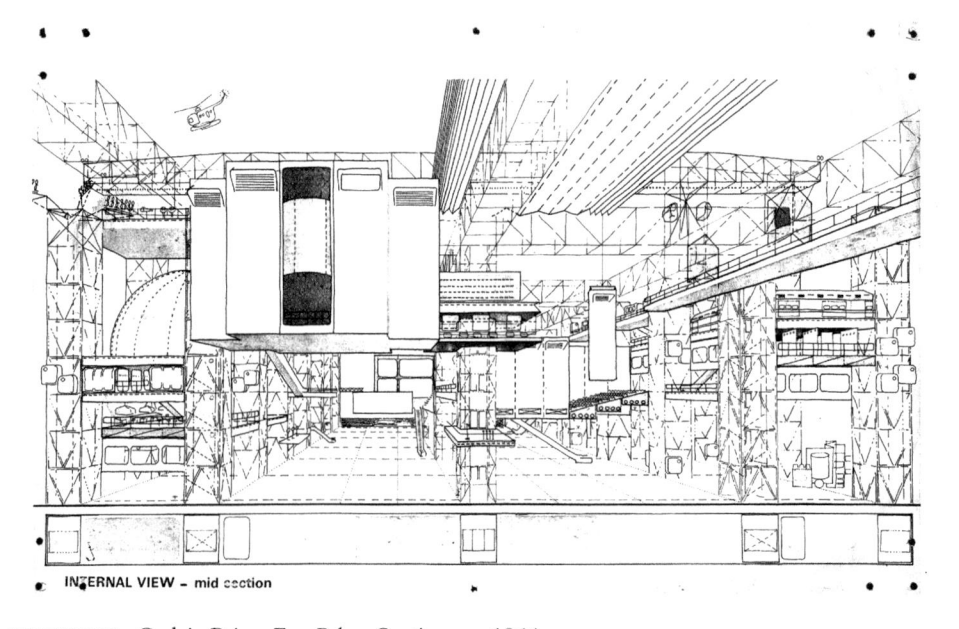

INTERNAL VIEW - mid section

FIGURE 2.15 Cedric Price, *Fun Palace*, Section, ca. 1964

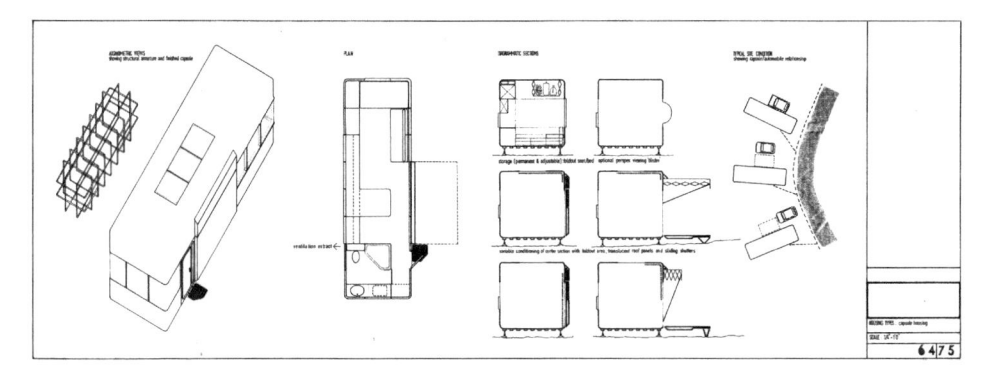

FIGURE 2.16 Cedric Price, *Potteries Thinkbelt*, North Staffordshire, England: Housing types, capsule housing 1963–1967

In both projects, Price used cybernetic and system technologies, which would facilitate constant changes in view of current needs, and the adjustment of architecture in view of the temporariness of social demands.[187] Enthusiasm over computer technology, game theory, and cybernetics coincided with the planning for unpredictable situations. Similar to Fuller's *anticipatory design*, Price's *calculated uncertainty* became the key "design" tool in his projects. These were the result of the work of expert groups, in which one of the key actors was an expert on programming and cybernetics. With its optimistic faith in science and technology, the *Fun Palace* project, was devised by Price in cooperation with the initiator of the project, Joan Littlewood, who was one of Britain's most influential and radical personalities among actors, directors, and producers. These two were joined by a group of enthusiastic scientists, sociologists, psychologists, cyberneticists, and politicians. Although Gordon Pask's cybernetic social control mechanisms installed in the project seem completely naive today, many had faith in the "purity" of technology, which should enable emancipation for everyone.[188]

This learning and entertainment machine was composed of a space-frame structure with "enclosures," or closed spaces, of two types. Although some of them had all the characteristics of the capsule, Price did not refer to them as such. Kitchens, restaurants, workshops, and lavatories were part of the category of a small-scale cell type with a lot of service equipment, while larger volumes, which need less equipment, were anticipated for programs of cinemas, auditoriums, and event venues.[189] Following many years of negotiations to sort out politics and financing to support the project, as well as finding a suitable location, the idea of a "mechanized shrine to *homo ludens*,"[190] as marked by Reyner Banham, with its initially undefined program, control mechanisms, and "frivolous" name of the *Fun Palace* fell apart in 1966. Prior to this, certain media also responded to the project with criticism. The editorial criticism of the *Daily Mail* in 1965 hints at a negative attitude to informal aesthetics, and fear of authoritarianism of the project, which looks "more like sanatorium than a fun palace. And more like George Orwell than Joan Littlewood."[191] The radical technological anti-monumentality of the *Fun Palace*, which was recognized and commended by Reyner Banham in 1964 as an advanced architectural expression, was not to the liking of the masses, although the "palace" was supported by certain representatives of politics and the local community, when it came to seeking a suitable location.[192] Banham described this "kit of parts," about which Price did not want to publish any images as to what it should actually *look like*, as its appearance was not regarded as important, as follows: "Seven nights of the week it will probably look like nothing on earth from the outside: the kit of service towers, lifting gantries and building components exists solely to produce the kind of interior environments that are necessary and fitting to whatever is going on."[193]

The *Fun Palace* example is important from the aspect of development, particularly as a project of *other*, technological architecture beyond representation and the environment of complete cybernetic control which, even as it emerged, caused discomfort and doubt about the reality of its socially liberating role. In the *Fun Palace* project, it was not the physical envelope of the building that was important, but the electronically completely controlled operation, including the activities of the participants, which would legitimately present it as a proto-capsular environment project, where electronics devised with "good intentions" could be used as the system of control and exclusion. Stanley Mathews also pointed out the irony of the acceptance of the *Fun Palace* project in connection with technology and "high-tech aesthetics," which Price rejected, since his main motivation was of a social nature.[194] It is hard to persist in the advocacy of the unambiguity of technology, since its results were frequently used in a negative way, and with disastrous consequences. Great distrust in technology was thus caused by its use for military destructive purposes, the consequences of which were nuclear weapons. Despite everything, skepticism did not halt the desire to make progress and use technology. After abandoning the canonic *Fun Palace* project, which was never realized, Cedric Price attempted to use the concepts developed within it in his further activities.

The substantive characteristics of the *Fun Palace* model were used by Cedric Price in the *Oxford Corner House (OCH)* project from 1965, which was not realized, and in the *Inter-Action Center* project, which was built in 1977. With the *OCH* project, Price planned the corner as a fusion of architecture and alternative education "unfettered by tradition – scholastic, economic, academic or class structure," which "permits and encourages self-pace exploration by the individual of his curiosity, skill and mental appetite."[195] A technologically advanced center, intended for individuals' development, included the division of programs according to McLuhan's division of media into "hot" and "cool," which were allocated design characteristics by Price. Organizational patterns for the "hot" programs were linear and rectangular, while the "cool" programs were organic and curvy—Mathews identifies "television viewing capsules" as the latter, and marks the *Center* as a predecessor of cybercafés.[196] In the *Inter-Action Center* project from 1977 (later known as *InterChange*), which was, similar to the *Fun Palace,* composed of a load-bearing space-frame structure into which larger and smaller units were installed, the latter were clipped on *Portakabin* prefabricated units, according to the system of clip-on capsules, although we do not notice this explicit denomination. The project was low budget, and materialized Price's conscious evasion of aesthetics, which makes this project different from Renzo Piano and Richard Rogers's famous *Centre Georges Pompidou* project, built that same year in Paris.

In the higher education facility *Potteries Thinkbelt* project from 1964, Cedric Price used capsule units, called as such, for housing. With this project, Price attempted to present architecture as a planning tool in the service of social progress and, unlike the fantastic schemes of mobile and megastructural cities of his friends from Archigram, he remained within practical and feasible frameworks. The *Potteries Thinkbelt* comprised cybernetic control of the territory and of transport, education systems, and, in addition to a radical alternative to the education system for the needs of applied science for 20,000 students, with mobile and fixed educational units; it also anticipated four basic mobile types of apartments, and named one of them "*capsule housing.*"

The types presented have various characteristics for them to be erected, in view of the conditions of the topography. The *capsule* type was to be stacked in linear layers on steep terrain, where other types would not be appropriate. The design of the *capsule* type anticipated a certain extent of personal selection of individual parts, and was planned for one person, or for short-term living of two people. Units from panel modular elements of the *sprawl* type had adjustable "legs" to be erected on various terrains. Modular units of the *crate* type were clipped onto the megastructural frame with various options of connection between units. Units of the *battery* type were designed in a similar way: The difference was that they were anticipated for "low rise" and equipped with adjustable legs, like *sprawls.*[197] The durability of individual elements of the whole regional *Potteries Thinkbelt* complex was anticipated, and Reyner Banham eagerly welcomed the fact that it was not concerned with aesthetics, and praised Price's engineering use of new modular container transport technologies as the only project which indicated the possibility of executing "goods handling aesthetics" without stylistic or cultural pretensions.[198]

In addition to the capsule architecture used in them, and their explicit iconoclastic tone, the *Fun Palace* and *Potteries Thinkbelt* projects are also important for their socially critical undertones. However, due to the social visionary approach, and the advocacy of individual freedom by means of modern technology and Price's explicit practicality, the projects are wrapped in a series of questions. Price was an extremely technology-oriented representative of the generation of architects of the 1960s, who stood up to the state of social systems and the traditional non-acceptance of technological discoveries with a scientific approach and lucid analyses, as well as with radical critical responses in the form of his own a-formal projects.

———————

In the mid-1960s, British media was awash with presentations and reviews of completely prefabricated functional units, most often made of plastics. David Kirby published in the April 1965 issue of *Architectural Review* a "historical review" which presented typical examples of the use of plastics in architecture between 1955 and 1964.[199] *Architectural Design* regularly presented prototypes, the production of prefabricated sanitary units, as well as the presentation of plans for Nicholas Grimshaw and Terry Farrell's spiral tower of clip-on plastic prefabricated bathrooms for the *International Student's Club* in Paddington in London, built in 1968 as a rare realization of the concept of smaller monofunctional capsules from that time in Great Britain.[200]

Over the course of a decade, the concept of the capsule underwent transformation from a single-space, fully equipped living cell, which could be connected to the infrastructure of a (megastructure) city from the first half of the 1960s, to a monofunctional space or piece of equipment connected to the infrastructure of a large or small living or activity environment, in the second half of the 1960s. After all, single-space living capsules in megastructures were part of the revolutionary tone of the transformation of society influenced by the technological development, while monofunctional capsules were becoming part of the pragmatic, immediately feasible reality, and remain, although not by the name of capsule, in modern architecture and construction as still the most economically acceptable manner of the construction of repeatable units, particularly bathroom and sanitary units, in the building of hotel complexes, housing, office, and other buildings.

Was the transformation of the concept caused by the undefined *subsistence minimum* or even *maximum* of the city of capsules for a potential *homo ludens,* or perhaps by an unexpressed need for such a typology of dwelling, although the proposed capsule dwelling may be understood as one of the first steps toward the formation of a new lifestyle through which this need could be expressed? Perhaps scientific and technological pragmatism was to blame, combined with the playfulness of the "why not" concept of angry young men, who indeed they were, if they had not accepted and enjoyed so vehemently the provisions of the capitalist system on the one hand, and lost their credibility, at least with certain critics, for lack of pragmatism on the other.

In a pile of pragmatic technological questions of mobility and adaptability of the city of capsules, and questions on economic, political, and organizational management mechanisms, including the marketing and sales of *Plug-in City* units, Denise Scott Brown pointed out the question of living patterns that change in the project under the influence of technological innovations and determine factors for the integrated design of living units—capsules.[201] She was surprised that no one had mentioned Richard L. Meier, for example his work *Science and Technological Development*, whose notion "Minimum Adequate Standard of Living—MASL" she deemed "quite pertinent to the encapsulated society."[202] In 1954, Meier, with an economic calculation on the assumption of equal opportunities of all people in the world, and the ability of their energy and other supplies, and taking into account the "physiological comfort, patterns of family life, the need to have contact with wider culture (magazines, books, television, probably phone, bicycle, etc.), the need to store, and other needs," arrived at a surprising result that, in a moderate or tropical climate, 6 m^2 of living area are enough for one person.[203]

Meier critically took up architects and their liberation attitude to space, and marked the position of the designer who thought that less than 20 m^2 of dwelling was not enough for an individual as scientifically unjustified, and, at the same time, mentioned that the Russians had managed to pull off the "economic approach" with 3 to 4 m^2 per citizen, or three persons in one room, with which the people responsible ensured just enough suitably equipped living space to enable adults to become reliable industrial workers, and prevented living outdoors in harsh climatic conditions.[204]

Nevertheless, we cannot accuse *Plug-in City* of a wasteful attitude to space, but it is clear that reference to a new lifestyle of consumerism and pop culture cannot be the only parameter to determine a suitable standard of living and dwelling, which seems technocratically determined and controlled, while the presentation of social relations is less clear. Meier is aware of the technocratic tone of his proposals, but he deems a more extensive scientific approach to the problem which, in addition to the review, and proposals of, new patterns of living, also comprises a detailed discussion of global needs for food and energy, the only approach acceptable.

Flexibility within a living unit was, undoubtedly, the topic of the described experimental practices, but we cannot expect great flexibility in compact living units, like capsules, owing to the smallness of space. In proposals where capsule units are anticipated as clip-on monofunctional elements, the flexibility of the remaining space is all the more emphasized. The key difference between Meier's proposals, and proposals for capsules and general designs by Cedric Price and, even more, by Archigram, is perhaps manifested in a focus on the need for individuality before collectivism and consumerism, and expendability of pop products, which is not in accordance with the calculated "sustainable" prudence. In Meier's opinion, prudence while consuming luxury products is possible in societies which have achieved political stability, and developed an elite group with almost puritanical standards, and perhaps his call for "a new international design aesthetic," which must "provide variety with economy and extract beauty from simplicity,"[205] is part of that puritan demeanor. On the basis of analyses, Meier summed up the proposals in the first half of the 1950s, which ran parallel to what the Smithsons had concluded, though not as universally radical, in the field of architecture with the New Brutalism, through existentialism and with completely different starting points.

Despite respecting Fuller and his universal engagement, the playful and swinging 1960s of Archigram were more focused on experiments than on finding genuine solutions to pressing global problems. Hence, the response to D. Scott Brown's question regarding created economic, social, political, and other relations in the *Plug-in City* of Archigram: "What is everybody doing up there together with everybody else in those megastructures?"[206] which is, half-satirically, offered by Reyner Banham, that they were "rearranging the equipment for the next game," is understood in that context.[207]

Japanese Metabolism and the philosophy of change

Invisible tradition in the context of the Modern Movement, technology, and Metabolism

At the end of the 1950s, reaction to the overpopulation of Japanese cities and faith in the power of technological progress produced an architectural movement with the philosophy of change, calling itself "Metabolism," and comprising, in addition to architecture, urbanism and industrial design. In the declaration *Metabolism 1960 – The Proposals for New Urbanism,* architects Kiyonori Kikutake, Fumihiko Maki, Masato Otaka, and Noriaki (Kisho) Kurokawa, critic Noboru Kawazoe, with designer Kiyoshi Awazu, present their position regarding human society as a part which, together with other living organisms, forms a permanent natural whole, and emphasize their faith in technology as an "extension of humanity," which they describe in the following way:

> We regard human society as a vital process – a continuous development from atom to nebula. The reason we use such a biological word, metabolism, is that we believe design and technology should be a denotation of human vitality. We are not going to accept metabolism as a natural historical process, but we are trying to encourage active metabolic development of our society through our proposals.[208]

Parallel to Archigram, the concept of the capsule in Japan is connected with cultural tradition, and transformed under the pressure of post-war social reality as a response to urgent needs in restoring and growing metropolises with parallel inefficient spatial planning, and faith in science, technology, and modernity in the newly defined Japanese society.

In the post-war period, ravaged Japanese cities were in need of complete renovation. In the early post-war years, this was carried out under the influence of the American occupation and, after 1952, under the influence of American capital. This helped Japan reestablish its industrial system, promoted as a barrier against communist expansion, and as a branch of the capitalist world and democracy in the Far East, and facilitated high economic growth. The post-war shortage of habitations was enormous—amounting to almost 4.2 million needed—which was almost a quarter of the apartments in the entire country, prompting an "era of self-construction" immediately after the war.[209] The post-war centralization of production and capital led cities, crowded even before the war, to an urban crisis with faster and less controlled development and unsuitable and inefficient urban measures, which manifested itself in endless proliferation of dense low-rise urban fabric. At the end of the 1950s, the pre-war system of land ownership and landowners opposing the already small areas to be used for public needs brought about the idea to acquire new land from the sea. After 1958, Tokyo Bay became an experimental laboratory for new proposals for floating cities, artificial islands, and infrastructural cities, which contributed to the image of the general global trend of megastructures in the 1960s and were, according to Raffaele Pernice, the origin of urban utopias (e.g. floating cities, artificial islands, and infrastructural cities), in modern Japanese architecture.[210]

In addition to the famous plan from 1960 for Tokyo Bay by Kenzo Tange, the most influential proposals, which mirrored the urban realities of Japan and self-confidently pointed to the future, include early projects of the floating cities of Kiyonori Kikutake's, which he developed from 1958 onwards, and Kisho Kurokawa's helix structures. Like other members of the group of Metabolists, both aforementioned protagonists were launched into the orbit of international architecture by their joint participation and manifesto, which was marked by Robin Boyd to be the "Japanese architects' declaration of independence," at the *World Design Conference*[211] in Tokyo in 1960.[212] Emphasized at the conference, the topics of mobility (movement), growth, and change, which were proposed by Team 10 for the CIAM Congress in Dubrovnik in 1956, lost their metaphorical distance or were "translated" into biological imagery in the context of the philosophy of Metabolism.[213] Another member of the group was Kenji Ekuan who, in addition to Kikutake and Kurokawa, paved the way for recognition of a modern prefabricated mobile living unit in Japan. It had different references for each of them. Kikutake even had a different name for it.

Japanese Metabolism was a movement co-created by autonomous individuals with frequently inconsistent views and interests. The extent of the work and influences of the group of Metabolists, and of their like-minded colleagues, had an unexpectedly significant influence, in view of the official, relatively short-term, functioning of the group, which had its swansong at Expo '70 in Osaka.[214]

One of the key starting points for the generation of the group of Metabolists was facing the defeat in war and the subsequent total destruction of Japanese cities. The main starting point was the modern dream of *tabula rasa* which was, in the case of the Japanese, made difficult by traumatic recent history. The new generation under the influence and mentorship of Kenzo Tange, who attempted to realize the dialectic synthesis between Japanese tradition and the "tradition of the new," which made him a representative architect of the Japanese post-war democracy, ventured to take a step forward, away from Le Corbusier's approach to architecture.[215] The group of Metabolists functioned parallel to their mentor, Kenzo Tange, exploring the concepts he began developing and, as feedback, inspired the older master. With shifts beyond the functionalist approach, Tange showed his interest in seeking a new meaning and advocating a "new tradition."

Both he and the Metabolists believed that prudent architectural forms contained "cultural meaning and national spirit," which they did not attempt to express by repeating traditional forms, but rather by abstracting the invisible cultural tradition and the tradition of understanding constant changes and renewal, although sometimes only at the symbolic level.[216] The Metabolists attempted, through critical revisionism of functionalism, to find a framework for the architectural functioning that would highlight the uniqueness of Japanese culture, and preserve it with the use of western engineering, modern technology, and economy. The name of the group—*nomen est omen*—clearly indicates the field of work, while, in Banham's Second

Machine Age, the biological metaphor of Metabolism becomes a product of modern technology as an extension of man. Kurokawa pointed out that this principle was different from the western one, where modernization is related to the opposition between technology and humanity, and the group of Metabolists strove to develop a new relationship between humanity and technology, based on the belief that technology is the extension of humanity.[217]

The term metabolism means the process of change, and comprises both breaking down as well as building up. In modern science, it also covers biological regeneration, and is related to the concepts of transformation and reincarnation in Buddhism. To members of the group, this title facilitated their own metaphorical interpretations in the field of urbanism and architecture. Despite the different approaches by the Metabolists, Kikutake and Kurokawa were prone to fantastic structures and the use of state-of-the-art technology, while Maki and Otaka focused on practical and contextual proposals. But they all have a common approach to architecture, which builds a city as a living organism, beyond traditional aesthetics. Kurokawa describes his aesthetics, which are very similar to the New Brutalist aesthetics and may generally also be attributed to his colleagues from the group, as an inclination to the natural, unadorned, plain, rustic, and slightly sad expression summarized by notions of the "the aesthetics of Metabolism" and "the aesthetics of time," which indicate a philosophy which points out the significance of preserving relationships between architecture, society, and nature, and constantly changes with time.[218] Important elements in the Metabolists' projects were constant change, the possibility of endless expansion and organic growth balanced by technological means, organizational flexibility with "public participation," replace-ability of individual architectural elements in view of their durability, the prefabrication and use of mass production, the significance of liberating mobility and of leisure time, and the design of clip-on and multicellular cluster structures as a product. Due to their megalomaniacal designs, Manfredo Tafuri critically marked them as the "academy of the utopian,"[219] since, in his opinion they completely lost touch with direct social reality.

Despite the fact that the Metabolists were aware of the utopian extent of their proposals, they did not perceive their works in the sense of classical utopias according to western understanding, since the latter seemed implanted in feasibly technical possibilities of time.[220] Metabolists' urban projects promoted political ideals and social ambitions, and like many intellectuals of the time, Metabolists required the social characteristics of the modern age. Requirements for democracy, equality, liberation from land, and freedom of movement were, frequently paradoxically, stuck in the classical utopian schemes of hierarchical organizations, central administration, and regulation with the ambition of merging classical contradictions between city and countryside, centralization and democracy, order and freedom, tradition and modernity.[221] But in Japanese culture, the conflicting pairs do not signify an intolerable situation, but rather potential. For Kurokawa, the coexistence of contradictions is an important contribution of eastern ideas to modernity, and a tool for devising its architecture: "Coexistence in architecture does not mean the resolution of conflicts; it means the development of a *third* space which enables conflicts to exist side by side, in harmony while remaining at variance."[222] Despite visionary utopian projects, his thesis that "the architect's job is not to propose ideal models for society, but to devise spatial equipment that the citizens themselves can operate" is also important for the concept of the capsule.[223] The realization of this thesis is different in individual projects and does not necessarily apply to all members of the group of Metabolists. Nevertheless, at least in a declaratory manner, by devising capsule architecture, Kurokawa and Ekuan managed to indicate the direction of non-representative dynamic architectural rhetoric which, in extreme situations, even encourages the anarchy of spatial and social structures.

Unlike in Archigram, in the group of Metabolists the building of a post-apocalyptic new world was not about their enthusiastic acceptance of the fetish of the new, but about the establishment of an organic relationship between individuals and the basic characteristics of culture not shown through materiality, style, scale, or form, but through the connecting basic spirit, through immaterial intangible characteristics of culture, tradition as a process, without a visual connection with the past.[224]

The process of constant changes in metabolic architecture is facilitated by its replaceable components with various life spans or durability. In traditional Japanese wooden architecture, Kitutake recognized the system of the possible assembly and disassembly of architectural elements with a recycling system, which is one of the important topics of the "Metabolist movement."[225] Modular and standardized Japanese wooden architecture was admired by western modernists. Gropius visited Japan in 1953, and Le Corbusier and Wachsmann visited in 1955. Under the influence of eminent western experts, the traditional wooden construction was revived and reinterpreted with new materials.[226] To western revisionists, Japanese architecture was a source of inspiration. Many parallels can be found between the New Brutalism and Metabolism, and not only related to style. Alison Smithson based the sources of the British New Brutalism on Le Corbusier's *béton brut* of the Unité in Marseille and on Japanese architecture, its basic ideas, principles, and spirit, through which form is derived as part of the entire concept of life, where the attitude to materials facilitates the establishment of a connection between a building and man, which is a key connection for Brutalism.[227]

Before and after the war, special roles of the Japanese national symbol and the prototype of Japanese architecture were played by the Ise Shrine, which was presented to the international audience by Kenzo Tange and Noboru Kawazoe as architectural tradition in the book, *Ise: Prototype of Japanese Architecture.* A permanent platform marks a space reserved for deities, a space which is still part of nature. A transient temporary dwelling of deities, in the form of a wooden shrine, is erected upon it, and has been renovated in the same form every twenty years, at least since 685, with a Shintoist ritual. The shrine, located in the middle of pristine nature, has two enclosed spaces located next to each other, where the ritual building and demolition of buildings of Shintoist shrines alternate. Cyclical changes are installed in the very design of the shrine, where physical buildings are not considered permanent, while the style, or more accurately the "intangible essence within the style," is.[228] In the book, Kawazoe explains that the Japanese were not interested in the preservation of old buildings as such, but in the transfer of invisible tradition from generation to generation, and points out the significant difference between the Japanese and western notion of art:

> The Japanese thought that life becomes eternal by being absorbed into the great stream of Nature. For them, it was not a case of "life is short, art eternal." They had only to look to the Ise Shrine—ever new, yet ever unchanging—to know that it is art, in truth, that is short and life that is eternal.[229]

The transfer of tradition to the modern age takes place in the form of a connecting spirit of Metabolism equipped with technical means. Solid permanent concrete infrastructural cores of "artificial land" are opposed by tiny, transient, and replaceable living units that are clipped onto them. The analogy is obvious. Physical human life is transient. Therefore, furniture—a monofunctional capsule or, in the most extreme case, the entire living space of a human (a capsule)—is also transient, while the platform where life takes place is permanent. But since nothing in physical nature is eternal, infrastructure and other components also have their different limits of durability.

The concept of the "artificial land," which served as a direct model for many projects of Kenzo Tange and the Metabolists, was first used by Le Corbusier for his urban visions when traveling in South America in 1929, and articulated in the *Plan Obus* for Algiers in the 1930s.[230] While Alison and Peter Smithson, Team 10, Yona Friedman, their patron and mentor Kenzo Tange in Japan and others are among the recognized influences of the Metabolists,[231] a special role was played by Louis Kahn. In his project for *Richards Medical Research Laboratories* in Philadelphia between 1957 and 1960, and its division into served and servant spaces, Metabolists saw a useful realization which corresponded to their analytical concepts.[232] The simple formula of the eternal metabolic process was recapped in a few points, summarized by Kisho Kurokawa as a recipe in how to design a metabolic building:

1.   Divide the spaces into basic units.
2.   Divide the units into equipment units and living units.
3.   Clarify the difference in metabolic rhythms among the unit spaces.
4.   Clarify the connectors and joints among spaces with differing metabolic rhythms.[233]

Despite the fact that none of the Metabolists referenced Buckminster Fuller—whose proto-capsule units *Dymaxion* should have been known in Japan—among direct influences on the development of the capsule as an "international symbol of Metabolism," his dome over Manhattan was placed by Kurokawa on the table of graphic reference material related to the concept of the capsule, in a thematic issue of *SD—Space Design* in 1969.[234] It is also significant that Fuller was presented to the Japanese audience by art critic Yoshiaki Tohno[235] in the context of modern art, not architecture, which is very similar to the case of John McHale from the Independent Group in Britain. Naming functional and living units as capsules appeared in Japan in the second half of the 1960s, while the concept of the capsule is also based on the recent history of demolished cities, and then on minimum shelters transformed for the needs of the unpredictable modern world, and with its precise ergonomics also in the legacy of pre-war Japanese eugenics.[236]

Japanese Metabolism had a prominent role in the tradition of megastructures. Reyner Banham attributes the first official definition of a megastructure to Fumihiko Maki: "Megastructure is a large frame in which all the functions of a city or part of a city are housed. It has been made possible by present-day technology. In a sense it is a man-made feature of the landscape,"[237] while a more complete definition in four points, by Ralf Wilcoxon from 1968, recalls the aforementioned Metabolist instruction by Kurokawa and, like Maki's, emphasizes the duality between a permanent framework and subordinate and temporary units. Wilcoxon defines megastructure as

Not only a structure of great size, but … also a structure which is frequently:

1.   constructed of modular units;
2.   capable of great or even "unlimited" extension;
3.   a structural framework into which smaller structural units (for example, rooms, houses, or small buildings of other sorts) can be built—or even "plugged-in" or "clipped-on" after having been prefabricated elsewhere;
4.   a structural framework expected to have a useful life much longer than that of the smaller units which it might support.[238]

Metabolists' early, largely urban designs were undoubtedly breaking new ground for the fascination with megastructures, while the realizations, particularly of buildings at the end of the 1960s, showed that the concept was wearing thin. Following Charles Jencks's remark about the influence of Archigram on Japanese advanced architecture, in the second half of the 1960s—while missing the grandeur and originality of their tradition of megastructures, particularly in the context of the Expo '70 in Osaka—Reyner Banham marked it as containing too much plagiarism.[239] The flow of ideas toward Japan in the 1960s was often provided in the visual sense, at the level of visual images. Therefore, in this context, we can agree with Banham's statement but, at the same time, it seems that the flow of ideas westward was carried out in a similar fashion, and that the philosophy of Metabolism, which ran much deeper than the perceived visual images, was frequently overlooked, despite the efforts of Günther Nitschke and others in their presentations in the western media.[240] As emphasized by the Metabolists, visual images as such are not as important as the organic metabolic whole used by Metabolism to think about, and contribute to, the perception of living in modernity from a conscious avant-garde position.

As Kikutake wrote about the existing city which tries to conceal its unhealthy nature, and requires individuals to adjust to this concealment, he emphasized a question of repression of the institution of a traditional city. He opened up a field for experiments where each individual would be aware of the community and have their own living space, and the city's adjustments to the life of individuals and the community would reject a situation which it considers unbearable.[241] By fragmenting architectural elements, the Metabolists even offered in certain experiments to plan or guide the development of the city at least at the level of community with the methodology of industrial design instead of with architectural means, while the basic megastructural designs were supposed to remain in the hands of planners. Regarding modern technology, the Metabolists realized the idea of architecture, which contains invisible tradition, facilitates endless metabolic changes of structures in direct relationship with a cycle of changes in a human life. The duality of permanence and transitivity is manifested in durable formations of megastructures of artificial islands or massive cores, from which cells—living units with a shorter life span, most of which are actually capsules or similar living or functional cells—"grow," or onto which they are "clipped."

In her study on radical decontextualized Metabolist architecture in Japan, Cherie Wendelken connects the Metabolists' rejection of the existing Japanese city and known architectural forms with the rejection of political rigidity and restrictions. The designs contained flexibility and adaptability, and an unconditional requirement for power and the autonomy of an individual; that is, the autonomy which the Metabolists assigned to an individual "capsule" or "unit," which is separate from a "frame," and refers, in her opinion, to traumatic personal experience with a totalitarian regime.[242]

Despite the optimism of certain Metabolists, Kawazoe and Arata Isozaki, who was influenced by Metabolists' ideas but was never a member of the group, show obvious ambivalence about the modern city, modern society, and the role of an architect in it. If the technological pragmatism facilitated social utopias of the Metabolists, Isozaki accompanied, from the early 1960s, his megastructural designs with skepticism. While the pragmatic utopian project, *City in the Air* from 1961, decisively denies urban and legal regulation, and requires only 10 m^2 of land to set up a core to which smaller units will be clipped, the famous collage, *Incubation Process* from 1962, expresses ambivalence with the presence of ruins from which technological megastructures grow. With this collage, Isozaki showed a dystopian view of the future of a "city as a ruin" as different from utopian concepts, distanced himself from the uncritical technological orientation of some of the Metabolists' projects, stating that they did not antici-pate possible catastrophic changes brought on by wars, and rejected the idea of a social revolu-tion by the use of technology.[243]

Artificial land and biological analogies—Kiyonori Kikutake

Kiyonori Kikutake, who became famous with the built *Sky House* project in Tokyo in 1958, established in his first urban and architectural projects the duality between the load-bearing infrastructure called "artificial land," and clip-on prefabricated living mobile units. As in the case of the *Tower Shaped Community* project from 1958 (see Figures 2.17, 2.18, 2.19, 2.20), Kikutake does not designate these units as capsules. His machine-like system of a living unit is similar to the concept of the capsule, but not the same. With the mechanism of change and movement, it differs from the capsule which is, by his definition, a compact and unchangeable whole. His living unit "has a more flexible system and can change itself" while, in his opinion "the capsule doesn't metabolize itself, because it doesn't have such a dynamic system."[244]

The difference between a living unit in the *Tower Shaped Community* and the concept of the capsule is in greater flexibility inside of the cell, and in terms of the representation of a "building as a living organism" on the outside. In genuine Metabolist architecture, Kikutake also sees symbolic potential, as he describes *Tower Shaped Community* as a "monument" to modern life, which connects an individual with the community, and architecture with the city.[245] To be more precise, it is appropriate to use his designations for movable architectural

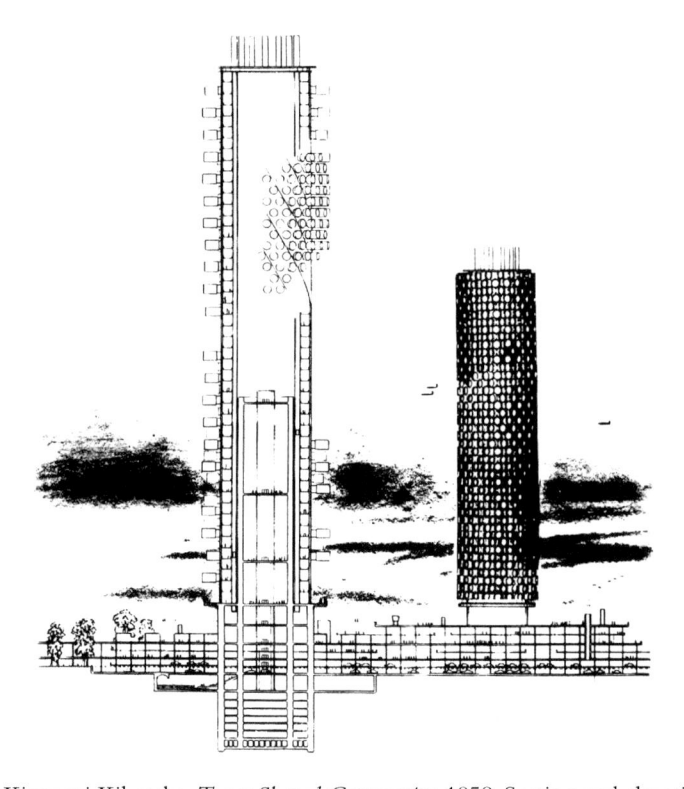

FIGURE 2.17 Kiyonori Kikutake, *Tower Shaped Community*, 1958. Section and elevation

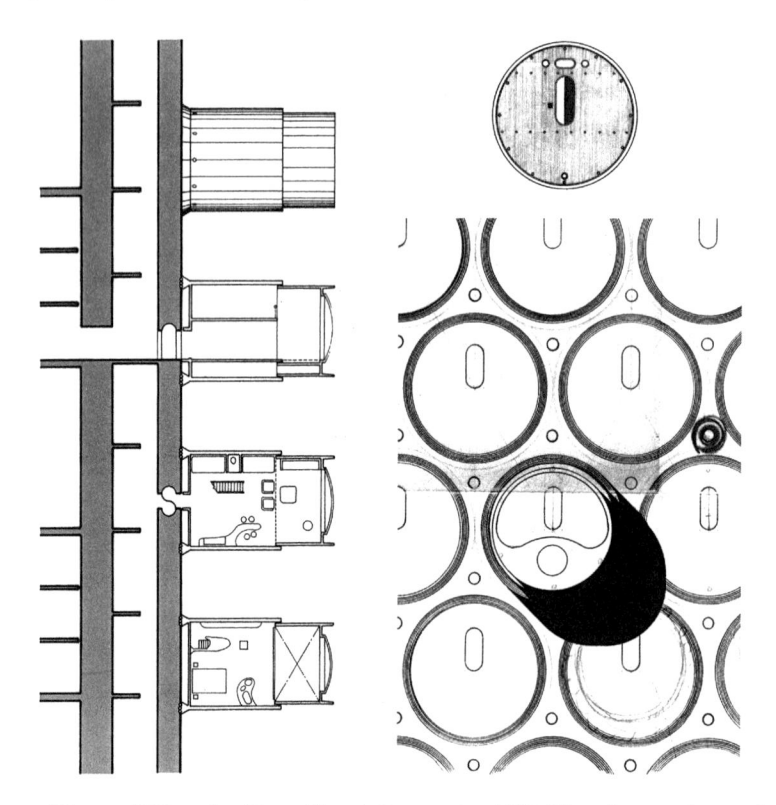

FIGURE 2.18 Kiyonori Kikutake, *Tower Shaped Community*, 1958. Elevation, section, and plan of the family space and parents' space; facade of the tower

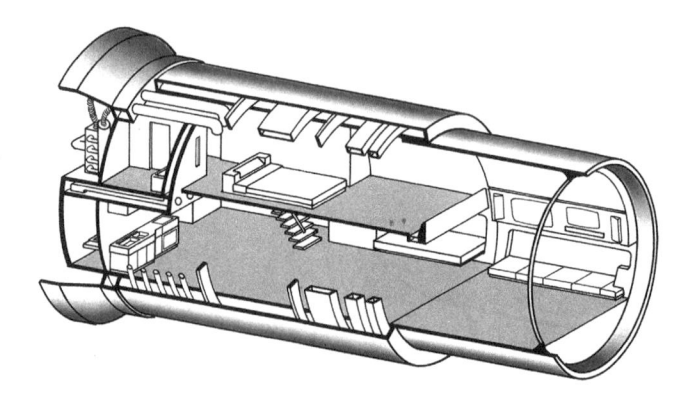

FIGURE 2.19 Kiyonori Kikutake, *Tower Shaped Community*, living unit which telescopically expands during the day and shrinks at night

structures according to the scale required. Functional equipment attached to infrastructure, which Kikutake calls "move-net,"[246] corresponds to the scale of a human life or its basic supply, a "mobile house" corresponds to the scale of family life, and the megastructure of a "mova-block" corresponds to urban life.[247] The units of the three scales are interrelated, since

FIGURE 2.20 Kiyonori Kikutake, *Tower Shaped Community*, use of the concept at the Ikebukuro location

smaller units support and comprise larger ones. According to the author's terminology, a living unit in, for example, the *Tower Shaped Community* or *Marine City* project from 1960 could be called a "mobile house" but, despite everything, Kikutake's living units could, in accordance with our definition, also be called capsules.

Kikutake's open "classical" spatial designs and mechanized capsule living units are equipped with elements called "move-net." Kikutake's neologism, move-net, signifies a comprehensive, technically equipped functional unit installed as movable furniture, which may be subsequently replaced with a technically improved model.[248] In view of our definition, Kikutake's move-net elements are actually monofunctional capsules, usually clipped onto main living spaces, and pursue the logic of serviced and servant spaces.

However, Kiyonori Kikutake was not an architect primarily interested in small-scale "capsule" living cells, and his theoretical explanations were not focused on them. Most of his early work referred to architecture and urbanism as tools of social change, with free and flexible designs of living spaces. To better understand his theoretical positions, it is extremely important to point out his attachment to family tradition on the island of Kyushu, in the western part of the Japanese archipelago, in the area of today's city of Kurume, where he was born, and where his family had been owners of a fertile plain for several centuries.[249] Kikutake is completely honest when using the philosophy of Metabolism, but also different, expressed by emphasizing his family history, social responsibility, and attachment to the land. Kikutake particularly highlights the social role of landlords, who selflessly helped people in difficult moments of hunger and war. Kikutake's functioning as a child of post-war Japan and his hope for a new society is completely attached to the social tradition of his wealthy landowner family, which lost most of its wealth through post-war reforms. He wanted to replace the traditional shortcoming with proposals of "artificial land" in tower shaped communities and floating cities on the sea. On the other hand, Kikutake's search for space for construction in the air and the sea enables us to follow the trend of the Japanese post-war generation, which responded to the aforementioned problems of scarce free land for construction in cities with proposals of US-style skyscrapers, which would facilitate concentration and limit uncontrolled proliferation of low-rise private dwellings, and establish a balance with the needs of infrastructure, particularly transport.[250] Kikutake states unambiguously that proposals for the city of the future are a response to the existing state of confusion and paralysis in metropolitan cities, and of inconsistency and lack of systems in cities which, in the given example, forced the group of Metabolists to prepare alternative proposals.[251]

Orientation toward technological solutions and megalomaniac dimensions of megastructures, which would facilitate quick solutions of social problems, placed the group of Metabolists, including Kikutake, in the realm of utopians, visionary architects, and rhetorical avant-gardists, although the Metabolists' interest in the prompt realization of proposals cast doubt on such a position. In the context of the perception and use of technology, the fact that Kiyonori Kikutake's floating cities, marked by Kenneth Frampton as "surely among the most poetic visions of the Metabolist movement,"[252] arose as a practical technical solution and an expression of disagreement with the construction of industrial plants on the coast, is very interesting. The first proposal for a floating building was made by Kikutake for the Bridgestone tire factory, while the project itself was a kind of an anti-proposal, used to demonstrate the unsuitability of the construction of such automated plants on the coast. Further proposals soon followed, such as those for floating housing buildings and cities with vertical constructive and infrastructure-equipped cores with clipped-on living units.[253]

In addition to designing "artificial land," Kikutake paid a lot of attention to architectural articulation of the flexible space of living units, which he linked with traditional Japanese space organization. In his own paradigmatic *Sky House*, Kikutake realized both the connection and break with tradition: A single-space design for a modern couple excludes the living of extended family from the pre-war period, but the architectural design reflects the design of a parlor with sixteen *tatami* mats, in his family house in the city of Kurume.[254] The main space allowed for various arrangements with respect to needs, while modern functional equipment was ensured by individual move-net units, such as a kitchen move-net, a sanitary move-net, and also a children's move-net, which was anticipated as a temporary element to be clipped onto the main space of the building from below, for the time when children need their own space.

The design of his capsule "mobile houses"—cylindrical dwellings in the *Tower Shaped Community* project from 1958, and circular living units for the *Marine City* project from 1958 and 1960, is a single space divided with partitions and functional "move-net" units. An important effect Kikutake wanted to achieve with both is the actual physical movement of units, as well as when installed in the load-bearing and infrastructure-equipped structure. While the cylindrical unit may be telescopically expanded during the day, creating space for day living, the circular unit, the design of which recalls Fuller's experiments *4D Timelock* and *Dymaxion House* with a central load-bearing infrastructural mast, facilitates the arrangement of individual living and functional spaces in the move-net form, according to desired peripheral conditions.

To achieve the cyclical characteristic of the renewal, and ensure constant changing of the metabolic structure, the anticipated durability of individual steel cylindrical living units attached to a permanent concrete framework is 50 years, which should correspond to the duration of the material and human life in it. The anticipated durability of the interior, which could be adjusted to potential changes in the living conditions of residents, and could be made of "friendlier" (to the touch) materials like plastics, was shorter.[255] The circular "mobile house" for two to eight residents in the *Marine City* project was designed to last for twenty-five years, which should correspond to the change of generations, but it was anticipated to be used for just five.[256] So for Kikutake, the main space was more important than mobile monofunctional move-net elements, which were treated as additional "devices" in his design. The design of the "capsule" living unit was conceived within the "traditional" framework of a house as a semi-public space, which is not intended solely for a family, but also for meeting other people and, according to Kikutake, is not intended to promote individualization.[257]

Unlike many visionary projects in the West in that period, Japanese projects were also technically well devised, despite Banham denying them this quality.[258] Kikutake anticipated the system of the lifting and attachment of the living unit produced in the tower to the rim of the tower, which should also have a symbolic meaning for the *tower community*, which he describes with a genuine utopian zeal:

> As if congratulating the newborn of a family, the new unit will [be] going up ... with slow rotation around the outside of the Tower to the higher part in the sky. All of the inhabitants of the Tower and the people in the vicinity of the tower will send their sincere and warm congratulations for the starting of [the] new life of a fresh couple, when they observe the lifting of [a] new unit.[259]

Kikutake concludes the metabolic cycle of the living unit with its metabolism, because the steel unit, which has fulfilled its purpose in the life cycle of its residents, was to be recycled into a new housing unit for a new family. The metabolic cycle is thus concluded, at least for the "anticipated temporary" housing units; but the question of the durability of the main structure, that is, of the vertical "artificial land" which, in theory and by the analogy to a live tree structure, is actually "eternal," remains. The problem of determining the durability of the concrete core lies also in the lack of experience of Japanese engineers with a relatively new material, which was then assumed to be more durable and resistant in various conditions than it actually turned out to be.

From a dwelling for extreme conditions to the generator of anti-bureaucracy—Kenji Ekuan and GK Industrial Design

According to Hajime Yatsuka, the story of modern Japanese concepts of capsules dates back to 1955, when Konrad Wachsmann presented a completely different approach to technology at a three-week workshop with students, at the invitation of Takashi Asada from the University of Tokyo.[260] Wachsmann who, after emigrating to the USA, achieved recognition when he participated in a prefabrication project with Walter Gropius, pointed out the modern meaning of modularity and standardization, which were part of traditional Japanese wooden architecture, with basic principles based on mass production and the achievement of greatest variability with a limited number of components.[261] In 1957, Takashi Asada, who was later appointed head secretary and organizer of the *World Design Conference 1960*, headed a Japanese group for the preparation of an international project for a research station in Antarctica. The purpose of the project, for the most extreme conditions, was to devise an autonomous and completely standardized facility with an entirely prefabricated panel system. Asada was joined in the project by a young student from Tange's research laboratory, Kisho Kurokawa, who later became famous for a unique concept of the capsule. In the course of events and experiments with prefabrication and the advanced use of technology for facilities in extreme conditions and in pragmatic studies fully in touch with a reality far from the general opinion of their utopian character, Hajime Yatsuka recognized rudiments of the capsule types from the group of Metabolists from the 1960s, particularly in the case of the Japanese base in Antarctica.[262]

In the early 1960s, Kenji Ekuan, who attended Wachsmann's workshop and established the GK Industrial Design Associates studio with his colleagues, was also active in the preparation of prototypes for minimum dwellings—capsules as products of industrial design. In 1964, the GK group carried out a series of experimental studies with a common title, *The Study of Tools*, which comprised various flat pack and systemically planned movable "appliances," from furniture to individual living units and a systemically designed "city." The *Pumpkin House* (see Figure 2.21), in the shape of a large pumpkin, was a flat pack single-family unit with additional components of capsule rooms and sanitary units, whereas the *Tortoise-Shaped House* was designed systematically with panels, while the *Dwelling City* interfered with urban scale with the basic constituents of capsules clipped onto a hexahedron megastructure.

In the western press, GK Industrial Design Associates made a great impression, with their proposals for mass-produced dwellings and components. They wrote that, unlike many representatives of flexible "throw away" architecture of the future, they did not get lost in the

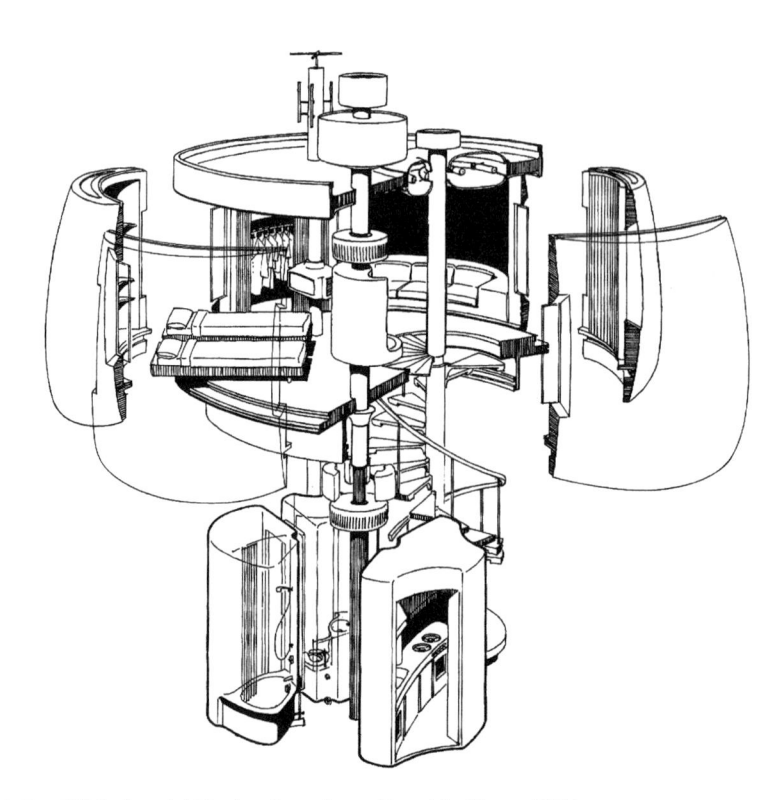

FIGURE 2.21 GK Industrial Design Associates, *Pumpkin House*, 1964

visionary dream world.[263] GK's interest in compact monofunctional or composite multi-function units paved the way for industrial design for the needs of planning and organizing space as a whole, which was traditionally a part of architecture. If prefabricated living units, with compact functional cores of kitchen and sanitary units, only indicated the concept of the capsule, the latter was realized in the *Komatsu ski lodge* project from 1962 (see Figures 2.22, 2.23, 2.24).[264] The shell of the capsule, made of fiberglass on a wooden structure, was much lighter than if it had been made of metal. A porch unit and a fully equipped sanitary service unit were clipped onto the main room of the capsule from the side, as monofunctional capsules. The ski lodge capsule was to be connected to the network of infrastructure, which perhaps reduced its potential to be completely independent, which GK Industrial Design Associates contemplated in the description of their approach and understanding of the concept. Similar is the subsequent *"YADOKARI" Hermit Crab Capsule Lodge* (see Figures 2.25, 2.26), which is an independent unit intended to provide flexibility and mobility for a modern family, mainly planned as a holiday dwelling in campsites, or as in Cedric Price's *Potteries Thinkbelt,* for the needs of mobile universities.[265]

In a thematic issue in 1969, the Japanese magazine *SD* published several features about the capsule, including the reflections and activities of the GK group. Their understanding of the capsule as a technological "extension" of man is similar to Kisho Kurokawa's understanding, but the GK group remains, with its speculations within design and technology and potential social consequences, without any of the historical and metaphysical derivations characteristic of Kurokawa. Designers in the GK group tried to find the common characteristics of capsules, which may look different, with key characteristics being functional autonomy, the provision of comfort "like in a womb," compactness and control, and mobility.[266] The capsule is presented as "packaging" or an envelope for humans who, as living organisms, require their own controlled environment. Encapsulation depends on external conditions, since a capsule is understood as a means to facilitate balance between a living organism and its environment. In the system by GK Industrial Design Associates, a living capsule is equipped with mono-functional units, such as an "eating" capsule, bedroom capsule, and sanitary capsule, which correspond to basic biological human needs. In addition to the common envelope, it enables survival and the performance of basic functions, even in the most extreme conditions.

FIGURE 2.22 GK Industrial Design Associates, *Komatsu Ski Lodge,* 1962

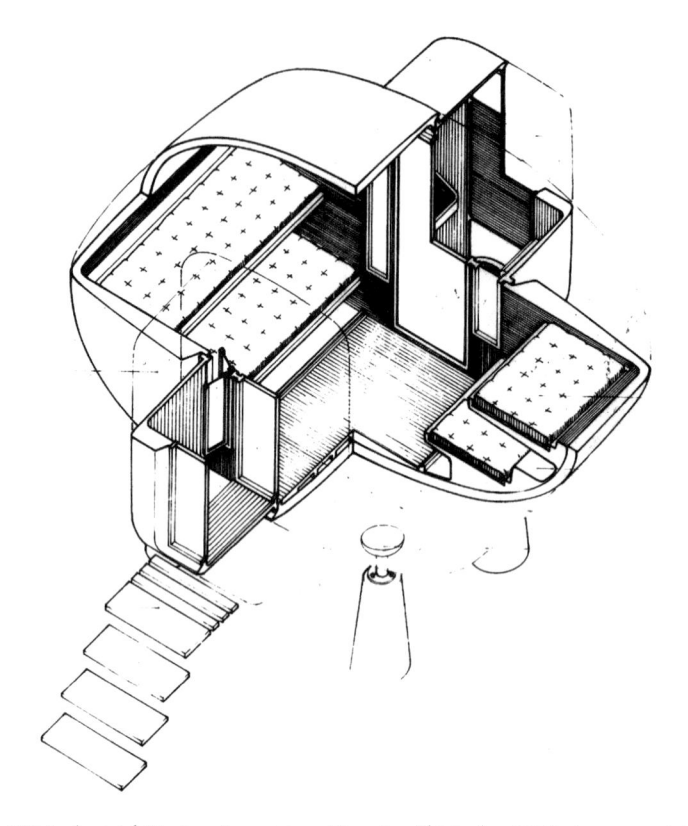

FIGURE 2.23   GK Industrial Design Associates, *Komatsu Ski Lodge*, 1962. Axonometric

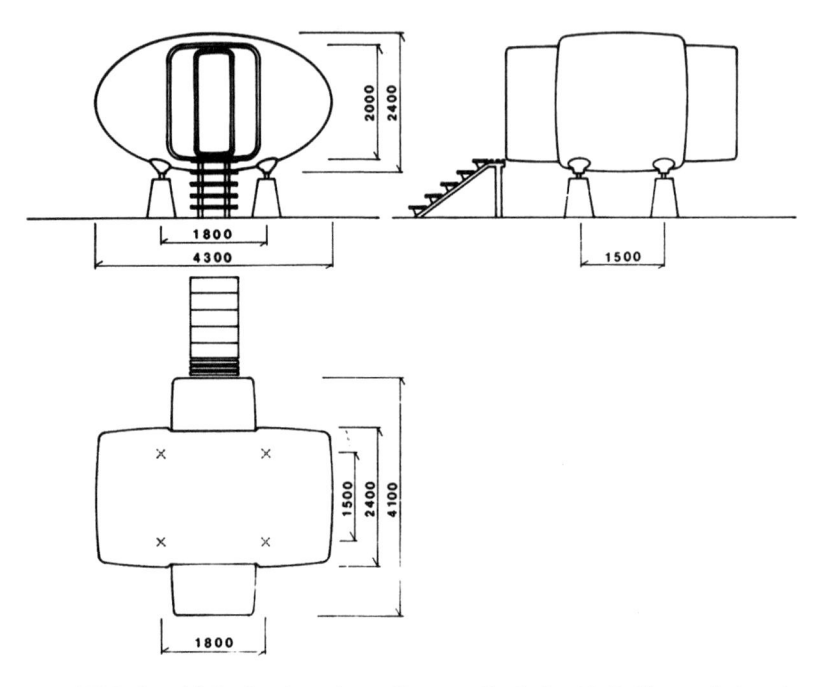

FIGURE 2.24   GK Industrial Design Associates, *Komatsu Ski Lodge*, 1962. Plan and elevations

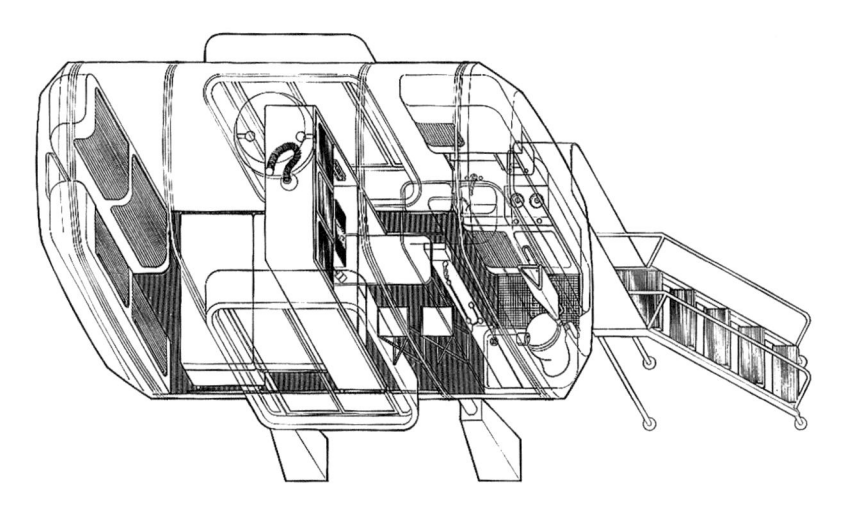

FIGURE 2.25 GK Industrial Design Associates, *"YADOKARI" Hermit Crab Capsule Lodge*, 1969, Nikko Kasei Co. Ltd. Axonometric

The GK group included movement among basic human needs, which determines the autonomy of the capsule and almost implies revolutionary bases for its spatial concept. The concept of the capsule put the striving for order and systemic arrangement of the built environment of certain Metabolists and architects of the young generation to the test, since the compactness makes capsules real objects, which may be proliferated almost into infinity. While many categories of a surveillance society are based on trust in total control of relations between humans and objects, capsules which depend on individuals and their activities are open to unexpected situations, such situations are more similar to "anti-bureaucracy."[267] The mobility of capsules, and their dependence on the individual's dispositions, is thus recognized as a threat to social order. Movable capsules may create temporary *ad hoc* arrangements, which are in total opposition to the basic aspirations of many other architects who attempted to prevent the uncontrolled sprawl of the city fabric in the post-war period, and to the doctrine of spatial planning which had already been established at the end of the 1960s. The space overgrown with capsules undoubtedly offers a liberating and poetic image, since it becomes fluid and its organization becomes temporary. However, this raises the question of the social consequences of such implicit latent anarchy. The autonomous capsule is a completely closed and controlled space, which evades the system of territorial control due to its individual mobile nature.

GK Industrial Design Associates carried on with their experiments to develop the concept of the capsule into the second half of the 1960s and, in cooperation with Kisho Kurokawa, designed capsules for one of the peaks of Japanese capsule architecture, i.e. the *Takara Beautillion* project, which was set between commercial pavilions at Expo '70 in Osaka. The commercialization and spectacular character of the world fair, with the commodification of "advanced ideas," pointed to the utopian character of speculations of other Metabolists, Ekuan, and the GK group, which even a year before had seemed almost revolutionary. Despite everything, this did not sway the optimistic zeal realized by the greatest protagonist of capsule architecture in Japan, Kisho Kurokawa, after Expo '70, though this was perhaps slightly uncritically undertaken, with a few "durable" designs.

FIGURE 2.26   GK Industrial Design Associates, *"YADOKARI" Hermit Crab Capsule Lodge*, 1969, Nikko Kasei Co. Ltd.

Cyborg architecture between tradition and modernity—Kisho Kurokawa

The 1970 World Exposition in Osaka was an event where many ideas, which matured during the 1960s in the form of visions of frequently utopian projects, were realized, materialized, and faced with reality. Expo '70, with the slogan "Progress and Harmony for Mankind" was, in addition to the Japanese pioneers of (proto) *high-tech* architecture, *structuralism* and world architectural *avant-gardism* in general, also attended by representatives of world experimental architecture. For the space-frame structure over the *Festival Plaza* designed by Kenzo Tange, various experiments with the typology of the capsule by Kiyoshi Awazu, Koji Kamiya, Moshe Safdie, Hans Hollein, Archigram, and naturally Kisho Kurokawa, were presented.[268]

In 1968, Robin Boyd described Kisho (Noriaki) Kurokawa as the most restless member of the group of Metabolists, and the group's verbose, prolific, brilliant, and often unintelligible representative, thanks to whom the metaphysics of Metabolism seem overblown, in view of the concrete examples, and thus hard to access.[269] Older colleagues were slightly restrained toward Kurokawa, who was the youngest member of the group since the *World Design Conference* in 1960, and the gap between them only increased as he shot to fame in Japanese mass culture.[270]

To what extent is capsule architecture, which was promoted by Kurokawa in the early stages of his career, the most representative product of Japanese Metabolism? Cherie Wendelken highlights the capsule as an "international symbol of Metabolism," but convinces us that the general opinion is wrong, by saying that "for other former Metabolists and architectural critics, the capsule represented the consumer commodification of architecture and the vulgarization of Metabolist philosophy," the symptom of which is the categorical distancing of other Metabolists from these concepts.[271]

At the end of the 1960s and in the 1970s, two important documents were produced in Japan, which round off theoretical discussion about the concept of the capsule: The aforementioned thematic issue of the *SD* magazine from March 1969 featuring various authors, and particularly Kisho Kurokawa's "Capsule Declaration" which was published in this issue as an article, but fully published in English in 1977, in the book, *Metabolism in Architecture,* was where his selected architectural works and articles were presented. In the preface to the *Capsule Declaration,* Kurokawa explains that the concept of the capsule stemmed from studies which used names such as "unit space" and "cell," which began in 1959. In the article, he assumed an iconoclastic position of penetrating existing order, breaking architecture down into units for individuals, and attempting to establish a new order. His thesis in the declaration also refers to his book from the same year, entitled *Homo Movens*, where he highlights endeavors for a new image of man and a new community in the middle of the flow of modern society.[272]

The *Capsule Declaration* is divided into eight articles, which address the concept of the capsule as an envelope for the protection of a living organism with heterogeneous approaches, a subject of mobility and leisure society, a mechanism of individuality and social diversity, an establishment of a different family system based on an individual, a subject of spiritual fulfillment of an individual in a metabolic city, a private protective envelope against unwanted information, a product characteristic of prefabrication and mass production, and as a tool aimed against systems and uniformity.[273]

Kurokawa defines the capsule as *cyborg architecture*, with which "man, machine and space build a new organic body," which is not an aid, but an appliance integrated into human vital function, which should enable people to survive.[274] It seems that the concept of the capsule announced the materialization of Le Corbusier's architecture as a device or a tool, expanded with McLuhan's call for a house as extension of the human body. With his faith in technology, which helps people survive and carry out their social functions even in unsuitable living conditions, Kurokawa, naively and prophetically, predicted the inhuman conditions of the modern world, since a capsule is "a device which has become a living space itself in the sense that a man cannot hope to live elsewhere."[275] In addition to technological enthusiasm, the first article also showed concern, which was understood by certain commentators as the result of his impressions of the complete destruction of Japanese cities after the war, a damage that was internalized by the group of Metabolists who wanted to surpass it with visions of the near future.[276] As well as being a physical envelope which could correspond to the metamorphosis of a bunker, the capsule is also a technical envelope or a "feedback mechanism," which enables individuals to reject unwanted or unimportant information.

Residents of the capsule are placed by Kurokawa in the environment of information industries, such as the "education industry," the "knowledge industry," the "research industry," the "publishing industry," the "advertising industry," and the "leisure industry," in which an individual needs a selective "filter"—a capsule so one could "recover his subjectivity and independence. The capsule is defined as a space which guarantees complete privacy for the individual," as well as one's physical and spiritual independence.[277] At the same time, the capsule, as a condition for the complete individualization of society, realized the need to ensure an independent shelter for an individual, where a resident may fully develop his/her individuality, thus allowing the diversification of society.[278] The capsule is presented as an instrument of personal freedom, the roots of which are in Buddhism. Therefore, oriental individualism should be understood differently than individualism in the West. Kurokawa supports the realization of the oriental individual who is called *jiga* in Japanese and, as explained by Kurokawa, is not an independent individual of the West, but "consists of a relationship in which the individual and society, while being contradictory, include each other."[279]

With the concept of the capsule, Kurokawa desired to reestablish the oriental individual, who had disappeared in the process of modernization and the introduction of the concept of abstract space, since an individual can no longer establish a relationship with space if it is abstract, which is present, for example, in the tea ceremony tradition in teahouses. According to Kurokawa, the minimum space of a teahouse coexists with the extensive world of nature, whereby the world of a teahouse and the world of nature do not exclude each other, but are part of each other. The principle of coexistence or symbiosis was applied by Kurokawa to the concept of the capsule since, in his opinion, "The capsule space, which is a representation of the oriental individual, is not a part of the piece of architecture to which it is attached. The capsule and the building exist in contradiction, yet mutually include each other."[280] So there is no hierarchical order between them. A whole is not more important than a part, and a part is not more important than a whole. Just like an individual contains the whole creation, in architecture, a part, a capsule, must be understood as a whole, because only as such can it be completely independent. The concept of detachment facilitates natural development, incompleteness, growth, adjustment, and change.

In addition to the focus on the (spiritual) liberation of an individual, it is the socially reforming component that came to the foreground in the declaration. The total freedom of modern social and spatial reality should be realized by the capsule, which is the habitat of a modern nomad. Kurokawa compares the capsule with a mobile house, whereby the building is free from contact with the ground. But he believes that a dwelling for *homo movens* does not need wheels, since it may be made of technologically easily assembled panels, or cast as one piece; the only important thing is that it corresponds to the lifestyle of the modern man, who will dedicate more and more time to leisure activities at different locations. The capsule becomes his status symbol.[281] Like many before him, Kurokawa used the comparison with a car, but not the car of standard mass production, instead using the car with many options, which instead enables diversity. A prefabricated capsule house should be "a qualitative change in the meaning of a building," as it would not be composed of *parts* or *elements*, but of replaceable *functional units*, such as *a bathroom unit* or *a toilet unit*.[282] The assembly of these units should express the will of an individual. Such division affects the system of composition which, in capsule architecture, explicitly shows functional units as *they are*, and affects the perception of the whole without any masking elements or decor.

As we have seen with English and American contemporaries, mobility was a key topic of both the profession, desiring to settle the situation, and of counterculture with entirely anarchist impulses. Connection between the concept of the capsule and mobility is undoubtedly a key category which distinguishes the concept of the capsule from other cellular designs. The possibility of capsules moving freely enables the changing society which Kurokawa aspired to, as he believed in the natural organization of the environment, which is the result of an individual's free will. Moreover, Kurokawa emphasized the significance of forming urban society and its environment which, in his opinion, cannot be created with technology by urban planners and architects.[283] At this point, and when defining a living unit, we can see in the group of Metabolists the different approaches of individuals. While Kikutake's and Kurokawa's "mobile houses" from the late 1950s and the first half of the 1960s are always installed in the load-bearing infrastructure, the capsules of Ekuan with the GK Industrial Design Group, and Kurokawa in the second half of the 1960s, similar to Archigram, break free from their attachment to the quay, and become truly mobile—at least in theory.

The realization of the capsules of Kurokawa and his contemporaries are, with exceptions, always installed in the network infrastructure. Naturally, Kurokawa is aware of the need for a system in spatial planning, but he advocates a non-repressive system, which puts emphasis on an individual and expresses itself as a self-organizing system of spatial units for individuals. A space should be divided into independent shelters, where each resident may fully develop his/her independence. Thus, in Kurokawa's system, independence is a key condition in the changing society, in which he, like many Utopians before him, anticipates that family will disperse.[284] The social formation of a family, with individual capsules for each member, could also be represented by merging in "cluster structures," which became a key topic for Team 10 in the 1950s, through the work of the Smithsons, and resounded greatly among Japanese contemporaries. Kurokawa's capsule city may be understood as a criticism of a modernist city of "four elements," and a fantastically diverse conglomerate called *metapolis,* or an urban settlement, which becomes part of a network city or a larger conurbation.[285]

In Kurokawa's theory, the metapolis installed in the network of communication and information flows—"the true home for capsule dwellers, where they feel they belong and where they satisfy their inner, spiritual requirements"—gets the function of seeking the meaning of life and a replacement of family tradition.[286] Despite being focused on an individual and his/her capsule space, Kurokawa anticipates the design of a "social space," which arises on the spot where the capsules are clipped onto the communal space, and anticipates, in a visionary manner, different types of public spaces with which an individual can identify. Kurokawa calls such a space a "spiritual haven," and describes it through feelings or moods expressed when people use public space, like a plaza or a square, or take part in a demonstration or hold a festival. It is reminiscent of the *ludic* visions of Situationists and of Archigram's *ad hoc* formations.[287] The nature of such a space of "spiritual fulfillment" should be multifunctional. Kurokawa states a few examples of such spaces, like hotels, universities, department stores, and terminals, which become information centers, meeting points, in-between spaces. This proposal, too, is visionary, since it predicts modern "non-places," which became anything but spiritual havens; the latter, as in the prophecy, constantly create a new type of community which merges individuals, and is organized like a "temporal community," which Kurokawa distinguishes from a "regional community."[288]

The layout of temporal communities also differs from the layout of place-related communities. Classical urbanism used a geometrical approach to establish order, while the Metabolist approach desires to create a dynamic, open structure of cities and buildings. Using the latter, Kurokawa hopes to surpass the role of architecture as a control mechanism of society. From then on, according to Kurokawa, "architecture is no longer a device to control men: It is a means whereby men control technology and machinery."[289] This position resembles Banham's advocacy of *une architecture autre*, which could direct the development of technology through its own concepts—*images*. But Kurokawa, with faith in the total fusion of the architectural capsule with an organism, does not say whether such a fusion is completely unconditional, and whether there is a possibility that one's adjustment to the capsule is greater than one would have wanted. This question is particularly relevant when reviewing designed and built capsule units, which function well below CIAM's subsistence minimum, and with less than 10 m^2, come closer to ideal technocratic calculations. But, due to the typology of units for individuals, they do not meet Meier's, or radical Soviet standards.

The conclusion of Kisho Kurokawa's *Capsule Declaration* leads us to another visionary understanding of architecture, which was justifiably pointed out by critics of the capsule as problematic, by transferring it to modern reality. Kurokawa's position that "architecture is nothing more nor less than an aggregate of countless functions (therefore, capsules) and may be defined as a group which comes into being when a number of capsules encounter each other"[290] sounds like an echo of the *group form* of Fumihiko Maki, who published an article with Masato Otaka entitled "Toward a Group Form," in the *Metabolism 1960* pamphlet. Of the four elements—*wall, shaft, floor, unit*—which constitute the group form, Kurokawa focused on the definition of the fourth element, i.e. on the unit which is defined as a cell or a block, which performs a certain function.[291] The connection between concepts of the capsule and the group is emphasized by Kurokawa in the description of the *Nakagin Capsule Tower,* built in Tokyo in 1972, when he describes capsule architecture as a "group form which expresses the individuum."[292] Fumihiko Maki disagrees with the "general" use of the concept of the "group" for capsule architecture, since the latter does not depend, in his theory, on a megastructure or attachment of a unit to an infrastructure.[293] Despite theoretical promises of independence, Kisho Kurokawa's designed or realized capsule architecture is usually connected to an infrastructure, attached to a megastructure, or part of a larger spatial design, where its mobility is, always and only, symbolic, despite potentially fulfilled technical conditions.

In the history of Metabolist realizations, the rationality of plug-in or clip-on designs was one of the main subjects of criticism, although they were, at least in the beginning, advocates of the movement. After the construction of the *Yamanashi Broadcasting and Press Center* in Kofu in 1964, and the *Shizuoka Press and Broadcasting Center* tower in Ginza in Tokyo in 1967 (see Figure 2.27), designed by Kenzo Tange with an explicitly Metabolist tone, a gap between theoretical proposals and realization came to light. The *Yamanashi Broadcasting and Press Center* very much resembles a drawing of a megastructure entitled *Incubation Process* by Arata Isozaki, from 1962, which critically pointed to the continuous demise of all, even modern, technological architectures. In Tange's project, the Metabolist principle of the possibility of change is

FIGURE 2.27 Kenzo Tange, *Shizuoka Press and Broadcasting Center*, Ginza, Tokyo, 1967

frozen in the economically still-acceptable phase at the first stage, and leaves unused parts of the building at the symbolic level of potential growth. In the following decade, some left-out voids in the "three-dimensional space network" have been filled with various additions, which signaled a success for the concept.[294] Conceptually similar is the *Shizuoka Press and Broadcasting Center* project, about which Günther Nitschke rhetorically wondered whether it signified a "prototype," or was it just the result of "wishful thinking" with its groups of, at least visually, "capsule" units clipped onto the vertical infrastructural mast, which show the concept as senseless, due to merely symbolic flexibility in reality.[295] Despite all criticism, these realizations may be understood as an introduction which directed the Metabolists and Tange to the realization of megastructural and more sophisticated capsule designs at Expo '70 in Osaka, and to rare applications at the beginning of the 1970s.

From the first attempt to use capsule units of a bathroom, kitchen, and children's room in the project for the *Prefabricated Apartment House* from 1962 (see Figure 2.28), Kurokawa, like Kikutake before him, endeavored to realize the metabolic life of a building, where the life span of various elements or functional sets varies. Projects of the concept of the capsule, realized at Expo '70 in Osaka, may have shown, perhaps owing to the temporariness of the world exposition, a more intensive poetics of transitivity and quasi naturalness of Metabolism.

The *Takara Beautillion* (see Figures 3.33, 3.34), designed by Kurokawa as a three-dimensional space-frame structure with inset functional elements—capsules—was, according to

FIGURE 2.28 Kisho Kurokawa, *Prefabricated Apartment House*, 1962. Model showing a capsule (bath unit, kitchen, closet) attached to main structure

Robin Boyd, by far the most ingenious pavilion, which represented a feasible future of construction, and put other proposals in the subordinate position of mere exhibitionism.[296] Since the changing and transient Metabolist architecture was devised as the architecture of the future, the future itself gains such qualities. According to Kurokawa, the flat pack *Takara Beautillion* pavilion with capsules, the interior of which was designed by the GK Industrial Design Group, could show its total beauty at the "event" of the exposition. Its assembly took only a few days, and its "disassembly was similarly easy to perform; it was like the falling petals of a cherry blossom tree," which in his words mirror Buddhist aesthetics: "In Buddhism it is considered noble to fulfill one's life and pass away beautifully, in accord with nature."[297]

At the temporary exhibition, the coexistence of contradictions of the spectacle of fantastic architecture and the transience of individual parts installed in the project is shown as a complete cycle of the metabolic wheel of life. The principle of parts being replaceable, which was emphasized by Japanese Metabolism, should be particularly of a practical, technological nature, and should not originate in the philosophy of a consumer approach, which was justified by the economics at the time, and in societies of mass consumption,[298] which is a principle that differs from the pop and consumer speculations of western colleagues. On the one hand, we perceive the beauty of transience, which is the result of technological pragmatism. On the other, constant changes and renovations are also driven by the inescapable mobility-based economic system. Yatsuka mentions that Kurokawa accepted the culture of consumer products of the 1960s and 1970s, which was not necessarily true of his older Metabolist colleagues, including architectural critic Noboru Kawazoe, who was a committed Marxist in the early 1950s.[299]

The absolute exchangeability of parts and mobility are shown in Kurokawa's second realized capsule project at Expo '70, called the *Capsule House in the Theme Pavilion* (see Figure 2.29). The *Capsule House* is a genuine realization of the *Capsule Declaration*, since it represents the fragmentation of the architecture of home in physical form, and creates space

FIGURE 2.29 Kisho Kurokawa, *Capsule House*, Symbol Zone, Theme Pavilion, Expo '70, Osaka, 1970

for an individual with its restructuring. Installed in the space-frame roof structure of the Festival Plaza at Expo '70, the *Capsule House*, which is comprised of three living capsules fully equipped, with sanitary and kitchen capsules clipped onto the main communal space, floats in the air like a spider in its web, waiting for an impulse that will lead it to new adventures. A living unit in the space-frame structure above the ground is automatically associated with Yona Friedman's endless cities above existing city fabric, with outdated living conditions. But as well as an object, Kurokawa's *Capsule House* corresponds to the image of a high-tech space station tranquilly floating (and providing physical conditions for the self-fulfillment of an individual, by clipping on individual units) above the metropolitan hustle and bustle far below it, rather than to Friedman's self-constructed infills. Parallels between the operation of a space station and space capsules, and the megastructural frame and living capsules, seem convincing enough. Although completely autonomous micro-units of living capsules would be an ideal solution, the division of specialized monofunctional elements also seems rational. Technically, completely autonomous capsules would include all the necessary installations and the processing of waste and sewage, while for much simpler capsule units clipped onto a megastructure, the latter is carried out by the megastructure itself.

For avant-garde groups and individuals, the technical aspect was just a means to achieve social or psychological effect. Robin Boyd accompanied the practical experience of entering an area of living capsule units detached from the ground, which he deemed to be Archigram's territory, at Expo '70, by saying: "When one climbs actually into Archigram territory – into some red and yellow capsules hanging on to Tange's giant space-frame over the Festival Plaza – one discovers an unexpected tranquility."[300] The separation of a living structure from the ground undoubtedly facilitated a different perception, while the view from the air of crawling crowds at the world exposition created the liberating feeling of being separated from everyday life. Like in formations at ground level, the definition of the critical mass, which enables or prevents the desired effects of isolation or integration, is also crucial in the "settlement" of the space-frame. If a space station floating in the air is becoming a model of an autonomous community, to which individual units are clipped, the rationality of a megastructure which, if it was to remain incomplete, wanted to compete with the vastness of the universe, was called into question.

Kisho Kurokawa's realized projects of capsule formations for Expo '70 were a test before the actual realization of the famous, iconic fourteen-story *Nakagin Capsule Tower*, built in the Shimbashi–Ginza business district in Tokyo in 1972 (see Figures 2.30, 2.31, 2.32, 2.33, 2.34, 2.35, 2.36, 2.37). The *Nakagin Capsule Tower* was not built as an apartment house, but particularly in order to provide single-bed rooms in the center of Tokyo for businessmen who live in remote suburbs, or as a hotel for businessmen who stay in Tokyo for short periods.[301] The tower comprises 140 capsules—minimum fully equipped living units with integrated sanitary units, which are clipped onto installation and communication load-bearing cores. Each steel prefabricated capsule was welded in the form of a rectangular solid, with dimensions 2.5 m × 4 m × 2.5 m, then clipped on independently of others. Therefore it was, at least theoretically, completely replaceable at any time. The capsule was equipped like a modern hotel, and comprised a bed with bedding, a space for clothing, a desk, a bathroom with sanitary aids, a phone, audio equipment and additional items, such as sheets, blankets, and even toothbrushes. The choice of interior finishing materials, colors, and equipment was up to the purchaser.[302] The absence of a kitchen and a dining area in the capsule is completely in accordance with the philosophy to activate the in-between space of the *metapolis*, a space for social activities. Nevertheless, Kurokawa also predicted the possibility of the merger of

FIGURE 2.30 Kisho Kurokawa, *Nakagin Capsule Tower*, Tokyo, 1972

individual capsules, each of which would get its own function, for example that of a kitchen, a bedroom, a bathroom, etc., and form a "usual dwelling" as a "group." The cluster structure of the tower produces a sense of growth and incompleteness and, at least symbolically, implies the metabolic process of creating a form, which is, in practice, "frozen" at some point. Living units/capsules were planned to be replaced after twenty-five years, however this did not happen. The tower is still standing, but its fate is uncertain. In 2012, approximately thirty capsules were used as apartments, while others were used as warehouses, offices, or were simply left to deteriorate. According to current standards, the unsuitable protection of the capsules, with a layer of asbestos, provides a rationale to demolish the building and replace it, in one of the most expensive parts of Tokyo. Kisho Kurokawa was actively committed to preserving the tower and to replacing the capsules with new suitable units. The initiative to preserve the tower by replacing the capsules or just reconstructing the old ones received a lot of support worldwide.[303] If the plan to preserve the tower is not approved, the most famous and perhaps the most representative capsule building in the world is set to be demolished.[304]

Capsules similar to those used in the *Nakagin Capsule Tower* were used by Kurokawa in his summer house *Capsule House "K"* from 1972 (see Figure 2.38), where the kitchen, two bedrooms, and the teahouse, in the shape of capsules, were clipped on to the main living space. The coexistence of contradictions is shown again in the ratios of the teahouse capsule, which assumes the dimensions of traditional teahouses 2.5 m × 4 m.[305] In 1972, Kurokawa also devised the *Capsule Village* (see Figures 2.39, 2.42), a settlement adjusted to steep terrains. Slightly bigger *Leisure Capsule* living units were clipped onto a horizontal megastructure

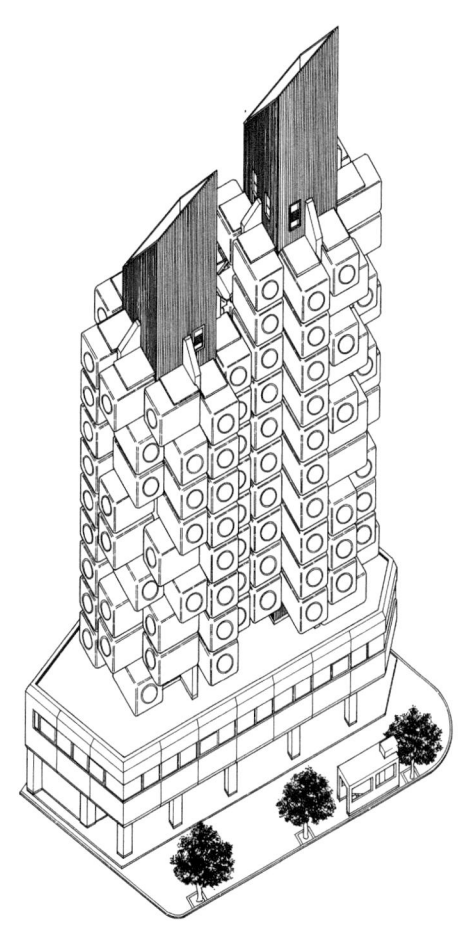

FIGURE 2.31 Kisho Kurokawa, *Nakagin Capsule Tower*, Tokyo, 1972. Axonometric

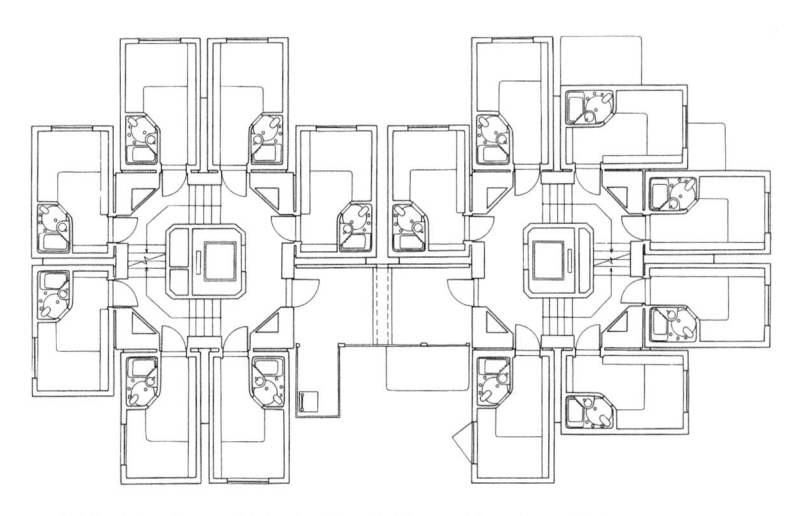

FIGURE 2.32 Kisho Kurokawa, *Nakagin Capsule Tower*, Tokyo, 1972. Plan

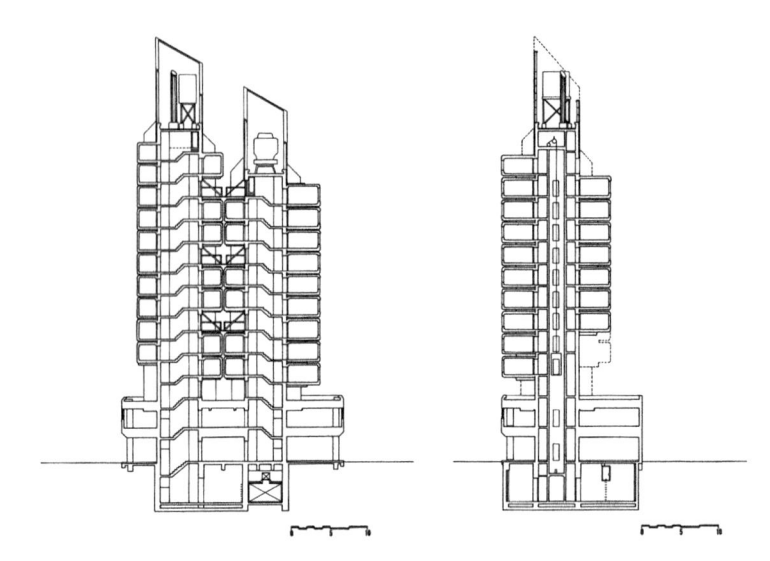

FIGURE 2.33 Kisho Kurokawa, *Nakagin Capsule Tower*, Tokyo, 1972. Sections

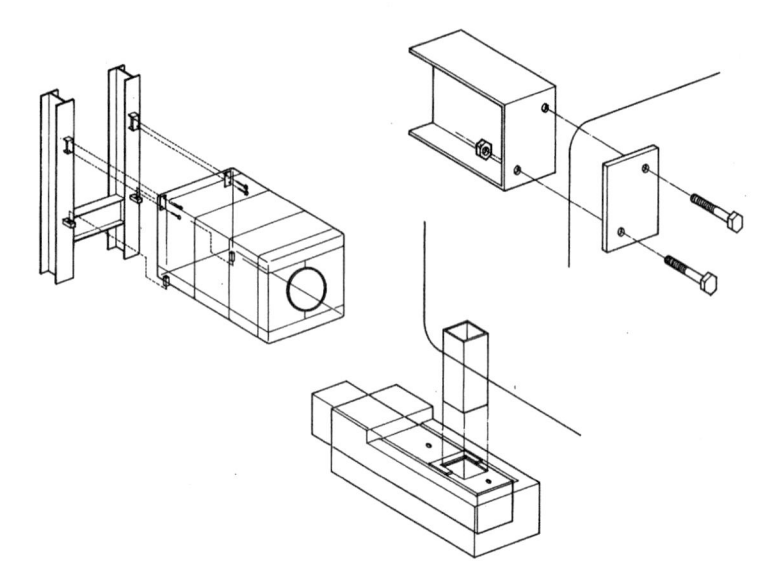

FIGURE 2.34 Kisho Kurokawa, *Nakagin Capsule Tower*, Tokyo, 1972. Detail of joining capsule to shaft

(see Figures 2.40, 2.41). Like a bridge above the terrain, the latter enables the attachment of capsules, which float above the ground and keep the vegetation on the slopes of the location. The capsule consists of a mechanical section with sanitary, kitchen, and energy parts, a living and a sleeping section, which are distinguished by dimension and chosen interior finish. The *Concrete Capsule House* from 1975, where capsules are not clipped onto a megastructure, but stacked to the height of three stories, is an experiment with self-supporting prefabricated capsules made of concrete. The size of the capsules is the same as in the *Capsule Village*

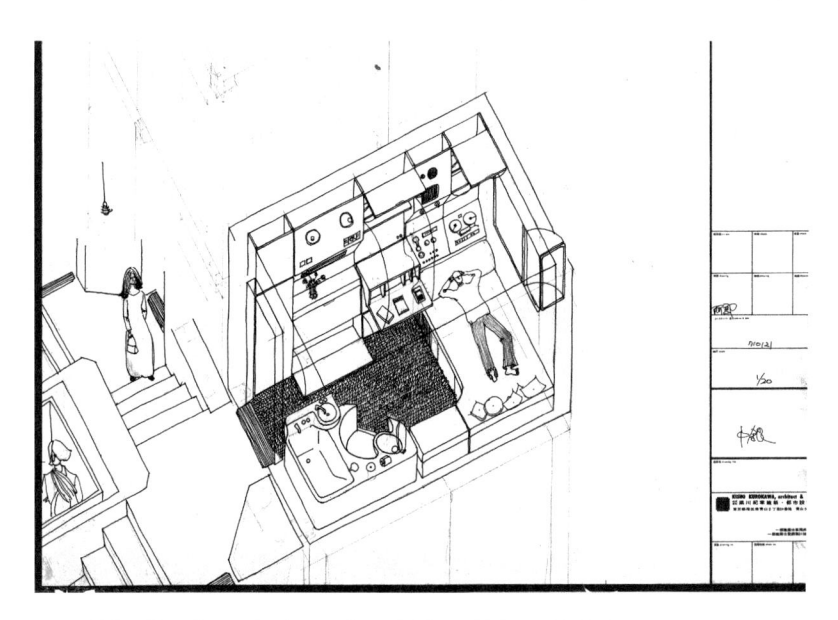

FIGURE 2.35 Kisho Kurokawa, *Nakagin Capsule Tower*, Tokyo, 1972. Axonometric

project, which is 3 m × 6 m. The functions of these capsules are not predetermined, and in view of the configuration of the whole facility may be randomly equipped. The concept of the capsule as a clip-on sanitary unit was also used by Kurokawa in the office buildings *Koito Building,* built in 1974, and *Sony Tower* in Osaka in 1976. In the latter, the concept of the capsule was also used as a representational means of vertical circulation on the facade. The *Sony Tower* was demolished in 2006. In the 1970s, the capsule as a monofunctional unit was a generally accepted solution, used in many projects, where a lot of identical units had to be provided. Kurokawa's project of the *Um Al-Kanhazeer* hotel, from 1975, with a central circulation core and rooms arranged on the external wall, is very similar to Kikutake's *Pacific Hotel* in Chigasaki, built in 1966 as a reiteration of Fuller's *4D Timelock* concept, this time with explicit "outgrowths" of capsule or move-net clip-on bath units on the facade.

In addition to the reviewed definitions, which are frequently wrapped in metalanguage through which we "should feel the theory behind them," according to advice by Noboru Kawazoe,[306] with designed and built facilities as a recapitulation, to fully understand the scope of Kisho Kurokawa's concept of the capsule, we should also take a look at the graphic reference material, which pursues Kurokawa's outlines of the *Capsule Declaration* entitled "Oh! The Code of Cyborg," in the thematic issue of the *SD* magazine on capsules, discussed by Kisho Kurokawa.[307]

Kurokawa's table with reference examples is divided into five lines, which are marked in alphabetical order from A to E. Line A entitled "Dwelling Capsule: Life Function for Everyday" shows: (A1) *capsule for exploration*—a space capsule, (A2) *capsule for a break*—*Komatsu ski lodge* designed by the GK Industrial Design Associates, (A3) *living capsule*, (A4) *erotic capsule (sanitary capsule)*, (A5) *environmental capsule*—Fuller's dome above Manhattan, and (A6) *leisure capsule*—*Living Pod* by David Greene from Archigram. In the first line, Kurokawa summarized a few basic, architectural manifestations of the concept of the capsule, which facilitate living in various external conditions. Line B expands the concept of the capsule by naming various

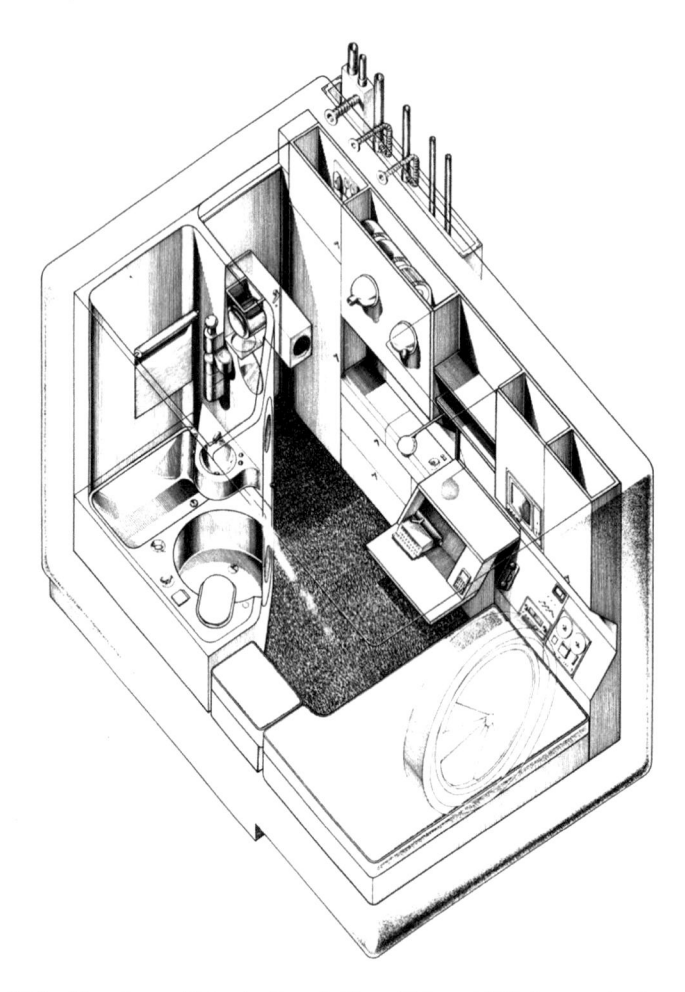

FIGURE 2.36 Kisho Kurokawa, *Nakagin Capsule Tower,* Tokyo, 1972. Isometric plan of capsule

mobile units, which are not necessarily intended for living. Line B, entitled "Capsule for Circulation: Mobility Function" shows: (B1) *travel capsule*—caravan, (B2) *sports capsule*—sports car, (B3) *docking capsule*—mobile jet bridge, (B4) *nutrition capsule*—bottles, and (B5) *transportation capsule*—truck with hermetically sealed cargo space. This is followed by line C with the dematerialization of the concept of the capsule entitled "Symbolic Capsule—Symbolic Function," which includes: (C1) *capsule for tactile feeling*, (C3) *capsule as a psychological barrier*, and (C4) *information capsule*. Line D entitled "Tool or Device Capsule: Displacement and/or Substitution of the Function of a living organism (Robot)" presents technological capsules of modern daily life as extensions of man: (D1) *translation capsule*, (D2) *air-conditioning capsule*, (D3) *engine capsule*, (D4) *projection capsule*, (D5) *music capsule*—jukebox, and (D6) *information capsule*—transmitter stations at sea. In the last line (E), entitled "Capsule of a Living Organism: Expansion of the Function of a Living Organism (Cyborg)," the concept of the capsule acquired biological and anthropological analogies, and ended with McLuhan's definition of a house as a dress—an envelope for the body: (E1) *capsule of living organisms*—placenta, which offers embryos complete protection and everything they need, (E2) *capsule of a corpse*—in the

FIGURE 2.37 Kisho Kurokawa, *Nakagin Capsule Tower*, interior of capsule

FIGURE 2.38 Kisho Kurokawa, *Capsule House "K,"* Nagano, 1972

shape of a casket, (E3) *capsule for covering*, (E4) *capsule for apothanasia*, (E5) *capsule for resuscitation*, (E6) *education capsule*—cybernetic helmets, and (E7) *homocapsule*.[308]

The reference framework of examples refers to the eight themes in the declaration, but not completely unambiguously, and not in a completely structural manner. It shows with visual images the phenomena and manifestations of the (then) modernity related to the concept of the capsule. While most of the aforementioned examples are recognized as having focused on

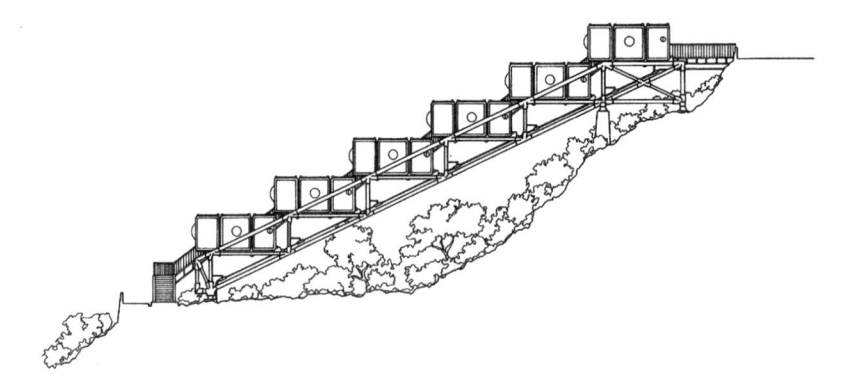

FIGURE 2.39 Kisho Kurokawa, *Usami Capsule Village*, Shizuoka, 1972. Section of the clip-on system

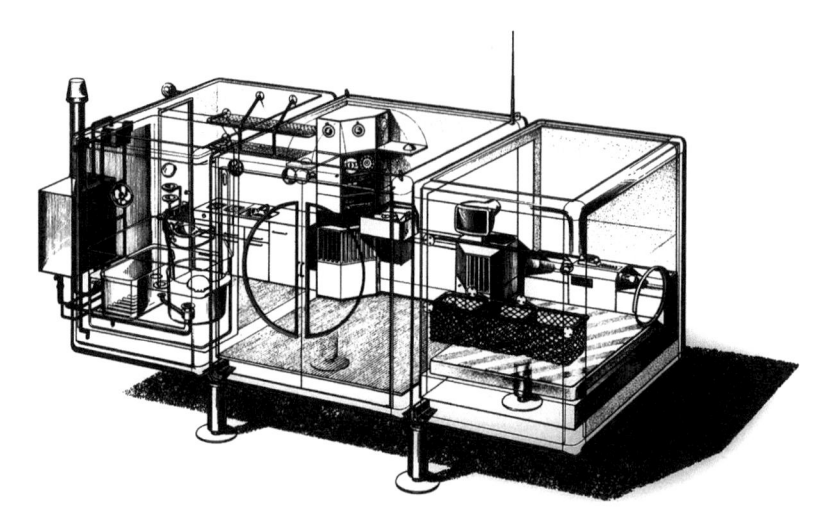

FIGURE 2.40 Kisho Kurokawa, *Leisure Capsule*, prototype for *Usami Capsule Village*, 1972 Drawing of the capsule with three sections

the realization of cyborg architecture, the table does not show a traditional example of the (proto-)capsule, which is included by Kurokawa in the *Capsule Declaration,* published in 1977. In the extended issue, "a traditional capsule for carrying people around"—the *Kago* litter serves as an illustration, which establishes a connection between tradition and modernity in various forms of typology. Interpreted with this example, the power and faith in the benefits of technology seem literally liberating.

Designs and analogies between euphoria and skepticism

After the period of heroic megastructural gestures of the Metabolists and Tange, the second half of the 1960s apparently saw direct transfers of ideas to Japan from the West, in the trend of "academic utopias" of the international scene, which is attributed, by Reyner Banham and Charles Jencks, to the influence of Archigram.[309] In Banham's opinion, the projects that

FIGURE 2.41 Kisho Kurokawa, *Leisure Capsule*, prototype for *Usami Capsule Village*, Shizuoka, 1972. Capsule composed of three different sections

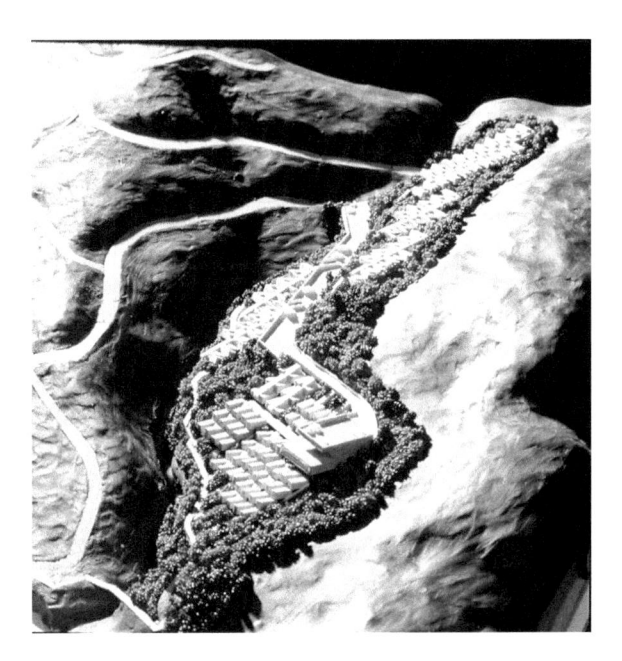

FIGURE 2.42 Kisho Kurokawa, *Usami Capsule Village*, 1972. Aerial view, model

participated in and won competitions organized by the *Shinkenchiku* (*Japan Architect*) magazine in 1966, with Kenzo Tange on the jury, and in 1967 were obviously influenced by Archigram, although one could be skeptical of such a scope of influence at that time. Banham writes that, as the result of these events with cranes and capsules, and "Archigram graphics and many Archigram usages," although they were closer to the tradition of Metabolism in 1967, the world was under the impression that the great and original tradition of Japanese megastructures was worn out, and had been replaced by academic elaborations of ideas that Archigram had already left behind.[310] Banham's review of events in the megastructure scene does not descend to the level of the organization of living spaces which are, in these proposals, different from those from the West. While Archigram broke society down completely into individuals—individual residents or childless couples—Japanese proposals show the fragmentation in the family visible in spatial organization; but within a housing unit, the family remains the basis for the concept of the basic constituents of architectural units. Most proposals anticipate rooms, bedrooms, and sanitary units as replaceable capsule units, which implies development toward specialized monofunctional units clipped onto the main communal space of a social cell; this is a principle that differs from that of the described proposals of the Metabolists from the early 1960s.

In Akira Shibuya's project, which won a competition entitled "Urban Residences and their Connective Systems" in 1966, and seems to focus on the automation of the placement of living cells on a megastructure, capsule units were clipped onto megastructural frameworks, and show the possibility for dwellings formed by clipped-on capsules to grow. Günther Nitschke condemned the megalomaniac feature of the proposed megastructures, since "as long as the actual buildings get heavier, harder, more and more monstrous in scale, as long as architecture is taken as a means of expression of power . . . the talk of greater flexibility and change-loving structures is just fuss," and puts traditional Japanese architecture, and the efforts of Fuller, Wachsmann, and Ekuan in Japan opposite to them.[311]

A rather different proposal came for Team Ancous housing (see Figures 2.43, 2.44, 2.45), which exceeded the preoccupation with the megastructure as such, and emphasized a social vision using technological rhetoric. Loosening family ties and individualization are the principles reflected in this project, which does not end its ambition with the fragmentation of traditional social structures, but facilitates the re-composition, or establishment of new social units. For each member of the family, their own cell/capsule living unit is anticipated within the *family unit*. Children's units, parents' bedroom, and separate units, "living rooms" for parents, are independent cells for each individual, while two bathrooms and a family "living room" are intended for all members. Twelve two-story family units are placed in a *team unit* with a vast communal space for 50 people, while sixteen *team units* form a *social unit*. When these social units are stacked on top of each other, they form an apartment complex.

The trend of the loosening of family ties replaced by daily contacts of the newly emerged *team* was understood by Günther Nitschke as a reaction to the traditional structure of the Japanese family, structures that did not allow an individual to have privacy and be independent. He explains the replacement of family functions within the *team,* with the influence of "Red China" on the younger generation of Japanese, which gave resistance to the modern Japanese capitalist competitive social system, in which everyone opposes everyone, a formal and structural expression. In addition to the social reform vision, the distinctly mechanical architectural expression in associations with space capsules of various scales is also convincing. The whole of the complex consists of *housing—social units* designed in the shape of a cylinder consisting of *team units,* and finished off with a "lid" in the shape of a cut-off cone, under which there is the communal space of an individual unit. Nitschke connects the whole form of the complex of "Sputniks put on top of each other" with the tradition of modern architecture, which was always influenced by pure technical forms.[312] A *team unit,* in the shape of a hexagonal pyramid, is a capsulized clip-on unit, which is clipped onto the infrastructural

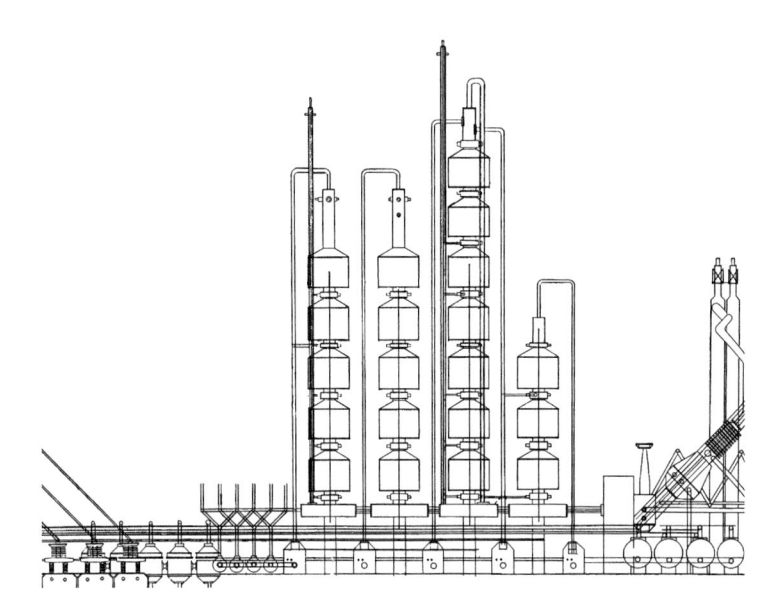

FIGURE 2.43 Tetsuya Akiyama, Iwao Kawakami, Norio Sato, Yuji Shiraishi, and Yoshiaki Koyama, Team Ancous housing: project for the *Shinkenchiku* competition (*The Japan Architect*) entitled "Urban Residences and Their Connective Systems" from 1966. Elevation of the complex

core of a *housing/social unit*. A *family unit* is a capsulized clip-on unit in the shape of a cylinder, which is clipped onto a *team unit*. The smallest *living units*, which may be called individual capsules, are spaces with round corners inserted into a *family unit*.

Capsularization of individual units is completely in accordance with the technological design inspired by the space technique. Capsularization, in this project, is the condition for the organization of social structure, which places an individual in a *team* and a wider *housing/social unit* through an optional contact with the family environment, which clearly points to the continuity of social utopias of the planning of communal spaces in apartment buildings, from the European utopian socialism at the end of the 19th century, to communist experiments at the end of the 1920s, and also Le Corbusier's megalomaniacal concept of *Unité d'Habitation* in the mid-20th century. The project contains sections for energy supply, production, and shopping, special functions, and a factory area. However, the project does not mention any larger communal spaces, since architects assumed that social activities should be limited to smaller groups.[313] Subsequent less "revolutionary" projects for the *Shinkenchiku* competition, entitled "Urban Residences for a High-Density Society" in 1967, continue along the way of the fragmentation of family living units to individual capsule units, paved by the project described above, and preserve a common family space as part of a family unit.

In the second half of the 1960s, the concepts of the megastructure and the capsule living cell were established and became a predictable practice among competition proposals in Japan. Despite the interest in capsules and capsule architecture particularly attributed to Kisho Kurokawa, the topic, which remained at the forefront at least until Expo '70, was also dealt with in intellectual, project, and critical terms by others. This is upheld by the aforementioned thematic issue of the *SD* magazine from 1969. In addition to articles by Fumihiko Maki,

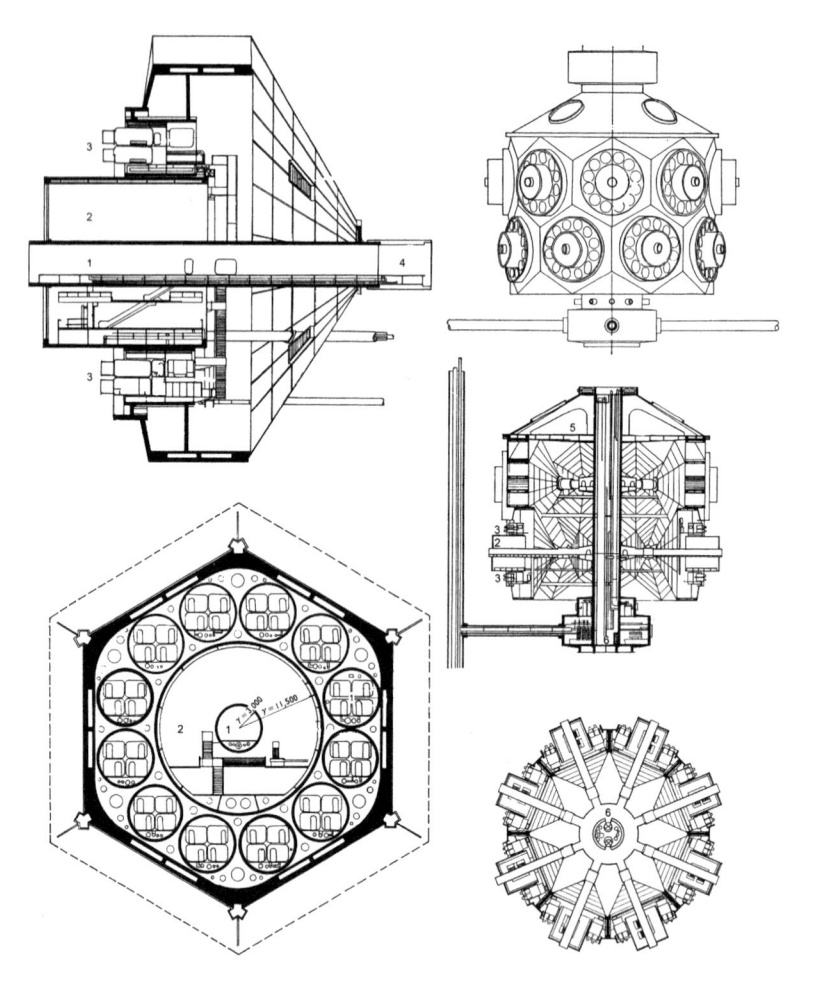

FIGURE 2.44 Tetsuya Akiyama, Iwao Kawakami, Norio Sato, Yuji Shiraishi, and Yoshiaki Koyama, Team Ancous housing, 1966. Plan, section, and elevation of the team unit: (1) access, (2) communal area/team space, (3) family unit, (4) connector, (5) common space, (6) access tower/duct for services

Kisho (Noriaki) Kurokawa, GK Industrial Design, Noboru Kawazoe, and a feature on Archigram, this issue also contains a substantial amount of reference and metaphorical visual material, which enhances the list, explains and illustrates (potential) origins, and establishes a system of analogies to the concept of the capsule.

The first reference is the development of an embryo in the womb as the primary biological capsule of a human. The use of the term capsule is illustrated by a French–Japanese picture dictionary, which shows examples from the human anatomy, examples from botany, engineering, and microbiology and, to expand the mindset, also a detail from Bosch's *The Garden of Earthly Delights*, where populated spherical "capsule" cells, without the technological equipment, seem even more illustrative than Dallegret's or Fuller's, and very much alive. A collage with examples from aviation, car, space, and military technology is graphically wrapped up in the form of a pharmaceutical capsule, which is surrounded by science fiction images, including

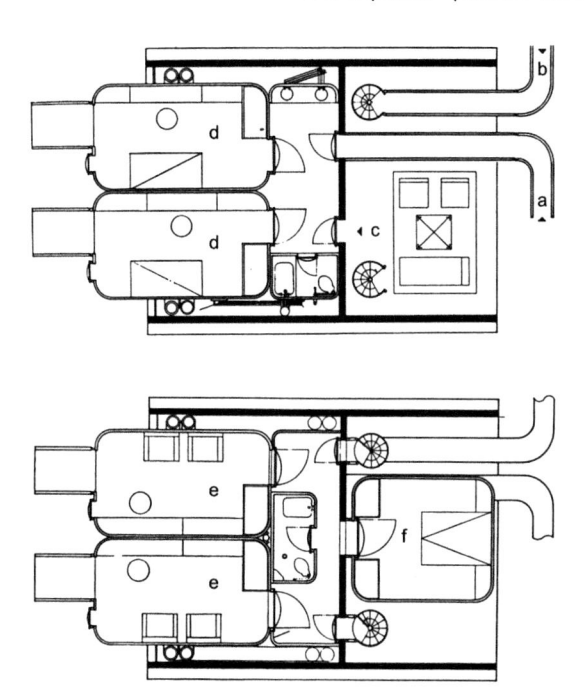

FIGURE 2.45 Tetsuya Akiyama, Iwao Kawakami, Norio Sato, Yuji Shiraishi and Yoshiaki Koyama, Team Ancous housing, 1966. Plan and section of living cells. Plans for both stories of family residential unit: (a) first floor children's entrance, (b) parents' entrance, (c) family unit/living room, (d) child's unit, (e) parents' individual unit, (f) parents' unit

Archigram's *Walking City* and Raimund Abraham's *Air-Ocean-City*, which corroborates the softening of edges of architecture as a discipline in Japan, and its legitimate coquetry or even coexistence with the fantasy world of science fiction. The transfer of the analogy to the field of architecture is presented on the subsequent pages. Historical examples of enclosed military camps, cities, settlements, and gardens with ground plan unicellular or related multicellular design expand the concept in the field of wider spatial designs. Drawings of space capsules highlight the most important mechanical analogy of capsules. A photo of an embryo in a womb is surrounded by "devices" that surround a grown man: Clothing, a space suit, a mini submarine, a pneumatic envelope, and a sci-fi attachment appears again, before the page with architectural examples, as a direct connection between the biological world of nature and anthropogenic aids, which is crucial in Metabolism.

The visual presentation of analogies introduces us to the capsule architecture examples, which include flat pack structures, like the *Tortoise-Shaped House, Nucleus Dwelling/Pumpkin House*, a sanitary-kitchen service block, and the *Komatsu Ski Lodge* by GK Industrial Design; a mobile shelter of a group from the Hornsey College of Art, the Imperial Chemical Industries (ICI) plastic bathroom and the *Imperial Chemical Industries Plastics Division* kitchen unit; Fuller's *Dymaxion* bathroom and the *Mechanical Wing* mobile unit, prefabricated and flat pack units of bathrooms and kitchen, a geodesic dome, and Archigram's *Suitaloon* and *Living Pod*. The display of autonomous and mobile organisms and machines ends with a list of analogies, which should stir, before written reflections, the understanding and scope of the field of the concept of the capsule, and its potential manifestations. But this concept is not completely unambiguous and devoid of risk. The other side of the euphoric display adds a critical note and a polemic collage with a text concerning the issue of the responsibility of designers, and establishes an analogy of the possibility of uncontrolled (architectural or urban) development, like that of cancer tissue. Fear of complete anarchy is present, at least latently. Biological analogies of growth and deterioration are part of the philosophy of Metabolism. However, the latter analogy of deterioration highlights the issues of the limits of freedom, the limits of system regulation, and whether the desired "form of a city," as a comprehensible and living organism, may be provided with the "planning tool of a capsule." Five essays that pursue, each in its own manner, the visual analogies, contextualize the concept of the capsule as such in relation to a wider space.

Fumihiko Maki acknowledges that a capsule space is actually a reflection of a developed information society with a high level of autonomy and free choice based on an individual, but places capsule space in opposition to neighborhood, which has the role of an open space for social interaction, as members of Team 10 and others had exposed. In Maki's conception, the basic capsule has, first and foremost, security functions provided by the envelope. Second, information functions are provided by the equipment, with information devices such as a television, a phone, terminal equipment, a teleprinter, a photocopier, and a typewriter, and these give meaning to the capsule as a place of rest, work, socializing, or learning. To ensure its autonomy, a capsule is supposed to be equipped with a battery and a self-propelled device, an air-conditioning device, a water supply, and a sewage device. Capsules also have a metabolic function of exchangeability, and can be merged into groups.[314]

Capsule units are, therefore, private spaces with high information density, which fill a city, a neighborhood, a place for spontaneous meetings, a fluid porous space which facilitates a flow of information and creates a special atmosphere. Maki perceives a capsule space as a fact of modern individualized society but, as in his philosophy about the *group form*, pays more attention to the in-between space, which may be a neighborhood, a place for informal spontaneous meetings, which actually makes a city into a vibrant and useful information center.

Noboru Kawazoe's article marks the 20th century as a century of "package culture," while it predicts the 21st century to be a century of "capsules."[315] In a Marxist tone, Kawazoe is critical of "package design" of modern "boxes of concrete, iron, and glass" which is in the service of marketing and added value, which changes products and architecture into dehumanized tools of capitalism. Maki and Kawazoe both believe that cities cannot be composed only of capsules. In Kawazoe's opinion, a capsule is the work of industrial designers, and is not architecture. In architecture as he knew it, the connection between space and equipment was blurred. Therefore, when capsules emerged, his goal was to emphasize space.[316] For Kawazoe, *space* is more important, but it may be defined only through the new spatial element of a *capsule*, which enables it to surpass former traditional relations.

It seems that, throughout the contextualization of the concept of the capsule and other Metabolist discourse, the duality between serviced and servant spaces appears and, in various contexts, attributes certain characteristics to various spatial elements. The diversity of aspects and positions of individual members of the group does not enable the determination of the common denominator since, for example for Kurokawa, capsules are more important, despite his awareness of the importance of the in-between space. Meanwhile, for Maki and Kawazoe, the in-between space is more important. At the same time, duality is emphasized between the industrial design domain, where capsules are classified, and architecture, which should be qualified, also critically, to deal with space.

Duality between industrial design and architecture is also implied by Archigram. In his presentation of the group, Toshio Nakamura points out its work in relation to the consumer culture, space mechanical tools, and expression from comics; this does not build a city as a permanent structure, but as a formation full of consumables, various expressive forms, and as a never-complete final form.[317] Nakamura describes Archigram's plug-in living capsule as a logical conclusion of its research of space and marine capsules, and compares it, perhaps with a Metabolist inspiration, to a living organism. In his opinion, a capsule is not a cell, but a unicellular organism. If we might consider unicellular organisms as extreme living organisms, then a living capsule may be considered an extreme living space. The meaning of this extreme is not to the extent a man can *improve* his living conditions, but to the extent he can *protect* his living conditions.[318]

The comparison of a capsule with a unicellular organism is very close to Kurokawa's definition of cyborg architecture, but Nakamura leaves out the significance of technology for the realization of the project in his analogy. A similarly incomplete analogy to traditional dwellings in extreme conditions, examples of which include Eskimo igloos and dwellings of Mongolian nomads, is later supplemented with Le Corbusier's concept of the house-machine and Fuller's realization of it, with the *Dymaxion House* and the *Monsanto House of the Future* in Disneyland. Nakamura divides Archigram's capsules into independent and clipped-on megastructures, and highlights their nature as consumable goods, in relation to the pragmatic parameters of the costs of the material durability, and requirements in view of the size of the family and fashion. Perhaps the approach of Kisho Kurokawa is closest to Archigram's, at least in certain segments, although his obsessive philosophical contemplations significantly differ from the colorful saturated ironic pop graphic speculations of the British colleagues.

Due to the economic crisis in the 1970s, which pierced the bubble of the Japanese economy, hardly anything remained of the initial theoretical contemplation about the liberating concept of the capsule as a program in its entirety, after a few built and partly realized promises, and several project solutions, except for its attractive name. In the first half of the 1970s, Kisaburo Kawakami hesitated between euphoria and doubt, asked himself several rhetorical questions about the concept of the capsule in the present and future, and pointed out the question of the possible formation of a community, and the question of individuality in the urban environment, as well as cultural determinism;

> Does the appearance of the capsule symbolize the flexibility of the Japanese people toward the exterior environments, with the irony of human beings inside the capsules and noise and pollution outside? . . . Will the capsule become the 21st century "brick" for the people in the internationalized city?[319]

Certain questions stem from doubts about the promise of manifestos, and others from completely pragmatic observations of the situation. Most answers remain in the form of optimistic good thoughts and revivalist rhetoric, as we cannot judge real consequences, because the number of realizations was very small. Several answers, in the form of the mutation of the concept of the capsule and commodified derivations to the last question, are provided by the reality of modern Japan itself, although perhaps not to the extent envisaged by Kawakami.

The trivialization of the revolutionary concept of the capsule emerged through a phenomenon which has kept this concept as part of the Japanese daily routine until today.

The substantive and conceptual derivations were provided for already by Kurokawa, when he designed the first capsule hotel, *Capsule Inn*, in Osaka in 1979,[320] with the popular typology of a sleeping unit, without which modern urban Japan cannot imagine an entertaining weekend or a workday prolonged into the night. Ironic is the fact that the liberating concept of the capsule turned into an emergency exit, which was predicted, albeit in a different tone, by Kurokawa in his declaration, saying that a capsule becomes a living space when a man cannot hope to live elsewhere.

In the modern reality of the Japanese daily routine, the capsule hotel became a dwelling for the homeless,[321] real-life modern nomads, residents of capsules. Capsule containers in the hotel are far from the anticipated technological prosthetics of a free individual. A capsule in a capsule hotel may be mobile, but is actually stacked firmly within the grip of the hotel program. The only one who is mobile is the individual for whom a hotel capsule provides minimum shelter, which is, unlike common dwellings, minimally individualized. A minimum space, with approximate dimensions of 195 cm in depth, 95 cm in width, and 95 cm in height, with minimum acoustic insulation, provides an individualized space for someone who withdraws from the city hustle and bustle to rest (see Figures 2.46, 2.47, 2.48, 2.49). It even offers the theoretical realization of the philosophy of inclusion, the coexistence of contradictions, since a man in the capsule is both part of the structure and an individual in his own living cell, at the same time. A plastic sleeping capsule is usually not equipped with high-tech devices, but with simple, nowadays outdated, equipment for fun and leisure time—a television

FIGURE 2.46　Capsule Hotel in Tokyo: the structure of the hotel does not show in any way the program inside

FIGURE 2.47 Capsule Hotel in Tokyo: communal access hallway with stacked sleeping capsules

FIGURE 2.48 Capsule Hotel in Tokyo: interior of the sleeping capsule—a view inwards

screen, a phone, a radio, and a built-in alarm clock, as it is envisaged as a short-term (night) dwelling. All other functions of the hotel are common, and vary from hotel to hotel. With increasingly greater mobility and their realization at certain airports, the trend of capsule hotels was transferred to the West.

With the aforementioned modern examples, headed by the capsule hotel, comes the trivialization and commodification of the original idea of the capsule. Kurokawa saw to the popularization of the name in the *Discothèque Space Capsule* project at the end of the 1960s. Even before the iconic realizations of capsules, a social space filled with futuristic aesthetics and technicalities tended to the transfer of the conceptual framework: "This stainless-steel space capsule is a place for the refining and smelting of information; it is a capsule for those who want to release what is pent up inside them."[322] Was Kurokawa's desire to expand the *modus operandi* of the concept beyond the sphere of an individual, by including this collective "capsule," which emerged in 1968 before the publication of the *Capsule Declaration*, but published together with the declaration in a book in 1977, among capsule spaces? In view of the

FIGURE 2.49 Capsule Hotel in Tokyo: interior of the sleeping capsule—a view outwards

last article of the declaration, we could corroborate that. In this case, the information aspect—the medium interior of the capsule is actually the key parameter of Kurokawa's *extended* concept of it. A capsule as an envelope, which prevents contact with unwanted information, may also be an envelope which facilitates a flow only of, perhaps unrealistically expected, desired information on the futuristic trendy fashion scene, in the space of avant-garde productions of poetry readings, a discothèque—artists' meeting point.

Despite partly different uses, a review of capsule structure and the responses of contemporaries of capsule architecture in the 1960s in Great Britain and Japan, even by its main protagonists, prompts consideration of the suitability of the use of the term "capsule" for spatial units of various sizes and with various delineations. Although the concept of the capsule in Japan, with metaphorical extensions, was not defined completely unambiguously, it particularly signified, at least in the early examples, as it did for their colleagues from Great Britain, a minimum, compact, mobile, fully equipped and ergonomically shaped living unit with prescribed durability and a monofunctional unit (sanitary units, kitchen block, furniture element) with the same characteristics, for which the following elements were defined: *Relative impermeability of the envelope; physical or simulated comfort of the introverted interior provided by the connection to the network; functional, spatial and visual integrity; time dependence or changeability; and smallness which enables mobility.*

Notes

1 *Existence minimum (Subsistence minimum)* has been conceived by the social scientists of the 19th century as the minimum requirements to support human life. It was related to quantitative standards for food, shelter, clothing, medical emergencies, etc. In the 1920s, architects defined it especially in relation to the smallest space needed to live (minimal dwelling) considering its social and hygienic consequences. See Susan R. Henderson, *Building Culture: Ernst May and the New Frankfurt Initiative* (New York, etc.: Peter Lang, 2013).

2 The topic of the dwelling for the subsistence minimum was specifically aimed at project solutions of the problem of high rents and low wages, i.e. at the smallest comfortable dwelling at the lowest price. See Eric Mumford, *The CIAM Discourse on Urbanism, 1928–1960* (Cambridge, MA and London: MIT Press, 2000), 27–44; Hilde Heynen, *Architecture and Modernity: A Critique* (Cambridge, MA and London: MIT Press, 1999), 43–70.

3 Hilde Heynen, *Architecture and Modernity*, 49.

4 Mumford, *The CIAM Discourse on Urbanism*, 31. The author is stating an example from Paris with a living area smaller than most living areas shown by the participants at the congress.

5 Ibid., 37.

6 Hilde Heynen points out that the terms which refer to modernist architecture are used differently in different languages, which also affects the concept. "The Dutch Nieuwe Bauen and the German Neues Bauen explicitly avoid the term 'architecture' (which exists in both languages), which hints at a desire for architecture which is not limited to representative buildings, but comprises the whole field of building and dwelling. This connotation is missing in the French term *architecture moderne* and the English term *modern architecture*." For H. Heynen to maintain the wider concept present in the Dutch and German terms, she uses the term "New Building," which was emphasized here in the context of ambiguity. See Heynen, *Architecture and Modernity*, 28; 230.

7 Ibid., 41.

8 Walter Gropius, "The Sociological Premises for the Minimum Dwelling of Urban Industrial Populations," in *The Scope of Total Architecture* (New York: Collier, 1970), 99. Gropius's basic requirements and goals are similar to the ones in the key document of the concept of the capsule in Kisho Kurokawa's *Capsule Declaration*, with the requirements being upgraded and adapted to new needs, 40 years after the CIAM Congress.

9 Mumford, *The CIAM Discourse on Urbanism*, 27–44; 285.

10 Nikolai Aleksandrovich Miliutin, *Sotsgorod: The Problem of Building Socialist Cities* (Cambridge, MA and London: MIT Press, 1974).

11 Regarding the issue of representation in architecture, one must distinguish between the representation methods that refer to graphical representations of architecture and space, and the notion of architecture as a representational system, a system for the production of meaning, which will also be presented through analysis in relation to the structure and function in individual selected cases.

12 See Heynen, *Architecture and Modernity*, 47–48.

13 The book was not published in English until 2002. Karel Teige, *The Minimum Dwelling* (Cambridge, MA and London: MIT Press, 2002), 32.

14 Ibid., 7.

15 Ibid., 346–370.

16 Ibid., 351; 354.

17 Teige even says (at least in the English translation) that communal houses or mega-houses will be, and that "collective houses are, essentially mega-structures." Ibid., 301, 360.

18 Stane Bernik, *Slovenska arhitektura dvajsetega stoletja* (Ljubljana: Mestna galerija, 2004), 101. The term was used by Bernik in his introductory text for the exhibition *Slovenska likovna umetnost 1945–1978* (Slovene Visual Arts 1945–1978) in 1978. See Stane Bernik, "Nekateri problemi predstavitve in vrednotenja sodobne slovenske arhitekture, urbanizma in oblikovanja," in *Slovenska likovna umetnost: 1945-1978: slikarstvo, kiparstvo, grafika, arhitektura, urbanizem, oblikovanje: '79*, ed. Stane Bernik et al. (Moderna galerija, Arhitekturni muzej, Ljubljana: Mladinska knjiga, 1979), 89–108.

19 See Max Risselada and Dirk van den Heuvel, *Team 10: In Search of a Utopia of the Present* (Rotterdam: NAi, 2005), 11–12.

20 Ibid., 13. Cf. Alison Smithson, ed., *Team 10 Primer* (Cambridge, MA and London: MIT Press, 1974), 3.

21 Barry Bergdoll, "Home Delivery: Viscidities of Modernist Dream from Taylorized Serial Production to Digital Customization," in *Home Delivery*, eds. Barry Bergdoll and Peter Christensen (New York: Museum of Modern Art, 2008), 12–26.

22 Although the need to reintroduce the standardization and harmonization of construction dimensions had emerged in the USA earlier, Europe became aware of the advantages of modular coordination only after the devastation of World War II. Tine Kurent, "Modularni princip," *Sinteza* 36, 37 (June 1976): 115–120. Cf. Tine Kurent, *Kompozicija modularnih mer* (Ljubljana: Univerza v Ljubljani, Fakulteta za arhitekturo, gradbeništvo in geodezijo, 1974).

23 Bergdoll and Christensen, *Home Delivery*.

24 This division is also pointed out by Bergdoll. Bergdoll and Christensen, *Home Delivery*, 12–26.

25 David Crowley and Jane Pawitt, in the introduction to the catalogue of the exhibition, "Cold War Modern: Design 1945–1970," emphasize that "if corporations, scientists, engineers, the military and others created the material world over and through which this conflict was fought, designers gave it form," pointing out the question of the designer's responsibility: "Should the designer be a technocrat, preparing expert designs in the service of State or corporation, or visionary,

independently pursuing a search for alternative ways of living?" David Crowley and Jane Pavitt, eds., *Cold War Modern: Design 1945–1970* (London:V&A Publishing, 2008), 21.

26 See Tomaž Brejc, "Modernizem: oris kriterijev," *Sinteza* 87, 88, 89, 90 (October 1991): 141–150.

27 Banham addresses the First Machine Age as the successor to the Victorian industrial age of "cast iron, soot and rust," while "machines of the First Machine Age of the early 20th century were light, subtle, clean and could be handled by thinking men in their own homes, out in the new electric suburbs." Reyner Banham, *Theory and Design in the First Machine Age* (Cambridge, MA: MIT Press, 1980), 11.

28 Ibid., 10.

29 In a letter by Richard Buckminster Fuller to John McHale, 1955. John McHale, "Richard Buckminster Fuller," *Architectural Design* (July 1961): 294.

30 The questioning of modernism after World War II included practices that referred to the systems theory, cybernetics, behavioral and social sciences, and also to the diversity or ambiguity of the perception of space, as found in Independent Group or Team 10 and positions and movements like New Monumentality, Neo-Liberty, and others.

31 "We must create the mass-production spirit. The spirit of constructing mass-production houses. The spirit of living in mass-production houses. The spirit of conceiving mass-production houses. If we eliminate from our hearts and minds all dead concepts in regard to the house, and look at the question from a critical and objective point of view, we shall arrive at the 'House-Machine,' the mass-production house, healthy (and morally so, too) and beautiful in the same way that the working tools and instruments which accompany our existence are beautiful." Le Corbusier, *Towards a New Architecture* (New York: Dover Publications, 1986), reprint of the publication from 1931 re-publication of the work originally published by John Rodker (London, 1931), 6.

32 John McHale, *R. Buckminster Fuller* (New York: George Braziller, 1962), 9.

33 Quoted in Michael John Gorman, *Buckminster Fuller: Designing for Mobility* (Milan: Skira Editore, 2005), 36–39.

34 J. Baldwin, *Bucky Works: Buckminster Fuller's Ideas for Today* (New York: John Wiley & Sons, 1996), 16.

35 McHale, *R. Buckminster Fuller*, 15.

36 Ibid., 10.

37 The name *Dymaxion* is composed of the words Dynamism + Maximum + Ion. In addition to his research and the development of the typology of dwellings, Fuller used the name *Dymaxion* for the famous *Dymaxion World Map*, and the self-propelled unit *Dymaxion Ground Taxiing Unit/Dymaxion Car* designed in 1933, a symbolic machine with which Reyner Banham announced the end of the First Machine Age in design. (Banham, *Theory and Design in the First Machine Age*, 304). The vehicle is an aerodynamically designed triangle for eleven persons, with a spacious interior, which is reminiscent of the interior of sailboats, and achieved a speed of over 160 km/h. It represents a stage in the evolution of a complex auto-airplane.

38 In *Your Private Sky: R. Buckminster Fuller: The Art of Design Science*, eds. Joachim Krausse and Claude Lichtenstein (Baden: Lars Müller Publishers, 1999), 173.

39 Richard Buckminster Fuller, "Lightful Houses," 1928, in *Your Private Sky: R. Buckminster Fuller: The Art of Design Science*, eds. Krausse and Lichtenstein, 73.

40 Flexible internal partitions, which also had the storage function, pneumatic folding door, automated laundry and dishwashing, incineration of waste, etc. The whole house was designed on the principle of modern "smart homes," with centrally controlled light, sound, and space.

41 Later, Fuller described the *Dymaxion House* as "designed to withstand all forces which seek to penetrate or destroy the human life process." Gorman, *Buckminster Fuller: Designing for Mobility*, str. 45.

42 Quoted in McHale, "Richard Buckminster Fuller," 316.

43 Joachim Krausse and Claude Lichtenstein, eds., *Your Private Sky: Discourse, R. Buckminster Fuller* (Baden: Lars Müller Publishers, 2001), 15.

44 Gorman, *Buckminster Fuller: Designing for Mobility*, 46.

45 Fuller was not even interested in making a handmade full-scale mock-up of the *Dymaxion House*, since it would affect his integrity. He reportedly replied to a potential investor who was interested in making it for the 1933–34 Chicago World Fair, that it would cost "100 million dollars." Fuller compared it to the total cost of a similar production in the automotive industry, where the cost of making just one new Ford Model A was $43,000 and the production of the second one would cost only an additional $500. Ibid., 49.

46 Krausse and Lichtenstein, eds., *Your Private Sky: R. Buckminster Fuller: The Art of Design Science*, 238.

47 Banham, *Theory and Design in the First Machine Age*, 326.

48 McHale, *R. Buckminster Fuller*, 18.

49 *Weissenhofsiedlung* was an experimental settlement in Stuttgart, built in 1927 as a building exhibition of Deutscher Werkbund (German Association of Craftsmen is a German association of artists, architects, designers, and industrialists, established in 1907) and was funded by the City of Stuttgart. Seventeen prominent architects formulated modernist ideals transcending the traditional ways of living of the preindustrial era. It is considered one of the most significant landmarks of the New Building movement.

50 Buckminster Fuller, "World Design Initiative, Mexico Lecture" (1963), in Krausse and Lichtenstein, *Your Private Sky: Discourse*, 270.

51 Ibid.

52 See Lloyd Kahn, ed., *Shelter* (Bolinas, CA: Shelter, 1973).

53 The dome was designed to include an inflated polyethylene envelope, and was built at Black Mountain College in 1949. See Baldwin, *Bucky Works*, 150.

54 The first equipped trailers and mobile homes have been used since the 19th century but, in the 1920s, they got a look that has not changed much to this day. In this segment, *Mechanical Wings* actually brings nothing new, but we have to admit that, as an equipment package, they open up opportunities for equipped living beyond the strict attachment to a means of transport—with the liberating setting of the dome, which becomes an equipped dwelling—anywhere in nature. Cf. Hans Ibelings, "Mobile Architecture in the Twentieth Century," in *Parasite Paradise: A Manifesto for Temporary Architecture and Flexible Urbanism*, ed. Liesbeth Melis (Rotterdam: NaI, 2003), 148–166.

55 Alastair Gordon, *Spaced Out: Radical Environments of the Psychedelic Sixties* (New York: Rizzoli International, 2008), 167.

56 Radical environments of the psychedelic sixties are presented in detail in Gordon, *Spaced Out: Radical Environments of the Psychedelic Sixties*. The study serves as an important reference in the contextualization of our topic.

57 Gordon, *Spaced Out*, 78.

58 Ibid., 23.

59 Ibid., 83. As shown below, formal and associative allusions to the womb as a primary shelter were constants also in the design of pioneer capsule units. The connection was especially pointed out in the Japanese magazine, *Space Design,* which discussed the topic of the capsule.

60 Ibid., 25.

61 Ibid., 17.

62 Gerald Heard used the name "intranaut" for a researcher who researched the interior by means of hallucinogenic substances. The term astronaut is compared to Timothy Leary's "neuronaut"— in the aforementioned derivatives of an explorer of the universe of one's own inner space. Ibid., 33.

63 Buckminster Fuller, *Operating Manual for Spaceship Earth (*1967), in Krausse and Lichtenstein, *Your Private Sky: R. Buckminster Fuller: The Art of Design Science*, 350–351.

64 The USCO group and other artists who, under the influence of McLuhan, adopted the idea of the transformation of society from Renaissance individualism to electronic tribalism, carried out multimedia events with light and audio impulses, and used all technical options to create a cosmic awareness in real time and space, and to redefine the relationship between space and time. Gordon, *Spaced Out*, 39. See also Felicity D. Scott, *Architecture or Techno-utopia: Politics after Modernism* (Cambridge, MA: MIT Press, 2007).

65 Gordon, *Spaced Out*, 87.

66 Ibid. Fuller's statement: "I made up my mind, at this point, that I would never try to reform man— that's much too difficult. What I would do is try to modify the environment in such a way as to get man moving in preferred directions"—B. Fuller, quoted in Krausse and Lichtenstein, *Your Private Sky: Discourse*, 17. Although counterculture seemed rather in tune with Fuller's mindset in the first half of the 1960s, the second half saw the movement inundated with skepticism. In 1974, the *Shelter* publication published quite a few doubts about Fuller's slogans, marked as misunderstandings. The aforementioned was brought into question with the following words: "Shouldn't that be the other way around?" Kahn, *Shelter*, 117.

67 Neke Carson's plastic bubbles, *Man-Moon-Fountain*, which looked like transparent pressure suits, contained bubbling water, imitating the sound in the womb. The radical gain of individual space is represented by Wendell Castle's *Enclosed Reclining Environment for One*. The comfortable interior, where there is just enough space for a lonely soul-searching individual, is enclosed in an amorphous bubble

sculpture of laminated oak and flocked fiberglass. "Time for Spaces, Monday," *Time,* Feb. 02, 1970, www.time.com/time/magazine/article/0,9171,878173,00.html?promoid=googlep (2009-3).

68 By rolling the cylinder, various elements of the furniture—bed, table in various positions—changed their purpose. The cylinder could also be spun more quickly, to get the feeling of weightlessness. Gordon, *Spaced Out,* 101.

69 Stewart Brand, the founder and editor of the legendary and influential "DIY" publication *Whole Earth Catalog* which, for many people, is a conceptual predecessor of the current world wide web, and which provided American counterculture drop-outs with a range of practical available tools, texts, and information for the creation of sustainable communities, wrote, in the June edition of *The Last Whole Earth Catalog,* in 1971, in the accompanying text to *Walden,* Henry Thoreau's book: "I believe that Thoreau would have accepted the idea. It costs sixty cents. The most important document of the currently-ongoing third American revolution." Stewart Brand, "Walden," *New Whole Earth LLC* (Last Whole Earth Catalog), www.wholeearth.com/issue-electronic-edition.php?iss=1150 (2009–3).

70 Gordon, *Spaced Out,* 134.

71 Ibid., 151.

72 Steve Baer, a fan of Fuller's mindset since 1963, came to *Drop City* in April 1966, and suggested sheet metal cut from waste car tops to be used as cladding for domes. At the same time, he developed an asymmetrical dome from panels of various forms, and called it "zome." Baer was also enthralled with sustainable systems, and invented the solar heating system, which is considered one of the first of such systems in the USA. Ibid., 175–182.

73 Gordon, *Spaced Out,* 190; Kahn, *Shelter,* 138–139.

74 Ibid., 199.

75 Lloyd Kahn, "Domebook 3," in *Shelter,* 110–111.

76 The heritage of Frederick Kiesler, who called conventional houses "voluntary prisons," and who erased corners and edges, and created smooth transitions between the walls, the ceiling, and the floor with biomorphous organic forms in the "Endless House," facilitating the endlessness of the house—the house in which all ends fuse together, was cut out for the countercultural movement's concept of space. Gordon, *Spaced Out,* 240.

77 The communities of Libré in Colorado, Lama in New Mexico, Farm in Tennessee, and Arcosanti in Arizona managed to develop with time, and prosper as potential alternatives to this day. Gordon, *Spaced Out,* 285; Lloyd Kahn, *Shelter,* 106–107.

78 The latter exhibit the stubborn persistence of modern purists and the softening of strict functionalists with picturesque detailing of non-picturesque urbanism, having organized the "Festival of Britain" traveling exhibition in 1951, and popularized the *Contemporary Style* which should combine the characteristics of past British design with a modern design look. For a more detailed presentation of the activities of the Independent Group in the context of Modernism and mass culture in post-war Britain, see Anne Massey, *The Independent Group: Modernism and Mass Culture in Britain, 1945–59* (Manchester and New York: Manchester University Press, 1995).

79 Certain "members" already collaborated in 1951, and also after the Independent Group ceased to exist. For a detailed review, see Massey, *The Independent Group;* Claude Lichtenstein and Thomas Schregenberger, eds., *As Found: The Discovery of the Ordinary* (Baden: Lars Müller Publishers, 2001). The chronicler and propagandist of New Brutalism in the 1950s was Reyner Banham, who published his own, momentarily ironic, "memories of a survivor" a decade later, with an accurate and extended review and description of the origins and derivations of the New Brutalism which, however, were not left without critical responses from the actors themselves. Banham, *The New Brutalism: Ethic or Aesthetic?* (Stuttgart: Karl Krämer Verlag Stuttgart, 1966). Cf. Alison and Peter Smithson, "Banham's Bumper Book on Brutalism," *Architect's Journal* (December 1966): 1590–1591; A. and P. Smithson, *Without Rhetoric–An Architectural Aesthetic 1955–1972* (London: Latimer New Dimensions, 1973).

80 See Massey, *The Independent Group;* esp. discussion of Expendable Aesthetics.

81 Nigel Whiteley, *Reyner Banham: Historian of the Immediate Future* (Cambridge, MA: MIT Press, 2002), 138–139.

82 Banham, *The New Brutalism: Ethic or Aesthetic?,* 68–69, 134. Due in his opinion to a not completely representative function of the text on the actual situation of the Brutalist movement at that time, he recommends to potential readers to read it "cum grano salis." Cf. Banham, "The New Brutalism," *The Architectural Review* (December 1955): 355–361; "The New Brutalism," *Architectural Design* (January 1955).

83 With the exhibition *Parallel of Art and Life*, Henderson, Paolozzi, and the Smithsons indicate, for the first time, the Brutalist sensibility, with a didactic collection of photographic images which show the toughness of everyday life in the emphasized coarse-grained structure, which led many critics to connect it with material roughness of the Hunstanton School. Banham, *The New Brutalism: Ethic or Aesthetic?*

84 Whiteley, *Reyner Banham*, 86.

85 Ibid., 117.

86 See A. and P. Smithson, "The New Brutalism," *Architectural Design* (April 1957): 113. Cf. Banham, *The New Brutalism: Ethic or Aesthetic?*

87 Banham, *The New Brutalism*, 355–361. According to Banham, these ideas complied with the so-called anti-academic aesthetics which were used at the time. He points out that they cannot be completely equated with the concept of Michel Tapié's *un art autre*, although the concept covers many Brutalists on the mainland, as well as Eduardo Paolozzi.

88 Ibid., 358.

89 Ibid., 358.

90 Ibid., 361.

91 Banham, *The New Brutalism: Ethic or Aesthetic?*, 68.

92 Whiteley, *Reyner Banham*, 253, 263, 395. Cf. Kenneth Frampton, "Towards a Critical Regionalism: Six Points for an Architecture of Resistance," in *The Anti-Aesthetic. Essays on Postmodern Culture*, ed. Hal Foster (Seattle, WA: Bay Press, 1983), 16–30.

93 See Massey, *The Independent Group*, 109–127.

94 Frampton, *Modern Architecture: A Critical History* (London: Thames & Hudson, 1980 (2002)), 265.

95 Jane Pavitt, "The Bomb in the Brain," in *Cold War Modern: Design 1945–1970*, eds. David Crowley and Jane Pavitt (London: V&A Publishing, 2008), 116.

96 In addition to a mutual connection between the projects, the historical cultural continuity of examples of exhibition pavilions is also symptomatic, where the *House of the Future* as a work of the third generation of the 20th century refers to Le Corbusier's pavilion *L'Esprit Nouveau* from 1925 from the first generation and an exhibition project of the Eames from the second generation. See Beatriz Colomina, "Unbreathed Air 1956," *Grey Room* 15 (Spring 2004): 28–59; Beatriz Colomina, "Paviljoni prihodnosti," *Oris* (IX-48-2007): 4–17.

97 A. Smithson, "Patio and Pavilion, 1956, Reconstructed U.S.A. 1990," *Places: A Quarterly Journal of Environmental Design* 7(3:11:1991): 8–15.

98 Ibid.

99 The chronology of the use of plastics for the needs of living units is comprehensively discussed in: Pamela Voigt, "Die Pionierphase des Bauens mit glasfaserverstärkten Kunststoffen (GFK) 1942 bis 1980" (PhD diss., Bauhaus Universität, Weimar, 2007). See also Arthur Quarmby, *Plastics and Architecture* (Washington, DC and New York: Praeger, 1974); Simone Jeska, *Transparent Plastics: Design and Technology* (Basel: Birkhäuser Verlag, 2008).

100 Openings in the axonometric display were there only for the needs of the exhibition. The ground plan clearly shows that, apart from the front door, there are no other openings in the outer wall. See also A. and P. Smithson, "England: House of the Future at the Ideal Homes Exhibition," *Architectural Design* (March 1956): 101–102.

101 A. Smithson, "Patio and Pavilion, 1956". The concept of the "unbreathed private air" of the *House of the Future* was used by Beatriz Colomina in the title of her thorough study of the project. See Colomina, "Unbreathed Air 1956."

102 See Colomina, "Unbreathed Air 1956," 40.

103 Simon Sadler emphasizes that Fuller's *Dymaxion* bathroom as a completely prefabricated and operating part of the house from 1936 to 1938 increased its value in avant-garde circles, by inspiring Alison and Peter Smithson's *House of the Future* from 1956. Simon Sadler, *Archigram: Architecture without Architecture* (Cambridge, MA and London: MIT Press, 2005), 107.

104 The association between the shape of rooms and the womb is pointed out by Sarah Williams Goldhagen. Williams Goldhagen, "Freedom's Domiciles: Three Projects by Alison and Peter Smithson," in *Anxious Modernisms: Experimentation in Postwar Architecture Culture*, eds. Sarah Williams Goldhagen and Réjean Legault (Cambridge, MA: MIT Press, 2000), 75–95.

105 To defend James Gowan's concept *the style for the job*, in relation to the issue of automobile aesthetics in architecture, Reyner Banham deals with the issue of styling in relation to the mass production and the possible rate of obsolescence for houses and mentions that the house was

designed and "stylized" similarly to automobile aesthetics. See Banham, "Stocktaking," *Architectural Review* (February 1960): 96; Cf. Banham, *The New Brutalism: Ethic or Aesthetic?*

106 They include *Appliance House*, 1956–1957; *Snowball House*, 1956–1957; *Bread House*, 1957; *Portico Row House* and *White Formica House*, 1957, and *Strip House*, 1957–1958. See Dirk van den Heuvel and Max Risselada, eds., *Alison and Peter Smithson: From House of the Future to a House of Today* (Rotterdam: 010 Publishers, 2004); Whiteley, *Reyner Banham*.

107 van den Heuvel and Risselada, *Alison and Peter Smithson*.

108 Le Corbusier, *Towards a New Architecture* (New York: Dover Publications, 1986 (1931)), 263.

109 A. Smithson, "Caravan–embryo 'Appliance House?'" *Architectural Design* (September 1959): 348.

110 See Colomina, "Unbreathed Air 1956."

111 Ibid., 47.

112 A. Smithson, "Patio and Pavilion, 1956", 13.

113 Peter Smithson, "Phenomenon in Parallel: Eames House, Patio and Pavilion," *Places: A Quarterly Journal of Environmental Design* 7 (3:11:1991): 22.

114 Banham, *The New Brutalism: Ethic or Aesthetic?*, 65.

115 Williams Goldhagen, "Freedom's Domiciles," 76. If, on the one hand, the freedom of social life in post-war western Europe was a generally accepted fact, endeavors for personal freedom of an individualized contemplative individual with an existentialist connotation became one of the key responses in British post-war artistic circles, brought on by the threat of unambiguity of mainstream mass culture and the awareness of omnipresent control mechanisms of the social system. Williams Goldhagen believes that the existentialist concept of authenticity is the concept that can help us clarify the Smithsons' endeavors, and particularly emphasizes Sartre's notion of authenticity, which became part of the fundamental discourse of the British avant-garde and, despite the fact that the Smithsons did not read Sartre in the 1950s, significantly influenced them.

116 P. Smithson, "Phenomenon in Parallel," 22. According to Peter Smithson, authenticity was the "obsession" of that time. See Williams Goldhagen, "Freedom's Domiciles," 78.

117 Williams Goldhagen, "Freedom's Domiciles," 78.

118 A. Smithson, "Patio and Pavilion," 13.

119 Colomina, "Unbreathed Air 1956," 52–53.

120 In literature, the author is cited as the Master of the Garden of Paradise assumed to be called Hans Tiefental. See Tomaž Zadnikar, "Mojster Bolfgang na Gornjem Porenju," *Zbornik za umetnostno zgodovino* (2004): 92. In Smithson's reference, he is referred to as "Master of Middle Rhine." See Colomina, "Unbreathed Air 1956," 53.

121 Saint Jerome (Eusebius Sophronius Hieronymus, 347–420) was one of four great doctors of the church, others being Saint Augustine, Saint Ambrose, and Saint Gregory the Great. His birthplace, the Roman Settlement of Stridon, is increasingly more often placed by church historians in the area between the Kvarner Gulf and Pivka, and between the peaks of the Učka, Snežnik, and Nanos. Certain sources also place it in present-day Dalmatia. He is known particularly as the author of the Latin translation of the Bible, called *Vulgata*. Rafko Valenčič, *Sveti Hieronim – mož s Krasa* (Ljubljana: Družina in ZRC TEOF Univerze v Ljubljani, 2007).

122 A. Smithson, "The Idyll and St. Jerome," *Places: A Quarterly Journal of Environmental Design* 7, Cambridge, MA: MIT Press, 3:11 (1991): 17. The article was written as a contemplation on the reconstruction of the *Patio and Pavilion* at the beginning of the 1920s, but the text does not explicitly refer only to that work. A more extensive text entitled "Saint Jerome: The Desert . . . The Study," which was published in 1990, was reprinted in *Alison and Peter Smithson – from House of the Future to a House of Today*, eds. van den Heuvel and Risselada, 225–229.

123 Ibid.

124 A. Smithson, "Saint Jerome: The Desert . . . The Study," 227.

125 Colomina, "Unbreathed Air 1956," 52.

126 A. and P. Smithson, "England: House of the Future at the Ideal Homes Exhibition," 101–102.

127 Whiteley cites openness, which was called "multiple aesthetics," "unifying but tolerant aesthetics," "the plurality of hierarchies," or in John McHale's words, particularly "both/and" instead of "either/or." Such a position is also succeeded by the neo-avant-garde of the 1960s—see for example Archigram. See also Whiteley, *Reyner Banham*, 104–105.

128 Banham, *The New Brutalism: Ethic or Aesthetic?*, 63; Cf. Le Corbusier, *Towards a New Architecture*, 227–265.

129 Banham, "Who is this 'Pop?'," in *Reyner Banham: Design by Choice*, ed. Penny Sparke (New York: Rizzoli, 1981), 94–96, article first published in *Motif* 10 (1963).

130 Whiteley, *Reyner Banham*, 137.

131 Peter Cook, "Time and Contemplation: Regarding the Smithsons," *Architectural Review* 1025 (July 1982): 40.

132 See Banham, *The New Brutalism: Ethic or Aesthetic?*, 61–67.

133 Irénée Scalbert, "Architecture as a Way of Life: The New Brutalism 1953–1956", TEAM 10 ONLINE, accessed December 2009, www.team10online.org/.

134 A. and P. Smithson, "The New Brutalism," 113; Banham, *The New Brutalism: Ethic or Aesthetic?*

135 If the *House of the Future* and the *Patio and Pavilion* are understood as explicitly Brutalist projects, the continuation of the tradition of surpassing differences, and diverse approaches characteristic of the position of the Independent Group is obvious also in the Smithsons' work of this period.

136 Nigel Whiteley highlights the duality of "engineering sensibility" and "mechanical sensibility," whereby the latter is connected with revived "architecture of technology"—which differs from the former in non-monumentality, and is intended for the everyman, the meeting of his needs and personal fulfillment—in the final consequence of the classless *Second Machine Age*. Mechanical sensibility should lay the foundations for qualitative changes in the relationship between people and machines. Whiteley, *Reyner Banham*.

137 Banham, "The Machine Aesthetic," *Architectural Review* (April 1955): 225–228.

138 See Anthony Vidler, *Histories of Immediate Present: Inventing Architectural Modernism* (Cambridge, MA: MIT Press, 2008), 107–155; Cf. Nikolaus Pevsner, *Pioneers of Modern Design from William Morris to Walter Gropius*, 1936.

139 Banham, "Sant'Elia," in *Architectural Review* (May 1955): 295–301.

140 Antonio Sant'Elia, "Manifesto of Futurist Architecture," in *Rethinking Technology: A Reader in Architectural Theory*, eds. William Braham and Jonathan A. Hale (Abingdon: Routledge, 2007), 21.

141 Whiteley, *Reyner Banham*, 48.

142 Banham, "Towards a Pop Architecture," *Architectural Review* (July 1962).

143 Sadler, *Archigram*, 177; Cf. Cook, *Experimental Architecture* (New York: Universe Books, 1970); Banham, "Towards a Pop Architecture," in *Reyner Banham: Design by Choice,* ed. Penny Sparke (New York: Rizzoli, 1981), 61, note esp. 141 (1979).

144 Banham, *Theory and Design in the First Machine Age*, 329.

145 Ibid., 329, 330.

146 See Whiteley, *Reyner Banham*, 167–185. Simon Sadler points out that the connection between avant-garde and popularity was perhaps the most important element of the avant-garde culture after World War II, and wonders: "If avant-garde activity was once defined by its very inaccessibility to the general public and its onslaught upon bourgeois culture, how could it survive the breakdown in distinction between the 'high' and the 'low' and the 'valuable' and the 'kitsch,' the 'authentic' and the 'inauthentic?' If the avant-garde was once considered to be, by its very nature, oppositional to the *status quo*, how could it even think about assimilating late capitalism, let alone imitate its operations?" Therefore, he marks the activity of new avant-garde groups with the term "neo"— neo-avant-garde, which distances them from historical avant-gardes. See Sadler, *Archigram*, 3–8. Cf. Peter Bürger, *Theory of the Avant-Garde* (Minneapolis, MN: University of Minnesota Press, 1984); Hal Foster, "Who's Afraid of the Neo-Avant-Garde?," in *The Return of the Real* (Cambridge, MA and London: MIT Press, 1996), 1–33.

147 See Lesley Jackson, *The Sixties: Decade of Design Revolution* (London: Phaidon, 1998).

148 *A Guide to Archigram 1961–1974* (London: Academy Editions, 1994), 37.

149 Sadler, *Archigram*, 6. The main actors of Archigram from 1961 to 1974 Warren Chalk, Peter Cook, Dennis Crompton, David Greene, Ron Herron, and Michael Webb worked within the group on individual projects, some of which supplemented each other or developed further.

150 Cook, ed., *Archigram* (New York: Princeton Architectural Press, 1999), 39.

151 Simon Sadler cites information on the shortage of apartments from Dennis Crompton and Michael Webb's lecture at the Bartlett School of Architecture in London on February 23, 1998. Sadler, *Archigram,* 37.

152 See "Polar Shelters," *Architectural Review* 716 (September 1956): 177–180; special topic "2000+," *Architectural Design* (February 1967): 55–101. For example, Archigram placed its experiments also in the underwater world. Warren Chalk's *Underwater City* from 1964 and Peter Cook's *Sea Farming* deal with the underwater world, while collages of spacecraft, together with heroes of science fiction comics, created an explicit rhetoric of design in the fourth issue of the *Archigram* magazine— "Amazing Archigram 4," 1964.

153 Cook, *Archigram*, 44–47.
154 In the chronological review of the work of Archigram in the November issue of *Architectural Design* in 1965, Warren Chalk's "clip-on living cell" is presented within *Plug-in City*, but not with the term "capsule." In this publication, "capsules" are called units of kitchen and bathroom next to the entrance. See "Archigram Group, London: A Chronological Survey," *Architectural Design* (November 1965): 559–573.
155 Cook, *Archigram*, 44.
156 Cook, *Experimental Architecture*, 63.
157 See n. 154.
158 Cf. Giles Sparrow, *Spaceflight: The Complete Story from Sputnik to Shuttle and Beyond* (London: Dorling Kindersley, 2007), 98–99.
159 Cf. Justus Dahinden, *Urban Structures for the Future* (New York: Praeger Publishers, 1972).
160 Banham, *Megastructure: Urban Futures of the Recent Past* (London: Thames and Hudson, 1976), 76.
161 Banham, "A Clip-on Architecture," *Architectural Design* (November 1965): 535.
162 Ibid., 535.
163 *A Guide to Archigram*, 72–91.
164 Sadler, *Archigram*, 53; Cf. Banham, *The New Brutalism: Ethic or Aesthetic?*
165 Ibid., 64.
166 Cook, *Archigram*, 16–17.
167 Cook, *Archigram*, 5. See also Denise Scott Brown, "Little Magazines in Architecture and Urbanism," *Journal of the American Institute of Planners* (July 1968). For a general theoretical framework or program of Archigram, Mechthild Schumpp proposed Peter Cook's book *Architecture: Action and Plan* from 1967, which perhaps lacks the expected "scientific" approach to the housing problem for D. Scott Brown. Mechthild Schumpp, *Stadtbau-Utopien und Gesellschaft: Der Bedeutungswandel utopischer Stadtmodelle unter sozialem Aspekt* (Gütersloh: Bertelsman Fachverlag, 1972), 162–176.
168 Banham, "A Clip-on Architecture," 535.
169 Ibid., 535.
170 Sadler, *Archigram*, 14.
171 Banham, *Megastructure*, 101.
172 Cook, *Archigram*, 46.
173 Banham, *Megastructure*, 98.
174 Cook, *Archigram*, 52.
175 A. Smithson, "Caravan–embryo 'Appliance House?'," 348; Banham, "Stocktaking," 94.
176 David Greene in Cook, *Archigram*, 52.
177 Banham, "A Home is Not a House," *Architectural Design* (January 1969): 45–48.
178 Banham, "Monumental Windbags," *New Society* (April 1968), quoted in Gordon, *Spaced Out*, 103.
179 Buckminster Fuller, part of lecture, *Megascope* 3 (November 1965) quoted in Whiteley, *Reyner Banham*, 185. In the introduction to "Stocktaking 1," Banham defines architecture from the technological point of view: "Architecture as a social service may only be defined as the provision of fit environments for human activities." Banham, "Stocktaking 1," *Architectural Review* 756 (April 1960): 93–100. Of course, Banham, as mentioned when the New Brutalism was discussed, distinguishes between architecture and merely functional construction (building).
180 Banham, "A Home Is Not a House," 45.
181 With his definition in the "Capsule Declaration," which is presented in the next subchapter, Kisho Kurokawa also relates the capsule with the notion of *cyborgs*.
182 Cook, *Archigram*, 80.
183 See Cook's "Metamorphosis – Control and Choice" plan from 1966, where the connection between a family and a robotized home is explained. See Cook, *Archigram*, 68–73.
184 Cook, "Capsules, Pods and Skins," in *Concerning Archigram*, ed. Dennis Crompton (London: Archigram Archives, 2002), 80–82.
185 Whiteley, *Reyner Banham*, 185. Cf. Beatriz Colomina and Craig Buckley, eds., *Clip/Stamp/Fold: The Radical Architecture of Little Magazines 196X–197X* (Barcelona: Actar, 2010).
186 Vidler, *Histories of Immediate Present*, 139.
187 See Stanley Mathews, *From Agit-Prop to Free Space: The Architecture of Cedric Price* (London: Black Dog, 2007).
188 Consultants to the projects included constructor Frank Newby, architect Yona Friedman, cyberneticist Gordon Pask, producer Robert Whitehead, and others. See Mathews, 76.

189 Cedric Price, *Cedric Price: Works II, Architectural Association* (London: Architectural Association, 1984), 56.

190 Reyner Banham was visibly fascinated with the technological address of the "anti-building" with the load-bearing structure as the only permanent component of this non-monumental building. See Banham, "A Clip-on Architecture," 535.

191 "Will This Be a Lot of Fun?" *Daily Mail*, April 19, 1965, quoted in Mathews, *From Agit-Prop to Free Space*, 156.

192 See for example a letter of support from residents—Millwall Resident Association Meetings. Ibid., 156.

193 Banham, *New Statesman*, August 7, 1964, quoted in Price, *Cedric Price: Works II*, 59.

194 Mathews, *From Agit-Prop to Free Space*, 176.

195 Price, *Cedric Price: Works II*, 65.

196 Mathews, *From Agit-Prop to Free Space*, 177–181.

197 In addition to the *capsule*, the remaining three types of living cells are called *sprawl*, *crate*, and *battery*. Cedric Price, "PTb: Potteries Thinkbelt," *Architectural Design* (October 1966): 483–497. See also Mathews, *From Agit-Prop to Free Space*, 222; Price, *Cedric Price: Works II*, 25.

198 Reyner Banham, "Flatscape with Containers," *Architectural Design* (November 1968): 510–511. First published in *New Society*, August 17, 1967.

199 David Kirby, "Plastics: Technical Prospects and Architectural Imagery," *Architectural Review* 818 (April 1965): 318–322; 392–398.

200 Gontran Goulden, "Points from IBSAC," *Architectural Design* (August 1964): 413–415; "Prefabricated Bathroom," *Architectural Design* (May 1965); Alexander Pike, "Product Analysis 3: Baths," *Architectural Design* (February 1966): 104–106; Alexander Pike, "Product Analysis 5: Heart Units," *Architectural Design* (April 1966): 204–212; T. Farrell and N. Grimshaw, "Bathroom Tower, Paddington," *Architectural Design* (November 1966): 577. The issue of a sanitary space and bathroom is not solely a technological problem, since hygiene, space for it, and services in general had an important role in the construction of the project of the Modern Movement, and of its widest social, psychological, artistic, and architectural implications. Cf. Nadir Lahiji and D. S. Friedman, eds., *Plumbing: Sounding Modern Architecture* (New York: Princeton Architectural Press, 1997).

201 Scott Brown, "Little Magazines," 223–233.

202 Ibid., 232.

203 Richard L. Meier, *Science and Economic Development: New Patterns of Living* (Cambridge, MA: MIT Press, 1964, first edition 1956), 164.

204 Ibid., 163–164.

205 Ibid., 183.

206 Scott Brown, "Little Magazines," 230.

207 Banham, *Megastructure*, 81.

208 Noboru Kawazoe et al., *Metabolism 1960: The Proposals for New Urbanism* (Tokyo: Bijutu Syuppan Sha, 1960), 6; Kisho Kurokawa, *Metabolism in Architecture* (London: Studio Vista, 1977), 27.

209 Noboru Kawazoe, *Contemporary Japanese Architecture* (Tokyo: Kokusai Bunka Shinkokai, 1968), 35. In the context of understanding the philosophy of work of the group of Metabolists, Kisho Kurokawa also mentioned the need to ensure 1.6 million dwellings annually with minimum costs, which required a response to a major social problem. Kurokawa, *Metabolism in Architecture*, 28.

210 An illustrative review of the situation in Japan after World War II, and the renovation and urban growth after it is provided, for example, by Raffaele Pernice: "The Issue of Tokyo Bay's Reclaimed Lands as the Origin of Urban Utopias in Modern Japanese Architecture," *J. Archit. Plann., AIJ*, 613 (March 2007): 259–266; "Metabolism Reconsidered: Its Role in the Architectural Context of the World," *Journal of Asian Architecture and Building Engineering* 3/2 (November 2004): 357–363; "The Transformation of Tokyo during the 1950s and Early 1960s: Projects between Planning and Urban Utopia," *Journal of Asian Architecture and Building Engineering* 5/2 (November 2006): 253–260. See also Robin Boyd, *New Directions in Japanese Architecture* (London: Studio Vista, 1968); Zhongjie Lin, *Kenzo Tange and the Metabolist Movement: Urban Utopias of Modern Japan* (Abingdon: Routledge, 2010).

211 The conference was also attended by foreign architects Alison and Peter Smithson, and Jacob Bakema from Team 10, and Paul Rudolf, Ralph Erskine, Louis Kahn, Minoru Yamazaki, B. V. Doshi, and Raphael Soriano. David B. Stewart, *The Making of a Modern Japanese Architecture: 1868 to the Present* (Tokyo and New York: Kodansha International, 1987).

212 Boyd, *New Directions*, 15. The international breakthrough also took place when Kikutake's and Kurokawa's project participated in the *Visionary Architecture* exhibition in the Museum of Modern Art (MOMA) in New York in 1960, where the young Japanese generation presented itself for the first time, along with famous masters like Le Corbusier and Frank Lloyd Wright.

213 See Stewart, *The Making of a Modern Japanese Architecture*, 177–182.

214 Kurokawa states that the group wanted to issue more publications after the *Metabolism 1960* pamphlet but, due to their inconsistent positions, disharmony, and disagreements between members of the group, and despite many meetings and discussions, nothing came of it. After Expo '70, the last project in which Kikutake, Maki, and Kurokawa collaborated was a competition project for low-cost housing in Peru, under the auspices of the United Nations. But, despite winning the competition, this was their last joint project. See Kurokawa, *Metabolism in Architecture*, 41–45. The Expo '70 also signified the realization of many designs Metabolists dealt with, which had thus far remained unrealized, and also a great disappointment and the disillusionment of high-flying ideas about their potential to transform society, as the event was totally consumed by the logic of capital, commercialization, and spectacle.

215 Hajime Yatsuka, "Architecture in the Urban Desert: A Critical Introduction to Japanese Architecture after Modernism," in *Oppositions Reader: Selected Readings from a Journal for Ideas and Criticism in Architecture, 1973–1984*, ed. K. Michael Hays (New York: Princeton Architectural Press, 1998), 255–287. The article was published in: *Oppositions*, no. 23, 1981.

216 Lin, *Kenzo Tange and the Metabolist Movement*, 56.

217 Kurokawa, *Metabolism in Architecture*, 27.

218 Ibid., 23–39.

219 Manfredo Tafuri and Francesco Dal Co, *Modern Architecture Vol. 2*. (Milano: Electa Editrice, 1976), 357–363.

220 In the description of his philosophy, Kurokawa points out that Metabolists did not consider themselves Utopians, and attempts to explain the difference between their proposals and utopian ideas. Owing to fast-changing cities, Kurokawa does not pay much attention to the immediate realization of technologically feasible proposals, and emphasizes that their proposals were not idealistic images from the notion of a general city, but that they discussed contradictions in the city and the possibility of placing ideas in realistic projects. Following publication of the manifesto, *Metabolism 1960*, the intention was to publish a collection with the topics of methodology and implementation which, however, was not realized, because of inconsistent views within the group. See Kisho Kurokawa, *Metabolism in Architecture*, 23–45. For a more detailed discussion of the utopianism of projects of the group of Metabolists and Kenzo Tange see Lin, *Kenzo Tange and the Metabolist Movement*. The utopianism of Metabolists' projects was committed to the urgency of social changes. Just like Kurokawa pointed out, although by denying the utopian nature of their projects, the special interest of the group in the realization of ideas in reality, the orientation was also confirmed by Kikutake, who explains his position in a terminologically not-quite-coherent statement that his projects are utopian and, at the same time, ready for the urgency to be realized as soon as possible. "Yes, although it was a dream, similar to Western utopias, in my case it was necessary to be realized." Kiyonori Kikutake, unpublished interview, Tokyo, June 18, 2009. Audio transcription and authorized text, author's archive; hereafter Kikutake, interview.

221 Lin, *Kenzo Tange and the Metabolist Movement: Urban Utopias of Modern Japan*, 74.

222 Kurokawa, *Metabolism in Architecture*, 140.

223 Ibid., 28.

224 Cherie Wendelken, "Putting Metabolism Back in Place: The Making of a Radically Decontextualized Architecture in Japan," in *Anxious Modernisms: Experimentation in Postwar Architecture Culture*, eds. Sarah Williams Goldhagen and Réjean Legault (Cambridge, MA: MIT Press, 2000), 279–299.

225 Kiyonori Kikutake and Maurizio Vitta, *Kiyonori Kikutake: From Tradition to Utopia* (Milan: l'Arca Edizioni, 1997), 9–15.

226 Before that, Japan was visited by important architects like Frank Lloyd Wright in 1922 for the *Imperial Hotel* project, and Bruno Taut in 1933, which resulted in his books on traditional Japanese architecture in relation to the principles of the Modern Movement. See Kawazoe, *Contemporary Japanese Architecture*.

227 "The New Brutalism," *Architectural Design* (January 1955): 290. See also Kawazoe's discussion, who explains Otani's call: "Concrete is ours!" as follows: "That is to say, traditional Japanese architecture

used wood; the new Japanese tradition should be based on the use of concrete. Therefore, not only by sheer imitation of wooden structures of the past, but from the very nature of concrete, new forms should be invented," Kawazoe, *Contemporary Japanese Architecture*, 65.

228 Kenzo Tange and Noboru Kawazoe, *Ise: Prototype of Japanese Architecture* (Cambridge, MA: MIT Press, 1965), 202.

229 Ibid., 206.

230 Tafuri and Dal Co, *Modern Architecture*, 360; Lin, *Kenzo Tange and the Metabolist Movement*, 105.

231 Wendelken, "Putting Metabolism Back in Place," 294. In the interview, Kikutake said that he first met Fuller in Iran in 1977, while he did not respond to the question about Fuller's direct influence on his work. Kikutake, interview.

232 See Boyd, *New Directions in Japanese Architecture*, 16. Kurokawa also speaks about the pair of a master space and servant space. See Kisho Kurokawa, *Metabolism in Architecture*.

233 Noriaki Kurokawa, "Two Systems of Metabolism," *The Japan Architect* (December 1967): 80, quoted in Boyd, *New Directions in Japanese Architecture*, 46.

234 Ibid.

235 Fuller's connection with modern art is explained by Hajime Yatsuka. (Hajime Yatsuka, unpublished interview, Tokyo, June 18, 2009. The audio transcription and authorized text are in the author's archive; hereafter Yatsuka, interview.) According to Yatsuka, Tohno was part of the avant-garde artistic group in the second half of the 1950s, when the main personality was Syuzo Takiguchi, who was a kind of patron to young avant-garde artists in the late 1950s, including Arata Isozaki. Hajime Yatsuka is considered an authority and a great connoisseur of the group of Metabolists and of modern Japanese architectural history and theory in general. He graduated with Kenzo Tange, and later collaborated with Arata Isozaki and Kisho Kurokawa. He is the author of two books on Metabolism, from 1997 and 2011.

236 Wendelken, "Putting Metabolism Back in Place," 294.

237 Banham, *Megastructure: Urban Futures of the Recent Past*, 8. The definition taken from Maki's work "Investigations in Collective Form," Fumihiko Maki, "Notes on Collective Form," *JA* (1994-4): 248–297.

238 Ralf Wilcoxon, *Council of Planning Librarians Exchange Bibliography* (Monticello, III, 1968), quoted in Sabrina van der Ley and Markus Richter, "Megastructure Reloaded. From Space Frame to Spatial Monad and Back," in *Megastructure Reloaded: Visionary Architecture and Urban Design of the Sixties Reflected by Contemporary Artists*, eds. Sabrina van der Ley and Markus Richter (Ostfildern: Hatje Cantz Verlag, 2008), 28.

239 Banham, *Megastructure*, 103.

240 See earlier presentations in for example: *Architectural Design* (October 1964): 496–524; *Architectural Design* (December 1964): 403–409; *Architectural Design* (May 1965): 216–221; *Architectural Design* (July 1965): 346–360; *Architectural Design* (March 1966): 116–156, etc.

241 See Kikutake, "Ocean City," in Kawazoe et al., *Metabolism 1960*, 7–39.

242 Wendelken, "Putting Metabolism Back in Place," 288. Discomfort with the American occupation until 1952, a conservative government after it, and security collaboration with the USA provoked great protests, in which the Metabolists participated. See Lin, *Kenzo Tange and the Metabolist Movement*, 37–68.

243 Lin, *Kenzo Tange and the Metabolist Movement*, 120–127; Günther Nitschke, "The Metabolists of Japan," *Architectural Design* (October 1964): 520. The comment does not apply to all projects and members of the Metabolists group—the awareness of the possibility of total destruction has been emphasized by Noboru Kawazoe also in his article "Material and Man" published in *Metabolism 1960*. Kawazoe et al., *Metabolism 1960*, 43–51. I thank Hajime Yatsuka for emphasizing this detail.

244 "A capsule is something to be fixed (packed or locked) compactly. Instead, the move-net is movable, changeable . . . the capsule doesn't metabolize itself because it doesn't have such a dynamic system . . . In that sense, move-net is different from the capsule. It has a more flexible system and can change itself." Kikutake, interview. The name of the project *Tower Shaped Community* is summarized from more contemporary sources, whereas in the manifesto *Metabolism 1960: The Proposals for New Urbanism*, it was stated as *Tower Shape Community*.

245 Kikutake, "Ocean City," 13.

246 The improvised solution of shoe boxes, which were placed on the external side of the window in the *Tonogaya Apartments* project (1956) due to lack of space, supposedly represents a prototype for

his version of the capsule—move-net. Rem Koolhaas and Hans-Ulrich Obrist, eds., *Project Japan: Metabolism Talks* (Köln: Taschen, 2011), 336. In certain publications, the term "movenette" or "Move-nette" is also used.

247 Kikutake, "Ocean City," 26–39.

248 Manfred Speidel, "Critical Remarks," *Bauen+Wohnen* 7 (July 1967): 259.

249 A brief autobiographic description of the origin of his family is also provided in the introduction to Kikutake and Vitta, *Kiyonori Kikutake*. Also in the interview, he first attempted to highlight his "difference" from other Metabolists by presenting the origin of his family and its social mission; Kikutake, interview.

250 In 1954, the Architectural Institute of Japan (AIJ) organized a research camp, in order to check the possibility of raising the Japanese restriction regarding the height of buildings to 31 m (100 feet in the old Japanese measurement system), and the possibility of a suitable urban response to great pressure brought on by a population boost in the metropolitan area, where one of the driving forces was Kenzo Tange's Laboratory at the University of Tokyo. In the early 1950s, architects Fumihiko Maki and Arata Isozaki, who were related to the group of Metabolists, were also active in the field of construction of tall buildings. The regulation regarding height restriction was withdrawn only in 1963, but only for a limited Tokyo area. Hajime Yatsuka, *Metabolist Nexus* (unpublished manuscript, chapters "6 Take-off: quiet and far from being utopian" and "12 Metabolist monadology" were sent to the author November 3, 2009; hereafter, H. Yatsuka, *Metabolist Nexus*).

251 Kikutake, "Ocean City," 10.

252 Frampton, *Modern Architecture,* 282.

253 When he visited the factory, Kikutake was surprised by the fact that production was completely automated: "When I saw it [new factory in Yokkaichi-city (in Mie Prefecture), which was to produce waterproof rubber material], I felt like, 'Stupid!' because there were only manufacturing machines. Everything was made automatically. I thought it would be better to build such a thing on the sea, rather than by the seashore. Therefore, the first study on the Marine project was focused on a prototype for a factory;" Kikutake, interview. Kawazoe also mentions that cities on water were a response to the criticism of artificial land on the coast for the needs of industry, which "deprives fishermen of their right for existence and creates an atmosphere unfavourable to outdoor recreation." Kawazoe, *Contemporary Japanese Architecture*, 74.

254 Kikutake and Vitta, *Kiyonori Kikutake*, 9–15.

255 See editorial "Proposed Tower-Shape Community," *Kokusai-Kentiku* 26/1 (January 1959) and Kikutake, "Ocean City," 13–19.

256 Kikutake, "Ocean City," 30–31.

257 ". . .in my project, this housing unit was thought to work as a semi-public space. It is not to encourage the individualization. A house, for me, must work as semi-public space, which is not only for that family, but for other people to meet each other;" Kikutake, interview.

258 The technical usefulness of Metabolists' projects was also emphasized by Yatsuka in his interview: "But comparing to them, both Tange and the Metabolists, were really concerned with the 'real stuff.' And even if some of their projects like Isozaki's *Cities in the Air* or Kurokawa's *Helix* might look quite extravagant in terms of feasibility, it was an outcome of a previous accumulation of the technical investigations, if not only done by them individually, but also after a long process of collective work; especially the development of the idea of the core, from core to megastructure in Tange's studio;" Yatsuka, interview. Cf. Banham, *Megastructure,* 98.

259 Kikutake, "Ocean City," 19. The text is quoted in the original.

260 Yatsuka, *Metabolist Nexus*. Takashi Asada was a principal assistant in Tange Lab.

261 Braham and Hale, eds., *Rethinking Technology: A Reader in Architectural Theory*, 127–128.

262 Yatsuka, *Metabolist Nexus*. Yatsuka also mentioned Asada's proposal for a circular cylindrical design, which was rejected by the research group. It was similar to the design of Vladimir Bodiansky for the French base. The significance of research projects for the development of the concept of the capsule was also pointed out by Yatsuka, in his interview: "Eventually, the Antarctic base was very, very pragmatic and had nothing fascinating, but I am sure that it was a sort of embryo of a Metabolists' capsule;" Yatsuka, interview. Due to their diversity and specificity, Yatsuka is also reluctant in the use of the word "utopia" for the Metabolist projects in general.

263 "Industrial Design in Japan: GK Industrial Design Association," *Architectural Design* (July 1965): 353.

264 Ibid., 356–357. *Komatsu ski lodge is also known as Plastic Ski Lodge.* An alternative history of the capsule could highlight Ekuan as the person who first detected, intuitively, the meaning of the

capsule as a hybrid of industrial design and architecture, and designed a phone booth in 1953, subsequently omnipresent in Japan. Koolhaas and Obrist, eds., *Project Japan,* 486. A cabin for traffic officers A. A. Guarell and F. Bini from 1954 have a similar design, but both units seem "permanently" installed in the ground, making them capsules only conditionally—in the metaphoric sense, or proto-capsules. Cf. "Applicazioni del cristallo 'securit,'" *Domus* (July 1955).

265 Kisaburo Kawakami, "Capsules-Capsules," *Architectural Design* (March 1973): 149–150. The "*YADOKARI" Hermit Crab Capsule Lodge*, 1969 is very similar to the capsule for Kisho Kurokawa's *Capsule Village* from 1972, which also points to the simultaneity of the needs and development of specific types of units.

266 "GK: The Proprieties of this Flawlessly Composed Organism" ("GK: Kono Ten-i-muhou na Kotai no Sahou"), *SD–Space Design* (03/1969): 54–55. Translation from Japanese by Urška Capuder, Hiroshi Kohno; author's archive.

267 Ibid.

268 More on Expo '70: "Expo 70," *Architectural Review* 882 (August 1970): 67–128; *Architectural Design* (June 1970): 271–284; Lin, *Kenzo Tange and the Metabolist Movement*, 200–232; Koolhaas and Obrist, eds., *Project Japan*, 506–548.

269 Boyd, *New Directions in Japanese Architecture*, 46–47. Charles Jencks describes Kurokawa as the third most popular Japanese, as a character from a success story, with an office with a hundred employees, 18-hour working days, and a monthly appearance on television screens in front of 30 million people. Kisho Kurokawa, *Metabolism in Architecture*, 9.

270 See Charles Jencks's Introduction to Kurokawa's book, *Metabolism in Architecture*, 9–22.

271 Wendelken, "Putting Metabolism Back in Place," 294–296. In an interview, both Kiyonori Kikutake and Fumihiko Maki implied that the concept of the capsule was mainly part of Kurokawa's creative field, despite the fact that parts of Kikutake's projects look like capsule architecture, and that Maki published substantive contemplation of capsules; Kikutake, interview; Fumihiko Maki, unpublished interview, Tokyo: June 19, 2009. Audio transcription and authorized text are in the author's archive; hereinafter, Maki, interview.

272 Kurokawa, "Capsule Declaration," in *Metabolism in Architecture*, 75. The declaration was published as an article for the first time in an abbreviated version as Kurokawa, "Oh! Saibogu no Okite" ("Oh! The Code of the Cyborg"), *SD–Space Design* (03/1969): 50–53. Translation from Japanese by Urška Capuder, Hiroshi Kohno, author's archive.

273 Eight points from the first publication read: "1. The capsule is cyborg architecture. 2. The capsule is a dwelling of *homo movens*, traveling people. 3. The capsule pursues society of diversity. 4. The capsule aims to create a future vision of a family, focusing on individuality. 5. The capsule is the metapolis of a hometown. 6. The capsule is a device composed of feedback which accumulates in society and, in certain cases, a device which rejects such feedback. 7. The capsule is prefabricated architecture—the ultimate figure of industrial architecture. 8. The capsule is opposed to integrity and systematic thinking." Kurokawa, "Oh! The Code of the Cyborg." Translation from Japanese by Urška Capuder, Hiroshi Kohno, author's archive.

274 Kurokawa, "Capsule Declaration," 75–76. The faith in technology and the influence of science fiction, which dealt with cybernetic organisms—cyborgs was upgraded by Kurokawa in relation to the architecture of personal liberation.

275 Ibid., 76.

276 Cf. Crowley and Pavitt, eds., *Cold War Modern: Design 1945–1970*; Williams Goldhagen and Legault, eds., *Anxious Modernisms.*

277 Kurokawa, "Capsule Declaration," 82.

278 Ibid., 79.

279 In his explanation of the philosophy of Metabolism, Kurokawa pays great attention to origins in Buddhism. "Jiga" is translated as "ego," understood in the context of differences between the Japanese and western psychology. Kurokawa, *Metabolism in Architecture*, 23–40.

280 Ibid., 36.

281 Kurokawa, "Capsule Declaration," 78.

282 Ibid., 83.

283 Ibid., 79.

284 De Cauter also points to the utopias of complete mobility of predecessors and contemporaries such as Chtcheglov, Friedman, and Archigram, in relation to the complete nomadism implied by the concept of the capsule, as well as to the disintegration of a family with Plato and Moore. Lieven

De Cauter, *The Capsular Civilization: On the City in the Age of Fear* (Rotterdam: NAi, 2004).

285 See Kurokawa, "Metapolis – The Hishino Plan," in *Metabolism in Architecture*, ed. Kurokawa, 67–74. Published as an article for the first time in *Kenchiku Bunka* (June 1967).

286 Kurokawa, "Capsule Declaration," 80–81.

287 Ibid., 81. In the interview, Yatsuka explains his amazement: "Constant and Situationists had been rarely known among Japanese until recently, maybe in the last ten years they were introduced. Of course, Archigram became very popular around 1967 or 1968 after Isozaki met them at the UCLA, they were teaching there at the same time . . . , they also met at the Milan Trienale [in 1968, author's comment]. Kurokawa was energetic about introducing the foreign, most recent fashion (at that moment), (and) might have been introduced to the work of Archigram even before that . . . But it was imported only as a (visual) 'image'," Yatsuka, interview.

288 Ibid., 82. Cf. Marc Augé, *Non-Places: Introduction to an Anthropology of Supermodernity* (London: Verso, 1995).

289 Kurokawa, "Capsule Declaration," 85.

290 Ibid., 85.

291 F. Maki and M. Otaka, "Toward Group Form," in Kawazoe et al., *Metabolism 1960*, 59.

292 Kurokawa, *Metabolism in Architecture*, 105.

293 In the interview, Maki limited his definition of the capsule to be understood as an artifact—like with Kisho Kurokawa's housing unit (in the *Nakagin Capsule Tower*); Maki, interview.

294 See Lin, *Kenzo Tange and the Metabolist Movement*, 179–188.

295 Günther Nitschke, "Prototype or Wishful Thinking," *Architectural Design* (May 1968).

296 Boyd, "Expo and Exhibitionism," *Architectural Review*, 882 (August 1970): 99–109. At the same time, the pavilion was a commodification of the original idea of the capsule—from a space for personal fulfillment to a luxury mini unit for the presentation of beauty products of the Takara company. Koolhaas and Obrist, eds., *Project Japan*, 528.

297 Kurokawa, *Metabolism in Architecture*, 101.

298 Ibid., 32.

299 To the question of whether the emergence of the capsule in Japan was related to pop culture and the influence of the Cold War, Yatsuka replies: "The answer is yes and no. 1960s were surely characterized by Cold War culture. Japan could enjoy economic rehabilitation, suspending the ideology and issues of national defence. This was to raise a culture of commodities in 1970s. This was welcomed by Kurokawa, but not necessarily so also for elder architects, and especially for Kawazoe, who was a convinced Marxist in early 1950s;" Yatsuka, interview.

300 Boyd, "Expo and Exhibitionism," 100.

301 Kurokawa, *Metabolism in Architecture*, 105.

302 Ibid.

303 There are also several online initiatives for the preservation of the tower: www.nakagincapsule.com (2014–1); www.facebook.com/SaveNakaginCapsuleTower (2016–11); www.facebook.com/NakaginCapsuleRenovation/info (2016–11); See also Kisho Kurokawa, "Recent situation about Nakagin Capsule Tower."

304 See for example Yuki Solomon, "Kurokawa's Capsule Tower to be Razed," *Architectural Record* (30 April 2007) http://archrecord.construction.com/news/daily/archives/070430kurokawa.asp (2016–11); Nicolai Ouroussoff, "Future Vision Banished to the Past," www.nytimes.com/2009/07/07/arts/design/07capsule.html?_r=1 (2016–11).

305 Kurokawa, *Metabolism in Architecture*, 113.

306 Parts of the text are completely abstract and difficult to understand. Therefore, we will not ignore Noboru Kawazoe's recommendation, mentioned by Boyd: "The reader should not be taken in by the words but should feel the theory behind them."—which is difficult to carry out in the scientific sense. See Noboru Kawazoe, *The Japan Architect* (December 1967): 78, quoted in Boyd, *New Directions in Japanese Architecture*, 46.

307 "Oh! Saibogu no Okite," *SD–Space Design* (03/1969): 51.

308 See *SD–Space Design* (03/1969): 51. Titles of individual fields in the table are in italics, while our description of the graphic material is in straight font.

309 Banham, *Megastructure*, 102–103; *Architectural Design* (May 1967): 207–216.

310 Ibid., 103.

311 Günther Nitschke, "The Metabolists," *Architectural Design* (May 1967): 215, 216. Cf. Dahinden, *Urban Structures for the Future*, 92–94.

312 Ibid.; Cf. Dahinden, *Urban Structures for the Future*, 80.

313 Dahinden, *Urban Structures for the Future*, 80.

314 Fumihiko Maki, "Anyone can be the King of the Capsule" (Fumihiko Maki, "Kapuseru deha Oh-sama de aru"), *SD–Space Design* (03/1969): 46–49 (translation from Japanese by Urška Capuder and Hiroshi Kohno, author's archive). The title could also be translated metaphorically as "A Capsule is a World for Its Master" or "A Capsule is a Space Where Anyone can be King."

315 Kawazoe, "Capsule as Countervalue," (Kawazoe, "Han-Kachi toshite-no Kapuseru"), *SD–Space Design* (03/1969): 36–45 (translation from Japanese by Urška Capuder and Hiroshi Kohno, author's archive).

316 Ibid.

317 Toshio Nakamura, "Archigram's Capsule" (Nakamura, "Akiguramu no Kapuseru"), *SD–Space Design* (03/1969): 56–60 (translation from Japanese by Urška Capuder and Hiroshi Kohno, author's archive).

318 Ibid., 59.

319 Kisaburo Kawakami, "Capsules-Capsules," *Architectural Design* (March 1973): 149–150.

320 See Syunsuke Kurakata, "Capsule-in-Osaka," *Nikkei Architecture* 23 (February 2009); ArchINFORM, http://eng.archinform.net/projekte/1869.htm (2016–11).

321 Hiroko Tabuchi, "For Some in Japan, Home Is a Tiny Plastic Bunk," www.nytimes.com/2010/01/02/business/global/02capsule.html (2016–11).

322 Kurokawa, *Metabolism in Architecture*, 95.

3

CATALOG

Typology and its manifestations

Two main types of capsule units may be distinguished, based on the analysis of pioneering examples of realizations and definitions of the concept of the capsule: *An autonomous,* self-sufficient type, which may be independent or composite, and *connective* type, which is connected to infrastructure or the frame of a megastructure, dependent on it, and appears in the form of a *plug-in, clip-on,* or *insert.*[1]

Today, the classification and labeling of building types are instruments for the recognition of various common characteristics or ideas for units or buildings, particularly in the field of residential construction, but they are not an end in themselves. Knowledge of the existing typology helps us to design and plan new realizations, and assess the existing ones from a new developmental perspective. To avoid the reinvention of established concepts, the knowledge of typologies enables us to work toward their upgrade. With the systematic treatment of the typology and examples presented, we wish to point to the openness of possibilities shown within individual types through diverse approaches, problems, and intentions; and last but not least their potential of spatial options, architectural expression, and the formation of social communities. In the examples selected, we will check the similarities, differences, relations, and openness of the concept in the physical and/or metaphorical sense—since not all of the examples unambiguously meet the characteristics of the capsule—and attempt to show the meaning, problems, and relevance of the concept and typology in contemporary theoretical and spatial reality.

In comparison with pioneering designs, the contemporary examples continue the tradition of typology set with a significant change in purpose: Instead of the utopian exit or focus on work outside the system,[2] most are operating within it, and function in the heterogeneous field between utilitarian pragmatism and potential subversiveness. The typology of capsule dwellings in contemporaneity is also interesting for its extensive use, which is not bound to only one discipline. Concepts and constructions of capsule structures are not only addressed by architects but, as in their pioneering times, they are also a subject of industrial design and enthusiastic self-construction, and of more or less subversive artistic practices. Products might include: Dwellings, additions to them, and mono- or multifunctional units for urban and anti-urban proposals; stimulators, and interventions in public space; environments for seclusion and contemplation, in the center and away from the city hustle and bustle, as well as exhibits and

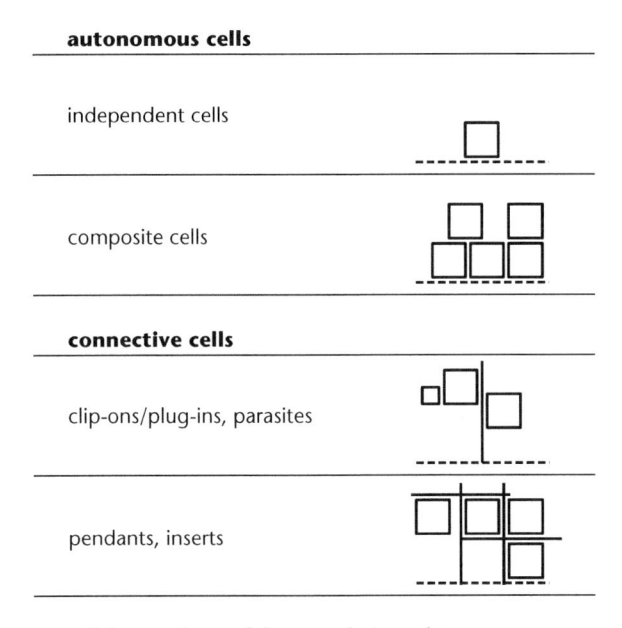

FIGURE 3.1 Taxonomy of the typology of the capsule in architecture

installations at exhibitions. Capsules may appear in all of the aforementioned environments, where they examine boundaries with their presence. The examples discussed also show that various forms of the capsule's typology in contemporaneity establish, although not necessarily explicitly, a transdisciplinary discourse, which rediscovers and discloses issues of an individual and a community, building and dwelling, structure, function and representation, and frequently relativizes the authority and autonomy of individual disciplines, opening the path for *other architecture for third cultures*.[3]

Autonomous cells

Autonomous cellular capsule units are independent living units intended for one person or a smaller household. In literature, the terms "shells," "containers," "pods," often also "bubbles," and of course, just "capsules" are used for them, but not unambiguously. There are two types of autonomous cellular capsule units: *Independent*, and agglomeration or *composite* units. The former are structurally completely independent units, whose structures are not adjusted to agglomeration, while the latter are completely autarkic and solid enough construction-wise, and of such form that they enable horizontal and/or vertical aggregation, facilitating the creation of more complex composite structures. Structurally speaking, autonomous units have *monocoque*, or frame and infill or panel construction, which can be completely prefabricated and preassembled, or may be assembled at the site. Their very structural logic usually determines their representation disposition.

Independent cells

Independent cellular capsule units are highly mobile, and represent the most appropriate implementation of the demand for complete autonomy and nomadism. These units are the most direct implementation of technology transfer,[4] from space engineering for needs on earth. The experimental field includes designs of *living units for extreme conditions* which, as *small houses,* imply entirely new social relations and community formation, the development and use of *new materials* and responding to the tendency for contemporary *nomadism,* established in the desire to transform society after World War II, and culminating in counterculture movements in the 1960s.

Living units for polar research designed by Japanese and French groups are proposals which set an example for many projects for temporary dwellings in less-demanding conditions, such as ski lodges, alpine huts, or more extreme underwater dwellings. The French group ATBAT worked on research projects for polar expeditions in the extreme conditions of Antarctica. Base (proto-)capsule units with obvious technology transfer should have a metal envelope with technical characteristics similar to that of planes, while the construction should be similar to that of a submarine. As in Fuller's *Wichita House,* the use of state-of-the-art aviation and ship technology was anticipated. The proposed circular dwelling for extremely low temperatures, wind, the possibility of fire due to static electricity, and other given climatic and geological conditions should exclude "sentimental or aesthetic purposes arising from the tradition concepts of a 'house' or 'home.'"[5] An exploratory (proto-)capsule unit is thus an engineering product beyond contemplation on visual representation and appearance. The latter is merely its non-conceptualized by-product. Despite the use of state-of-the-art technology, the technically most suitable circular design corroborates the knowledge of nomadic people pointed out by McLuhan: "Men live in round houses until they become sedentary and specialized in their work organization."[6] Nomadic life in unpredictable conditions that are not suitable for permanent living, and requirements for mobility, the ability to be assembled and disassembled, dictate similar requirements and forms for dwellings, albeit more durable ones, in extreme or adverse conditions.

In addition to Archigram's *Living Pod* (see Figure 2.13) or even *Suitaloon,* the *Komatsu ski lodge* by GK Industrial Design Associates in Japan (see Figures 2.22, 2.23, 2.24) and the Swiss

FIGURE 3.2 LEAPfactory, LEAPs1, Gervasutti bivouac, Fréboudze Glacièr, Mont Blanc, 2009–2011

FIGURE 3.3 LEAPfactory, LEAPs1. Transport and assembly

FIGURE 3.4 LEAPfactory, LEAPs1. Interior

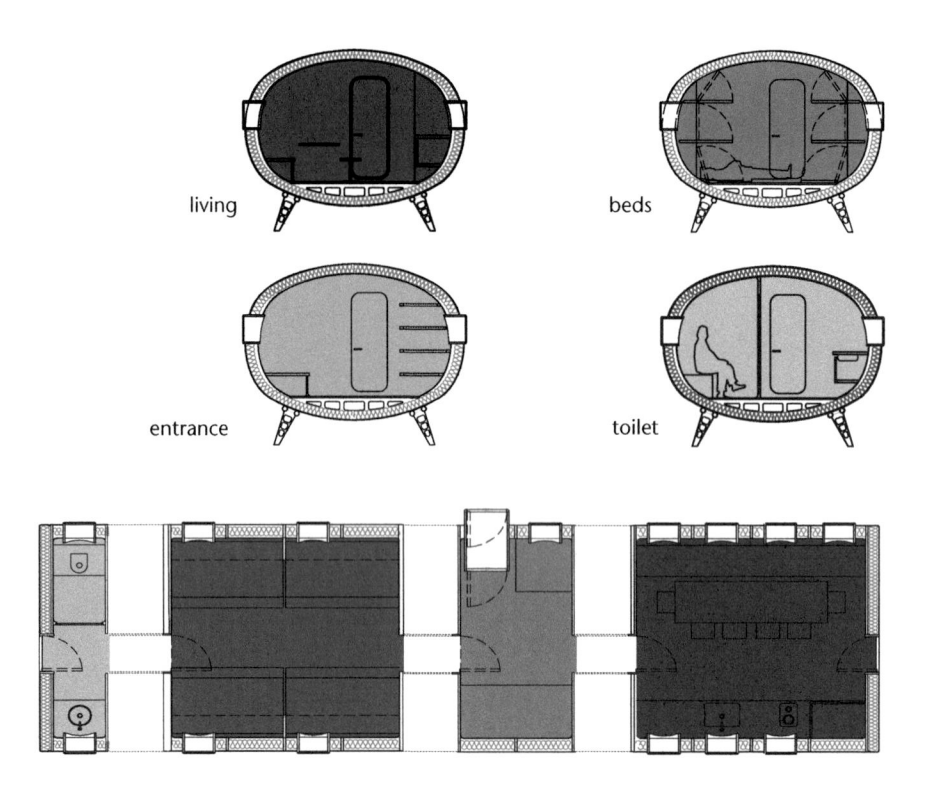

living   beds

entrance   toilet

FIGURE 3.5 LEAPfactory, LEAPs1. Function modules

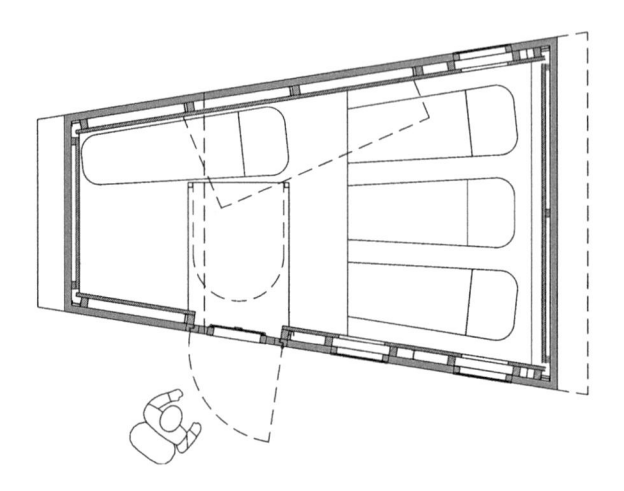

FIGURE 3.6 Miha Kajzelj, Bivouac below a Boulder, Kotovo sedlo, 2004–2005. Plan

pod *Rondo* by Casoni & Casoni, Matti Suuronen's *Futuro House* from late 1960s, is a paradigmatic and famous example of such a living unit. The circular design with prefabricated parts, which may be assembled into a dwelling in only a few days, continues the tradition of Fuller and ATBAT, but brings freshness with the use of new plastic materials and form.[7] The *Futuro*

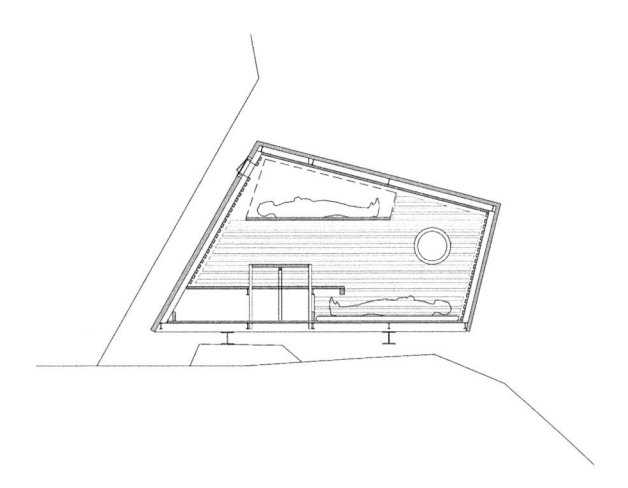

FIGURE 3.7 Miha Kajzelj, Bivouac below a Boulder, Kotovo sedlo, 2004–2005. Section

FIGURE 3.8 Miha Kajzelj, Bivouac below a Boulder, Kotovo sedlo, 2004–2005. Air transport

FIGURE 3.9 Miha Kajzelj, Bivouac below a Boulder, Kotovo sedlo, 2004–2005

House, which was initially designed as a ski lodge and included, within a uniform volume, space for a small kitchen, a bathroom, and a bedroom, was used in various permutations as a kiosk, a holiday house, a gas-station building, and even a lighthouse.[8] It was also anticipated, in the more dependent typological configuration of a clip-on, in the case of the *Futuro Hotel*. With the plastic *Futuro House*, Suuronen managed to realize the single-volume architectural space "without walls and foundations," which Frederick Kiesler strove for.[9]

Contemporary examples, which follow the tradition of dwellings for extreme conditions, include proposals and permutations that differ in design and structure, such as Richard Horden's *Ski Haus*; Lovegrove Studio's *Alpine Capsule*, a self-sufficient *monocoque* construction from fully transparent acrylic glass which does not hide its pretensions for the "new way of living off-grid," which is like "a sanctuary of peace and tranquility; a place to think and wonder in awe at the changing nature;"[10] a contemporary realization of Fuller's domed Garden of Eden; or a mere commercial deviation of a shelter for extreme conditions in Antarctica, like the *Polar Capsule* by the Arqze architects—architecture for extreme zones. Operative examples of prefabricated capsule structures are bivouacs for the alpine world, such as bivouacs by LEAPfactory (see Figures 3.2, 3.3, 3.4, 3.5), Miha Kajzelj (see Figures 3.6, 3.7, 3.8, 3.9), and many others, which are made completely in the valley and delivered to the location by helicopter.

Shelters that solve accommodation problems in cases of natural disasters, shelters for refugees, displaced persons, and the homeless are extreme cases of autonomous capsule units, but are only rarely called *capsules*. Just as containers are used to solve housing problems, their use in crisis areas for various purposes has long been established. For the affected, they are shelters which provide physical, emotional, and social safety, and can also play a role in the establishment of a community, in a manner which cannot be achieved with any other humanitarian means. In addition to the building of permanent shelters, temporary mobile units which have plenty in common with capsule units for daily or occasional use are frequently used when a need arises for the immediate arrangement of at least minimum living conditions.

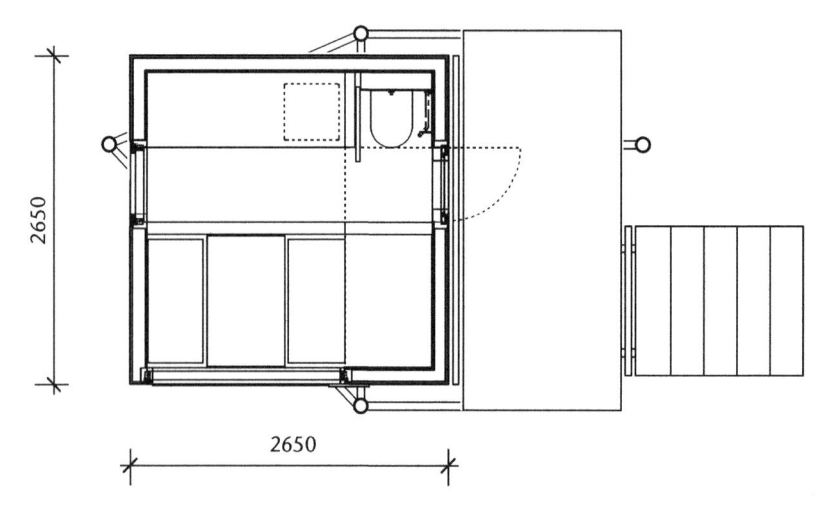

FIGURE 3.10 Richard Horden, Horden Cherry Lee Architects, *m-ch* (micro compact home), 2001–. Plan

An example which upgrades independent appropriations of usually disused or abandoned living containers, which can be seen worldwide, is Sean Godsell's *Future Shack* which, with strictly functional additions, flirts with the archetype of a primitive hut, and also operates at the symbolic level. In terms of accessibility and purpose of use, the differences between capsule units fully comply with diverse possibilities and the fates of individuals, and the involuntary and desired lifestyles characteristic of contemporaneity. As in most examples of mobile architecture, it is characteristic of many capsule units that, after being placed in a space, potential mobility becomes secondary and part of the field of metaphor—mobility remains a possibility only rarely realized.

———

We have seen great interest in small houses in recent years, which may be attributed to the increased energy awareness of individuals and architects, and an increasingly more-individualized and mobile lifestyle, which does not require large living places for a relatively

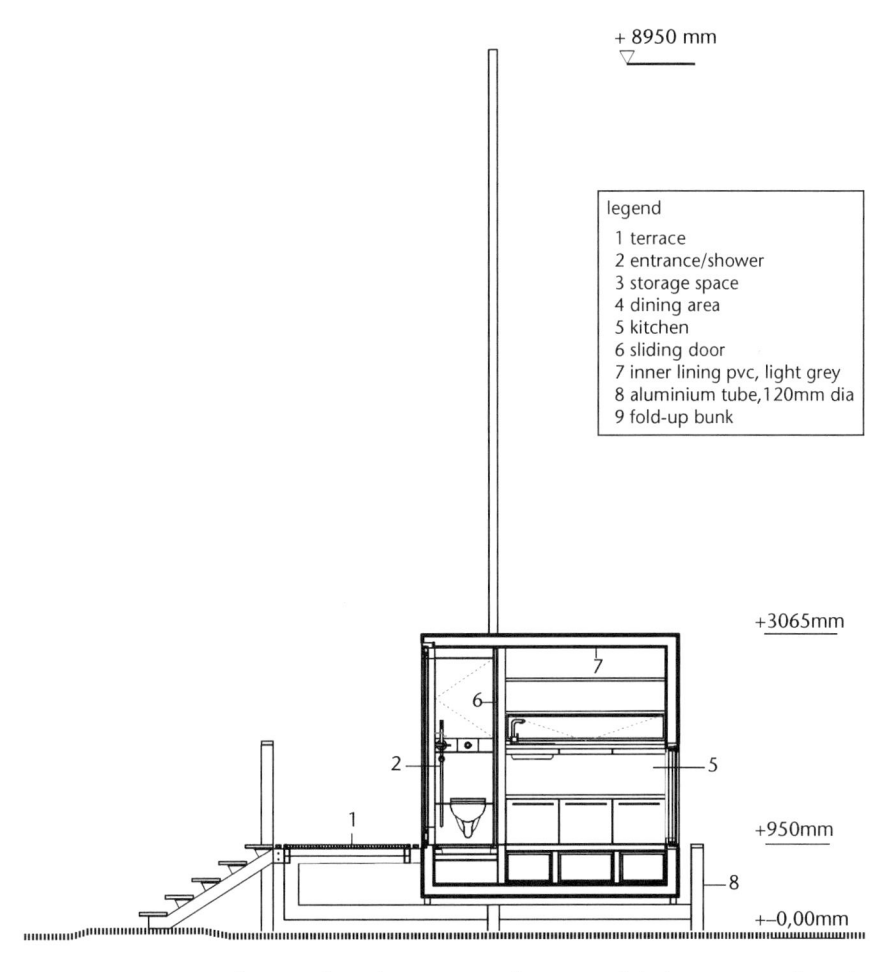

FIGURE 3.11 Richard Horden, Horden Cherry Lee Architects, *m-ch* (micro compact home), 2001–. Section

FIGURE 3.12 Richard Horden, Horden Cherry Lee Architects, *m-ch* (micro compact home), 2001–.

FIGURE 3.13 Richard Horden, Horden Cherry Lee Architects, *m-ch* (micro compact home), 2001–. Interior

short period of living at home or in a holiday house. At the same time, these examples can be designated as a continuation of the discourse on subsistence minimum. The interest in prefabricated and minimum dwellings, which appear in contemporary publications, with various designations such as *microarchitecture*, *minimal houses*, *small houses*, *tiny houses*, and *nano houses*, which share the identifiable format of the building type, may also be understood in this context.[11]

We need to point out that many publications particularly focus on the smallness of dwellings in terms of dimension, and although prefabricated and mobile capsule living units are also presented and classified among them, they are rarely so labeled. Contemporary examples of such capsule architecture include an extremely small 3.0 x 3.0 x 3.0 m cube named PACO, by Jo Nagasaka/Schemata Architects, the three-story prefab pod *Shelter No. 2* by Broissin Architects, or experimental tubular housing *Roll-it,* devised by the University of Karlsruhe.

The distinct successor of pragmatic prefabrication, which managed to go beyond the strict container logic and expression, is the *m-ch – Micro-Compact Home* by Richard Horden and collaborators from 2001 (see Figures 3.10, 3.11, 3.12, 3.13, 3.14, 3.15), with 2.65 x 2.65 x 2.65 m dimensions, which is intended for temporary or student dwellings, and was inspired by the Japanese teahouse.[12] The anticipated use fully complies with the tradition of mobile capsule units: From an independent cell in the wilderness, in a city, or in water. Units in the group setting served as homes to students in Munich, and they were also anticipated as inserts into a vertical structural framework. *M-ch* seems to be a formal successor of utopian and operative capsule autonomous cellular and megastructural formations of the 1960s, which attracted great interest from local authorities, organizers of events, and of the professional and general public. The question that arises is whether it will manage to justify the potential to surpass social conventions, the real redefinition of home and perhaps of "liberation" inherited from the past. With *m-ch* and many other prototypes, "objects which are physically lifted off the ground" and follow Fuller's maxim "more with less," Richard Horden brings architecture close to industrial design, and uses the "intermediacy" between "habitation and transportation, land and water, mountain and sky, aerodynamics and architecture, ecology and technology, and more important than all the above, between man and nature" to stir new experiences.[13]

FIGURE 3.14 Richard Horden, Horden Cherry Lee Architects, *m-ch* (micro compact home), 2001–. Air delivery

FIGURE 3.15 Richard Horden, Horden Cherry Lee Architects, London and Haack Hopfner
Architekten, München, *m-ch* (micro compact home), O_2 student village,
seven units, placed at the Munich Technical University, 2005

Richard Horden calls his architecture, which is distinguished by all the characteristics of a capsule, *microarchitecture*, and justifies it with distinctly pragmatic, technological, and sustainable principles, for a fuller life within a city or in nature. Microarchitecture is factory-built and mobile and, like a car, fully equipped with integrated communication and energy systems. For Horden, the foundation of microarchitecture is not architecture, but nature, and its results are products of industrial design for the environment. Nature serves microarchitecture as an inspiration for design, an imitation of the characteristics of successful forms of living organisms in specific environments and conditions, and through the awareness of the need to preserve the earth and natural resources. Therefore, it focuses on the philosophy of the Aborigines of "touch(ing) the earth lightly," which was brought into architectural discourse by Australian architect Glenn Murcutt, and is summarized by Horden, saying: "So the perfect micro architecture project enhances its natural setting and makes the least disturbance to nature, at the same time consuming less energy and the least carbon in its production."[14] Like many designs in capsule architecture, microarchitecture also strives to surpass dualism. When producing the best combination of form and function, Horden highlights the significance of intermediacy between inspiration from nature and production, and technology. Like Kurokawa in his capsules, Horden connects technology with the principles of traditional construction, home, and transport, architecture and design, etc., and with the paradigmatic and poetic placement of an object between the earth and the sky.

In the 1920s and 1930s, both Buckminster Fuller and Frederick Kiesler devised their designs by using materials which had not been tested before. Although attempts to realize conventional plastic houses could be observed in the interwar period, the material was not recognized until the mid-1950s, when the fall in oil prices, new generations of plastics based on better production processes, and recognition of the potential in the construction industry contributed to the availability and perception of a plastic house as a mass product, and triggered a formal and aesthetic revolution. The use of plastics influenced designs and design options in various living environments and, with its attractive characteristics, like the distinct lightness of the material, many experiments were conducted in transportable or generally mobile architecture.[15]

Structurally, independent units are types of prefabricated constructions of a uniform *monocoque*, framework or panel realizations—mass-produced, stable, and lightweight and transportable constituents or whole volumes, also facilitated by the use of new materials—of plastics, whereby the design of living environments also became the subject of industrial design. Ionel Schein's prototypes of plastic *monocoque* single-space modules for hotel cabins and mobile libraries are considered to be the first prototypes of completely plastic houses (1955–1956) (see Figure 3.16).[16] British pioneer in the use of plastics in architecture, Arthur Quarmby, paradigmatically described cabins as

> a brilliant exercise in the development of a living capsule to cater for ten hours of night and eight hours of daytime. It includes twin-beds, which convert for daytime use into a couch and a table, and a splendidly compact top-lid bathroom with W.C., shower and washbasin.[17]

The second type follows the tradition of prefabricated construction from constituents—panels. Ionel Schein's *Maison Plastique* from 1956, from the Paris household exhibition *Salon des Arts Ménagers*, is a proposal for a "growing" flexible house made of plastic panels with a conventional construction system of load-bearing and mounted elements. Some of the earliest and most recognizable examples are plastic houses designed by Cesare Pea which, in addition to Quarmby's shells for the British railways and Fuller's older experiments, and traditional prefabricated houses and caravans, were a direct reference for Archigram, when devising the issue of expendable architecture, and responses to it. Prefabricated fiberglass houses could be independent or combined, forming typologies of agglomerates, which is part of the second type, i.e. knockdown or *composite* cellular units.

Projects of potential emancipation took the form of container dwellings that can be disassembled, like units designed at the Hornsey College of Art and independent plastic units, the

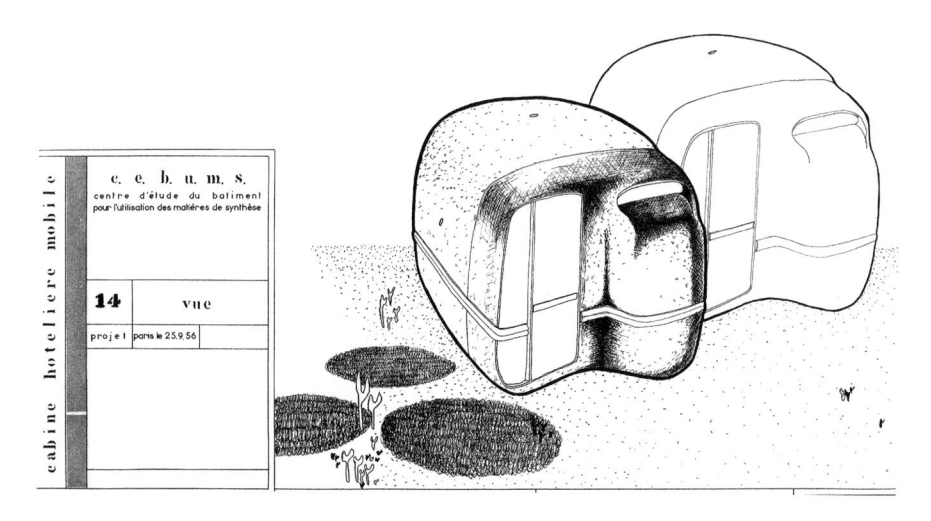

FIGURE 3.16 Ionel Schein, Cabine hôtelière mobile (Mobile Hotel Cabin), 1956

most recognizable of which were the *Bulle six coques* (Bubble made of six shells) by Jean Maneval from the mid-1960s, which could also be used as a dwelling, the aforementioned Suuronen's *Futuro*, and, last but not least, the pioneering Slovenian product by Saša Mächtig, the *K-67* kiosk.[18]

Technology transfer in high-tech realizations of contemporary dwellings and environments, and formal derivations of space idolatry and technological stylization, gave a recognizable expression to many capsule structures. Like Archigram's *Living Pod*, Kikutake's telescopic unit of the *Tower Shaped Community*, or Suuronen's *Futuro*, Richard Horden's *Ski Haus* and *m-ch* are all genuine capsule units in contemporaneity which—in order to create a suitable ambient of interior and an undoubtedly desired recognizable exterior, determined by technological and construction logic—continue the tradition of playful mimetic constructions modeled on space capsules, spacecraft, and aviation in general. Due to air transport and the demanding placement of the former into a high mountain natural environment, its construction logic, as a consequence of technology transfer, is at the formal level distinct. According to Horden, the coexistence of oppositions and the transfer of the "spirit of culture" devised, in pioneering style, the connection between "helicopter technology and the traditional Zermatt mountain hut or grain store."[19] On the other hand, in the search for alternative ways of living, and of the opportunity to assemble units and create small communities, the example of the *m-ch* micro-dwelling aims to be a response to the needs of modern lifestyles.

The *Miele Space Station*, which is not an a priori capsule unit, but a potential one, goes a step further, and is completely anchored in the problems of the present, and is thus characteristically multilayered. As an architectural installation, it is a knockdown multifunctional unit comprised exclusively of parts of washing machines, which is where its name comes from (the brand Miele). Connective elements intended for living or working are placed among fully equipped modular rings with installed hardware (warehouse, kitchen/shower/toilet facility, electronics, archive). With the impulse to use waste as building material, which designers 2012 Architecten call "recyclicity," by ensuring complete independence, with a self-sufficient energy and heat system and a water system, the ironic installation pointed to the parallels between living in extreme conditions and the representation of space engineering, which infiltrated our daily routine with technological transfer, burdened it with waste, and did not liberate it at all. A parallel with the domes of drop-out counterculture, which employed disused sheet metal from cars as building materials, and aimed at complete independence, was clearly expressed in this project. Back to the future, or the constant search for freedom, was the motto surpassed by the *Miele Space Station*: During the *Parasite Paradise* exhibition in Utrecht in the summer of 2003, it functioned as an office for mobile architects, and a research laboratory for flows of construction waste.[20]

A third reference for the designs of independent cellular capsules could be attributed to the desire to create the most suitable dwelling for a modern nomad. Following the example of Fuller's *Mechanical Wing* caravan from 1940, capsule environments for the needs of a nomad were fully equipped mobile dwellings. The first caravans, which were popularized in the USA in the early 1930s, and which permanently housed 200,000 families by 1937 (as a result of the Great Depression), were not fully equipped with toilet facilities until after 1950.[21] The American caravan has never really been used as a mobile home. Therefore, projects of genuine mobile dwellings for modern nomads in the 1960s were indeed an attempt to make use of the possibility

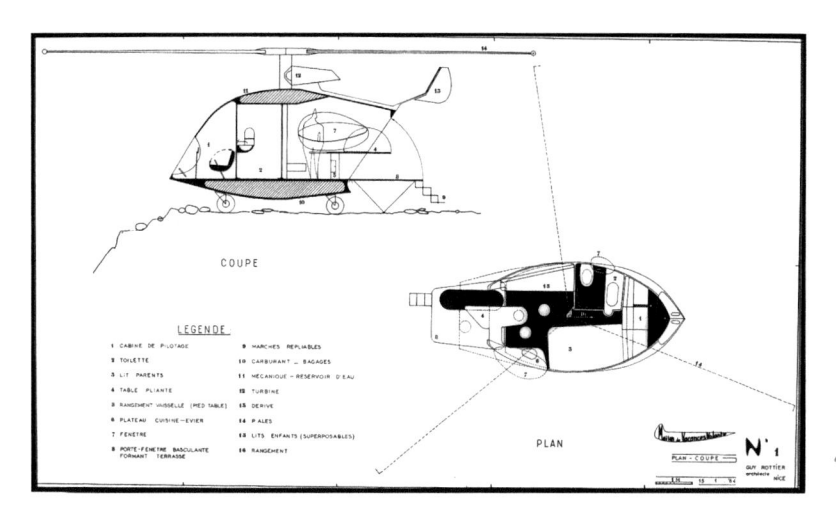

FIGURE 3.17 Guy Rottier, Maison de vacances volante (Flying Holiday House), 1964.
Plan and section

of true liberation.[22] The apotheosis of a fully equipped mobile dwelling, which irrevocably obscured the boundary between a private dwelling and a completely independent self-propelled means of transport, is Guy Rottier and Charles Barberis's flying home (see Figure 3.17).

Does the question arise again, following the example of the Japanese GK Design group, about the relationship between anarchy and freedom, and the possibility of resisting the system within the system itself? Are Archigram's *Rokplug* and *Logplug* actual equipment for a modern nomad to plug in, or mere accelerators of the omnipresent commodification of space?

If most proposals for nomadic independent cellular units, until the mid-1960s, are distinctly productive in nature and playful "extensions of a human body," more unclear, ambiguous, ironic, and even diametrically opposed responses to the social reality and the functioning of architects and designers in it, were provided by Italian designers and architects in the late 1960s and the early 1970s. Products of industrial design, manifestos, and rhetorical projects of negative utopias of "radical architecture" and "anti-design" opened up a complex field of operation at the exhibition *Italy: The New Domestic Landscape*, in the Museum of Modern Art in New York in 1972. The exhibited environments, which include examples of the typology of the capsule, presented two creative aspects, or two opposite approaches to design. While the "design as postulation" perceives design as a problem-solving activity which, at the physical level, is capable of creating solutions for problems in natural, social, and cultural milieus, the "counterdesign attitude" emphasizes the need to restore the philosophical discourse, and political inclusion as a path to changes in society.[23] Certain designers in the first group were tasked with creating environments which will not only be self-sufficient units, but should also research and develop ideas on living and housing. With special attention to the use of changing lifestyles in modern conditions, more informal family and social relationships, developing notions of privacy and territoriality, and research into new materials and methods, their proposals, contextually or explicitly, interfered with capsule architecture. Most designs with flexible functions, which enable various possibilities of use, can usually be assembled and disassembled, and are equivalent to monofunctional capsules or Kikutake's move-nets, operational upgrades of container dwellings, or tools for the creation of atmospheres and information environments. By influencing behavior patterns and the use of space, the latter's purpose could be compared to the art of dislocation, and to events or "happenings" of American counterculture.

Ettore Sottsass Jr.'s monofunctional movable capsules facilitate micro-nomadism within a living unit. A proposal for knockdown monofunctional capsules, and Joe Colombo's "total furnishing units," assembled in their basic compact form, also hint at micro-nomadism, while Alberto Rosselli's *Mobile House* is an expandable capsule made of materials which are the result of technological research in the automotive and aeronautical industries. Similarly, Marco Zanuso and Richard Sapper's mobile dwellings continue the tradition of the use of completely equipped independent or knockdown container capsule dwellings, which are primarily intended for temporary accommodation and accommodation in extreme situations of natural disasters, and are equipped with devices which facilitate complete independence.[24] In the accompanying publication, Manfredo Tafuri highlighted the significance of the design approach of the neo-avant-garde in the field of planning for personal fulfillment:

> For, in fact, it is only in the composition of architectural microcosms that it is possible today to hold forth the promise (without any pretense at credibility) of subjective liberation through the reconciliation of "man" with "the soul of things," and with the unfathomable depths of his own repressed impulses.[25]

From more static container dwellings and similar minimum shelters, in contemporaneity, the tradition of genuine mobility and nomadism is supplemented with two main types of units: Low-tech anti-design DIY examples, and high-tech machines as the technologically most advanced derivations of the concept, which aim at complete mobility and autarky.

Examples of, and proposals for, the former capsule shelters can be encountered particularly in the urban environment where, in addition to their practical function, they also have the function of informing the public, and are usually a subject of contemporary artistic practice and installations in interaction with the real conditions and actors. They may be knockdown, inflatable in the tradition of pneumatic structures, simply transportable, movable, or preset at a certain location. Krzysztof Wodiczko developed the *Homeless Vehicle Project* in cooperation with the homeless in New York, who collect plastic bottles and cans for recycling. A cart with a unit for sleeping, and carrying luggage and the collected material, enables the homeless to be mobile without being on the grid, since the latter is replaced by their independence and coexistence within urban space. In addition, looking like a food cart or street cleaning cart, it is adjusted to the environment and has a utilitarian character. It enables the homeless to be beneficial to the city, pointing out problems and influencing changes in the perception of the homeless in public.[26]

The *room-room* project by Encore Heureux and G. Studio responds to the emergent phenomena in contemporary cities, especially in the case of natural disasters. A minimum living cell with a small storage space, this is a cart that may be drawn by a wheel or yoke. Capsule units, in the sphere of useful artworks, are also intended for voluntary modern nomads. While the *Walking House,* by the Danish collective N55, is a smaller prototype of Archigram's *Walking City,* the rolling cylinder-shaped *Snail Shell* is a low-tech shell for a modern nomad, who may live in it on land or at sea, and it appears to be a paraphrasing of the famous barrel of Diogenes. During occasional situations of being on the grid, the capsule's WiFi connection is the only necessary and regular connection for contact with the outside world. Similarly, the environmentally conscious project, *The Exbury Egg*, by artist Stephen Turner, Space Place & Urban Design (SPUD) and architects PAD Studio was a temporary, energy efficient and self-sustaining workspace for artistic research in the estuary of the River Beaulieu, with 200 blog posts, produced during a twelve-month residency.[27]

The other type of genuinely mobile dwelling is usually technologically more complex, and part of the interdisciplinary field of architecture, industrial design, and mechanical engineering, ensuring movement on the ground, in water, and in the air. Recreational vehicles (RVs), caravans, and vessels are part of our usual or holiday routine; these gained variations with prototypes of special flying dwellings, at least from Guy Rottier's proposals. In the tradition of capsules as technological achievements, with installed comfort and the character of consumer products, these variations are intended for voluntary nomads, people who, in accordance with Kurokawa's forecast, create, and give meaning to, their lifestyles with such dwellings. For example, Jean-Michel Ducanell's capsule vessel, like many capsule units by Future Systems architects, *Mercury House One*, by Architecture and Vision, or the self-sufficient *Ecocapsule* (see Figures 3.18, 3.19, 3.20), which includes solar cells, a wind turbine, and rainwater collection, are part of this category. State-of-the-art house-machines utilize and use options provided by technology, in order to achieve the greatest self-sufficiency and independence possible, and are intended for escapes from urban chaos, into the lap of "pristine" nature. However, most of them remain at the level of prototypes or designs. If, at the beginning of the 20th century, the concept of dwelling wished to be reduced to the environment of a house-machine, capsule architecture added a new dimension to the latter. Kurokawa required that it fuse itself completely with the organism, to become cyborg architecture, McLuhan's extension of man. In the contemporaneity of the 21st century, when the period of production and unlimited consumerism is

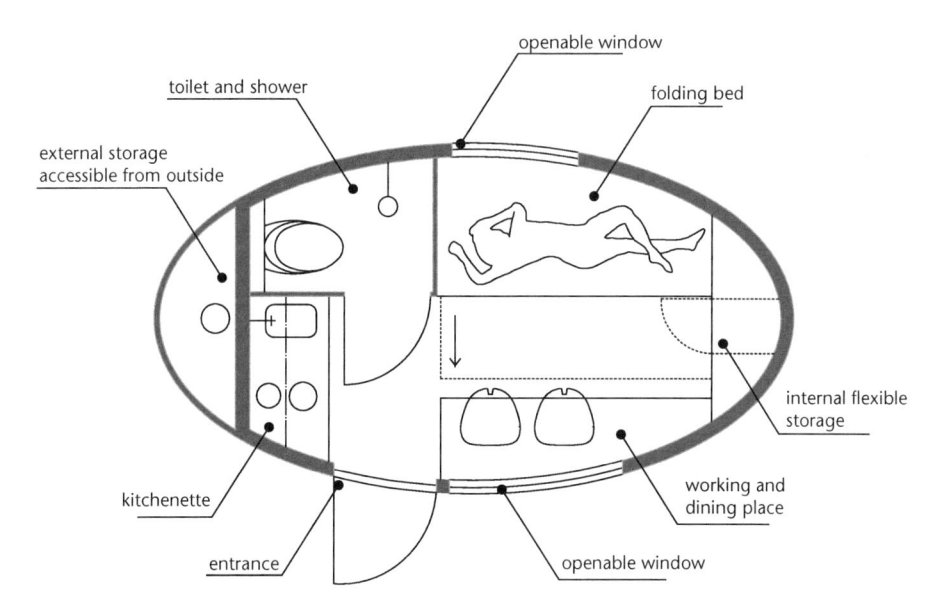

FIGURE 3.18 *Ecocapsule*, 2008–. Plan

FIGURE 3.19 *Ecocapsule*, self-sustainable smart living unit powered solely by solar and wind energy

FIGURE 3.20 *Ecocapsule*, interior

recognized as ecologically and morally problematic, the need for self-sufficient dwellings which respond to local economic, technical, social, and cultural conditions and, at the same time, function in the global information and communication network, seems an encouragement to think and function in architecture, to seek *other architecture* as an inclusive and unconditionally interdisciplinary activity which, in its extended role, is (re)defined as a relevant discipline.[28]

The fourth reference for the designs of independent cellular capsules is a product of the technological and electronic revolution of simulated environments, and personal protection against effects of climate impact, and of the technological- and media-stimuli saturated environment. A similarly rhetorical and ironic, but more playful, position than that of Italian "radicals" was nurtured by their Austrian colleagues who, particularly in the field of the use of pneumatic structures, designed environments which otherwise correspond with certain characteristics of the capsule, but intentionally remain at the level of distinctly provocative temporary use or technological prosthetics. From 1967, the Haus-Rucker-Co group wanted, according to member Laurids Ortner, to utilize architecture by using technical innovation as a "benevolent transformer capable of directly influencing the consciousness of its users," as it seemed that the "dream of being able to tangibly steer consciousness through architectonic devices seemed to have been shifted into the realm of the feasible, by the demonstrated experience of space travel and hallucinogenic drugs."[29] A series of projects entitled the *Mind Expanding Program* was completely focused on the urban environment, the increase in the sensitivity of senses, the stimulation of communication in the human microenvironment, and the possibility of perceiving and experiencing relationships without using drugs.[30] In search of a "better world," the basis of the Haus-Rucker-Co could be compared with the starting points and activity of their American contemporaries. However, the Central European specificity of the former is, despite the seeming complete radicalism, symptomatic. Despite being separate from the locus, their projects and prototypes are related, and depend on the social framework and structures of the existing traditional city, which they expand and expose, and are actually opposite to the utopian superstructures of many contemporaries since, according to the authors' intentions, they do not signify a new beginning, but further development, not resorting to utopia, but an instant feasibility.

Unlike the *Mind Expander* project's focus toward the outside of the urban environment, the pulsating pneumatic structure, *Gelbes Herz* (*Yellow Heart*) (see Figure 3.21), is more introverted. According to a member of the group, Zamp Kelp, *Yellow Heart* provides an environment which is completely different from the natural one, and facilitates temporary withdrawal: "The optical and acoustic impressions help the users achieve a new type of relaxation. The soft, pulsating movement of the interior of the cell effects a general loosening of how users feel. One returns to everyday life feeling relaxed and calm."[31] Although *Yellow Heart* is basically a simple transportable home for nomads or for a weekend break, a pulsating space for two people, or a nest or "cell" for lovers, its placement in the environment had a wider sociopolitical and critical intention, despite the introverted orientation of the project. In the summer of 1968, it was pulsating on the construction site of the police station at the Vienna Ring Road, i.e. in the area where one would expect to find cells for people who were deprived of their liberty.[32] Electronically or mechanically simulated environments inside cellular units were designed as an alert to general numbness and the increasing

FIGURE 3.21 Haus-Rucker-Co, *Gelbes Herz (Yellow Heart),* set on the construction site of the central police station at the Vienna Ring, 1968

FIGURE 3.22 Marko Peljhan, Projekt Atol, *Makrolab,* 1997–2007

individuality of modern man, who should become aware of his senses, the environment in which he lives, and of the significance and pleasure of communication with other people, by using playful devices.[33]

By direct participation of users in the functioning of architecture or the environment, experiments by certain Italian and Austrian groups are also important, because of their desire to establish a conscious attitude of an individual to the environment and social reality. Like the art of the dislocation of American multimedia performances, the projects described wished to achieve, with direct stimulation of the senses, a new awareness in an individual which, however, is in total opposition to the meditative isolation and the control of stimuli, which Kurokawa attempted to achieve within capsule units. At the level of technological prosthetics, we can

FIGURE 3.23   Marko Peljhan, Projekt Atol, *Makrolab*, 1997–2007. Interior

notice a great divide between the purpose of simulated environments of the interior in various projects of capsule units; however, these do have a common purpose—to develop the potential of an individual, influencing social transformation.

An example of complete realization of an extraterritorial unit equipped with technological communication devices is Marko Peljhan's self-sufficient mobile laboratory *Makrolab* (see Figures 3.22, 3.23), which was set up at several locations worldwide from 1997 until 2007. *Makrolab* is an autonomous self-sufficient communication, research, and living unit, which connects with the outside world through electronic media, and where up to eight people can live and work in physical isolation. By producing its own energy and recycling water and waste, *Makrolab* only depends on a food supply. The technological potential of the otherness of this project is not in the structure of the facility, but rather in its content. According to Peljhan, *Makrolab*, in the Situationist spirit, is "a declarative position outside of the spectacle, also outside of society (I stress the wording declarative) and is designed as a closed and isolated space-time, which will, in its inner logic and structure, function as a communication center and reflective tool."[34] Moreover, it is also a social experiment, since the perfect combination of a limited number of individuals in an isolated space should create more "evolutionary codes" of social relations than large social movements.[35]

The experiment of voluntary isolation is reminiscent of experimental isolated drop-out communities in the USA in the 1960s. Neverrtheless, in this project [*Makrolab*], the use of isolated technological and media-equipped interiors has been used in a different way. Instead of filtering information and seeking individuality or intimacy, residents of the *Makrolab* capsule were intensely and literally connected to the events of the global space of flows, and used their own isolation for in-depth scrutinizing and observation. In its isolation and simultaneous media connection, the contemporary capsule environment of *Makrolab* is an autonomous area of the recognition of the structure of powers and the strategies of resistance. The representation of the envelope in the field of space idolatry hints at flirtation with a spaceship or satellite, which has a similar function of collecting and processing information. *Makrolab* is a capsule unit with a heterotopic character, functioning outside the system while at the same time essentially connected to the system. It represents a genuine example of the use of the liberating potential of the capsule in contemporary space.[36] At the same time, the use of the concept of the third culture, otherness or the third path, also makes Marko Peljhan's work significant. The third culture he co-creates arises in the intersection between art and science, which are connected through technology, and between creators called artists–scientists or scientists–artists.[37] This is also a characteristic of surpassing the *either-or* duality, which frees science from the strict utilitarianism with the liberating status of art.

Composite cells

Composite cells are units with such internal structure that they can be assembled into cell agglomerates, i.e. composite structures of a higher order. Units are generally modular and structurally stable structures with a *monocoque* or frame and infill construction, and are adjusted to either horizontal or vertical agglomeration. Composite cells, which can be assembled vertically, do not need separate load-bearing structures, since their envelopes are also load-bearing structures. Like autonomous cells, the composite cells are fully equipped for the most independent functioning possible. Ideal cellular agglomerates would be composed of cellular units, each with its own service and sewage processing equipment. Justus Dahinden points out that the "growth" of cellular agglomerates was frequently inadequately compared with natural growth, since natural growth of plants results in the final state of maturity.[38] The growth of cellular agglomerates hides the problem of being completely uncontrolled and, particularly with vertical agglomeration, hampers or completely negates the basic possibility of further mobility of such cellular units. Therefore, we can distinguish two versions of *composite* cellular agglomerates, which will be called *operative* and *frozen*. While the former includes agglomerates which can be assembled and easily disassembled, the latter are structurally composed of self-bearing cellular units, but following the final setup, they remain in such a state and function in the form of a cellular structure only as a stable composite whole. In the operative version, the concept of the capsule is also fully preserved in individual agglomerates, while in the frozen version it changes, following agglomeration, into a less definite, metaphorical concept of composite *capsularity*.

The operative version most often appears in the form of lightweight prefabricated container units,[39] and their temporary setups usually up to a few stories high. Experiments with plastic cells offered a more picturesque path in the development of prefabrication which, in places, led to fully factory-made individual living cells, and following transport to the construction site, to their relatively simple stacking, one on top of the other. In many projects, the pragmatism of container compositions as designer products had the opposite effect from the "dictate of the Swinging Sixties" in the field of Brutalist sensibility and materiality, beyond the emphasized representation. This can also apply to many other examples of container dwellings, which co-created a more "serious" side of *operative* and potentially feasible general mobility and nomadism, in the second half of the 1960s.

The frozen version is usually based on units made of more permanent, conventional, and heavyweight materials, which are assembled into compositions with the rhetoric of an *open structure*, growth, incompleteness, fragmentation, or even organic structure. In the history of architecture, it was an attempt to establish a relationship between built structure and social structure, with a common denomination of *structuralism*. Despite the fact that individual parts explicitly composed a whole in structuralist compositions, and that these parts, in view of the focus of the living cell, were prefabricated and mobile up until construction, if they cannot be disassembled they cannot be unambiguously attributed to the concept of the capsule, due to their permanent installment in the megastructure's composite.

A characteristic and famous example is Moshe Safdie's *Habitat '67*, with its distinctly structuralist design and tone. Reyner Banham described the development of the project and its implementation, but constantly referred to living cellular units comprising the megastructure as "habitable capsules," "house-capsules," "concrete-box capsules," or "stacked capsules." This does not correspond to our definition of capsules as developed from pioneering examples, since living units no longer satisfy the necessary criterion of mobility after they are built in.[40] Fragmented megastructural formations named with a version of *frozen* cell structures crossed over to the field of the metaphorical concept of *capsularity*.

Composite cellular capsule units show the actuality of capsule architecture in conditions which require the greatest pragmatism possible, with many examples and projects, especially in the field of container architecture. It is interesting, however, that such minimum units, as pragmatic tools for solving the housing situation, are not only used for the needs of temporary dwellings for seasonal workers, or in cases of natural disasters, but particularly as dwellings for students. Cedric Price's "non-architectural architecture" from *Potteries Thinkbelt* became a reality in even more compact compositions.

The story of the development of containers for goods transport has a long history, but contemporary containers are the result of a patent from the 1950s.[41] At first, containers were used for needs beyond the basic purpose, in places where the need occurred due to their characteristics, such as weather resistance, resistance to fire and earthquake and, at least in the 1970s and the 1980s, as architectural and artistic manifestations, and homes for urban nomads, with their availability in terms of price, sustainable principles, and characteristic rough functional appearance giving them the status of trendy, cosmopolitan architecture.[42] Therefore, it is not unusual that the capsule units in the *Nagakin Capsule Tower* were manufactured by a factory for containers. A container may become an independent cellular capsule unit, if it meets the criteria regarding the comfort of the interior and connections to the network, since it meets all other characteristics of the capsule. While containers may be used in various ways, they can function as independent units, constituents in large compositions, or as connective cells. The use of containers and related knockdown living cells for the needs of student housing flourished in the Netherlands, where numerous more or less successful examples, in terms of architecture and urbanism, are located.[43]

A composition of modular container units can be easily disassembled, unlike, for example, Safdie's *Habitat*, but we cannot speak about the potential to constantly change the environment, the emerging functioning of an individual, and the co-creation of the built environment which, at least in theory, is provided by mobile capsule units. Such container compositions are temporary, transportable, and changeable, but are subject to management's decision. Designs are no longer equipped with cranes and mechanisms which promised dynamic megastructures with individualized units in the schemes of Archigram, the Metabolists, and others, although the problem of their management was frequently pointed out and criticized. Pragmatic compositions of modern capsule units, if we can still call them that, are set and moved by the force of capital. The problem of immobility lies in the absence of a megastructure, which was recognized as uneconomic, since the external structure of a container enables units to be stacked in several stories. Tempohousing, a Dutch company which manufactures container living cells and processes superfluous containers in China, and which built a settlement with a thousand living units for students, called *Keetwonen*, in Amsterdam, the biggest container city in the world, advertises its products as ideal: As you move, you take your house with you.[44] For diverse needs of the market and users, several versions are available, which differ in their size and equipment of a living cell, and are called: "Traveler," "Starter," "Manager," "Professor," "Master," "Director," and "Bachelor."[45] By investing in the megastructural framework, the emphasized motto of complete mobility in contemporaneity would probably be realizable.

Container architecture became a global trend, and is indispensable, if accommodation problems must be urgently solved, in cases of natural and other disasters, and mass migrations of refugees. Many student projects, realizations, and publications contributed to the popularization of container architecture, which represents affordable modular construction with particular emphasis on individuality and eco-friendliness—with recycled containers, quick setup, and minimum noise pollution, and activity at the site of their setup as eco-friendly construction.[46] In addition to changing the container into a suitable living unit, with lighting, insulation, and materials of the interior, they also provide contemporary solutions that promote the development of personal style.

Contemporary container units may be found in all types, analyzed and deduced on the basis of historic examples. Capsules, which usually have a monofunctional purpose in the wider environment of a dwelling, are as established a standard in mass construction as prefabricated sanitary units which, however, lose their capsule character when they lose mobility upon construction. Following the example of popular Japanese capsule hotels, the trend is moving to Europe. At Gatwick and Heathrow Airports in London, Charles de Gaulle in Paris, and Schiphol in Amsterdam, you can rest, for a few hours or more, in slightly more luxurious capsule units of various categories at the Yotel hotel which, however, lose their mobility once they are sited, just as in Japan. We could mention many prefabricated units placed in larger structures in contemporary built environments, but they are farther and farther away from the original concept.

Many small dwellings in contemporary concrete buildings of metropolises around the world do not exceed the quality of living in a container which is, on top of everything else, cheaper, transportable, and recyclable. However, container architecture has been entering our everyday routine and, in the field of spatial regulations, paves the way for the erection of temporary structures, which could, by providing interior comfort and mobility, perhaps realize the liberating potential of the concept of the capsule and other architecture.

Connective cells

The second main type of capsule units, depending both on the load-bearing and other infrastructural systems, is the *connective* type.[47] In view of the manner in which a unit is connected to the load-bearing and infrastructural system, *connective cells* may be divided into *clip-ons/plug-ins*, which include *parasites*, that are clipped on or plugged into the core, infrastructural framework, or a "host," like a plug is plugged into a socket; *pendants*, which are hung onto the basic frame; and *inserts*, which are placed in the megastructural framework or set onto the established platform.

Connectives can be largely independent, autarkic living units, similar to *autonomous* ones, and only use a megastructure as a physical load-bearing and communication platform, while most of them depend on their connection to the megastructure's service conduits. The type of capsule units which may be connected to a megastructure depends on the design and the availability of services of the megastructure. Connectives are usually compact units, which are placed in the megastructural framework as prefabricated living environments, attached by cranes, tracks, or hoists.

Clip-ons/plug-ins and "parasites"

Stemming from the relationship between the megastructure and the equipped living capsule, Archigram's *clip-on/plug-in* concept denotes a pragmatic system for solving housing issues with the simultaneous creation of a new lifestyle, "liberating" anarchism, techno-fetishism, and occasionally an ironic undertone of the view into a brave new world. On the other hand, the Japanese Metabolists express this relationship through social and political commitment inspired by a technologically conditioned "natural growth" and "cyclicality" and, due to the issues of managing such megastructures, also in an explicitly bureaucratic and problematic manner. By analogy with the stem of plants, many units in early projects of the Metabolists and Archigram are attached to the core, like branches. Therefore, clip-ons/plug-ins are sophisticated elements, in terms of construction, since a connective and cantilever-like load-bearing structural framework, or any other system for clipping or hanging on, must be installed in them. Paradigmatic and pioneering examples of such designs include Kikutake's *Tower Shaped Community* (see Figures 2.17, 2.18, 2.19, 2.20) and Kurokawa's *Bamboo Type Community* from the end of the 1950s, or the 1964 *Capsule Homes* by Archigram's Warren Chalk (see Figure 2.9), which were realized in Kurokawa's *Nakagin Capsule Tower* in 1972 (see Figures 2.30, 2.31, 2.32, 2.33, 2.34, 2.35, 2.36, 2.37) and his *Capsule House "K"* (see Figure 2.38) from the same year.

Specific proposals for clip-on/plug-in realizations came from Austrian architects, who were active in the field of inflatable structures. *Villa Rosa* of the Coop Himmelblau from 1968 (see Figures 3.24, 3.25, 3.26), and *Pneumacosm* of the Haus-Rucker-Co from 1967 (see Figure 3.27) designed the envelope of a clip-on living cell as a pneumatic structure. Unlike more pragmatic examples of Japanese and British proposals from the early 1960s, the nature of proposals by the Austrians is distinctly provocative.

The concept of random clipping of units onto the megastructural core or framework also promoted the development of a subversive type, which may be called *parasite*. A paradigmatic

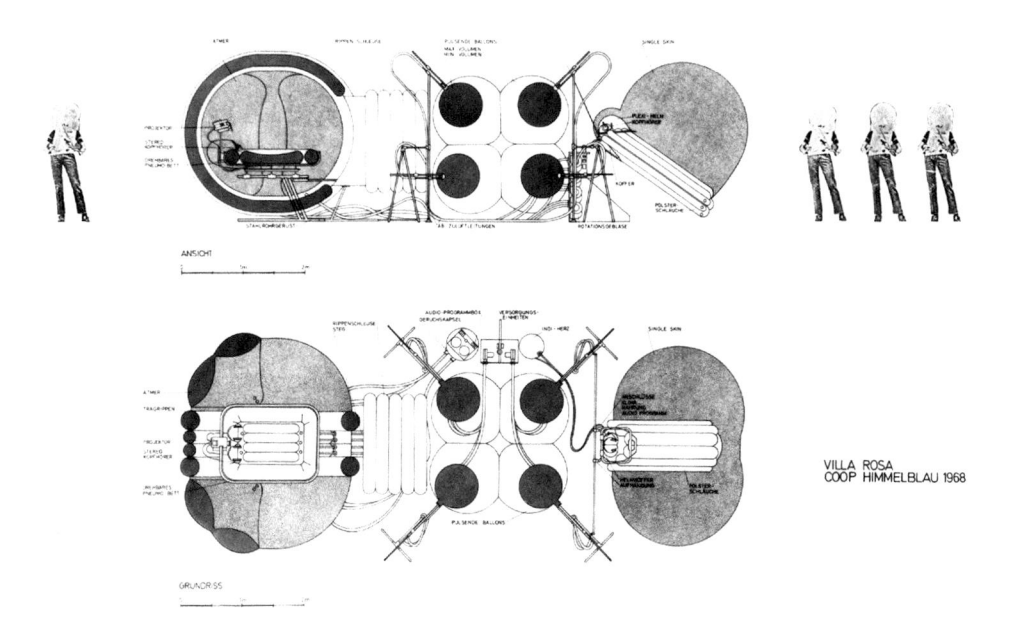

FIGURE 3.24 Coop Himmelb(l)au, *Villa Rosa*, 1968. Pneumatic living cell. Plan and section

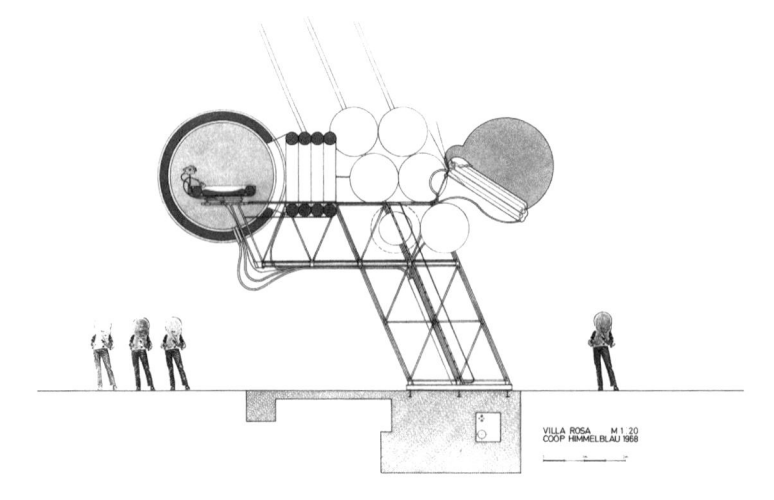

FIGURE 3.25 Coop Himmelb(l)au, *Villa Rosa*, 1968, Pneumatic living cell. Section

FIGURE 3.26 Coop Himmelb(l)au, *Villa Rosa*, 1968. Pneumatic living cell

example of the *parasite* is Chenéac's proposal from 1968, in which "cellular parasites" randomly extend the interior of individual apartments in modern block-like living structures (see Figure 3.28). Similarly, Claude and Pascal Häusermann wanted to disable urban regulation which, according to them, hindered the process of the transformation of the urban environment, to satisfy the needs of postindustrial leisure society, as a result of demographic and urban evolution. In their opinion, the realization would be possible by flooding the market with huge quantities of affordable housing living cells which, if used extensively, would help to establish the lifestyle of "intellectual and cultural urban community," and to overcome urban monotony.[48] Two years later, this proposal was actually realized by Chenéac's student, Marcel Lachat, who clipped a parasitic unit onto the facade of his apartment, and changed the bedroom window into the door of a womb-like chamber with its own window.[49] Similar examples were pneumatic parasites *Baloon for 2* from 1967 (see Figure 3.29) and *Oasis Nr. 7* by Haus-Rucker-Co from 1972, which was clipped onto the facade of an art institution as part of *Documenta* 5 in

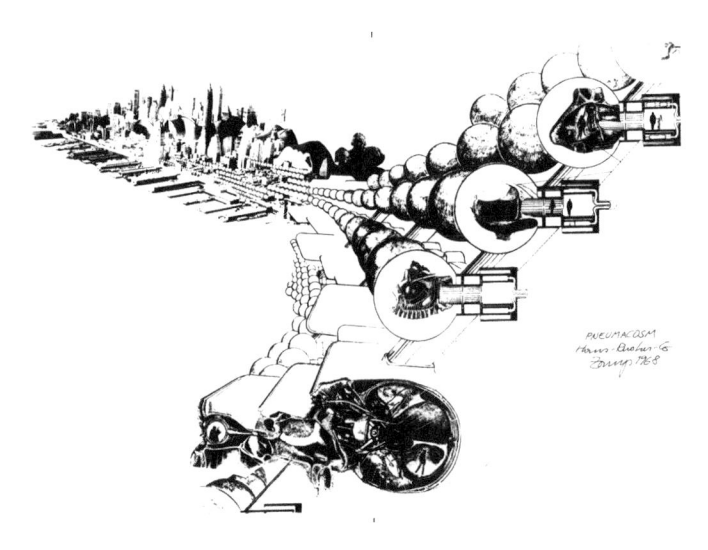

FIGURE 3.27 Haus-Rucker-Co, *Pneumacosm*, 1967. Visualization of the urban structure of clip-on units on a diagonal megastructure

FIGURE 3.28 Chenéac, Cellules parasites (Parasite Cells), 1968. Aerial view

Kassel (see Figure 3.30). It provided urban residents with a capsule-like image of dreams about nature represented by capsularized palm trees, within the transparent sphere with a diameter of 8 meters, which was attached to the main facade on the Fridericianum Museum building.

The aforementioned examples have their own operative field within a system, and their subversive functioning opens up possibilities for changing the system. The example of Lachat's polyester parasite of a children's room, on a residential building in Geneva, ended up rather miserably, as a fire officer established that it was dangerous and ordered its removal.[50] Technical arguments have always been in the service of structures of power.

Among contemporary parasites, we should point out Stefan Eberstadt's *Rucksack Haus* (see Figures 3.31, 3.32), which is still in the field between art–sculpture and architecture. The empty space in the *Rucksack Haus* parasite which is to be arranged by each individual hangs

FIGURE 3.29 Haus-Rucker-Co, *Baloon for 2*, Apollogasse, Vienna, 1967

onto the facade of a residential building. The comfort of the interior is provided by basic lighting and views, while its whole functioning is facilitated by its attachment to the "host."

Michael Rakowitz's inflatable shelters for the homeless *ParaSITE*[51] are *capsular* structures, since the characteristics of the concept of the capsule are only conditionally met—to ensure minimum comfort of the interior, they utilize the source to which they are attached. Humanitarian, rhetorical, and subversive inflatable structures are an awareness-raising intervention in public space, and enable the homeless to survive in adverse weather conditions. In terms of space, an inflatable *capsular* structure is a completely independent facility, the spatial existence of which is facilitated by its parasitic attachment to the exhaust of an air conditioner of a public building—and could be attributed a similar status, just like any other capsule unit attached to an energy source, although this one is explicitly determined to be a *parasite*. In addition to the "sucking of unbreathed public air" from the exhaust of an air conditioner, the presence and visibility of the *ParaSITE* parasites, in the urban environments of Boston and New York, alert us to the problem of the homeless in urban environments, and call for action by transforming social programs and ensuring affordable housing for people who are forced to live on the

FIGURE 3.30   Haus-Rucker-Co, *Oasis Nr. 7*, Fridericianum, *Documenta 5*, Kassel, 1972

street.[52] The promise of the capsule is indicated by the type of closed space within an equipped interior, such as, for example, the *A-Z Escape Vehicle* which, in the tradition of micro-nomadism, may be used for random activities: Reading, contemplation, work, etc., providing complete privacy when the hatch is closed. Andrea Zittel, who works in the field between art, architecture, and industrial design, does not intend her products to be mass-produced—although they seem to be adjusted to being so, thus silently resisting the consumerism of modern society—and encourages individual collectors to adjust the interior of units to their desires and needs.[53] Mobile facilities of the escapism of the interior are places of isolation, places where you do not have to adjust to anything or anyone. Symptomatically, this example also shows that the need for individuality and withdrawal into complete privacy, even within a family housing unit, arises from art, reaches into industrial design, but returns to art again. A commercial deviation from the concept, the micro-nomadic *sleepbox* by Arch Group, in any interior provides a private napping or workplace cabin, which offers private, secure, and soundproof accommodation of slightly more than 4 m^2, and with easy plug-and-play installation.[54]

Additional contemporary units or dwellings, which occur on rooftops, in front of, or behind buildings on the first floor, are among the most wanted, due to their attachment to infrastructure, and are classified among parasites, because they differ from the structure of a house. Due to their small size and simplicity, according to local regulations, many of them are realized without having to acquire any permission. Also from the field between art and architecture, *Zusatzraum*, by Exilhäuser architects, with its attachment, expands existing residential building or business premises, while the minimum living unit, *Minibox* by Holzbox, with its

FIGURE 3.31 Stefan Eberstadt, *Rucksack Haus (Rucksack House)*, Cologne, 2005

FIGURE 3.32 Stefan Eberstadt, *Rucksack Haus (Rucksack House)*, Bamberg, 2011

own heating with firewood, is a mobile unit which gained space as an addition to a rooftop in Innsbruck. It could have been set or inserted into any other environment or platform, like Werner Aisslinger's *Loftcube* or the completely independent unit, *Blob VB3* by dmvA, which emerged as a response to strict local building regulations, as well as many of the aforementioned examples. Like dwellings of desert American counterculture drop-outs in the 1960s, and avant-garde designs of their contemporaries, many contemporary realizations, which comply with the definition of capsule units, frequently avoid attachment to traditional values, creative disciplines, and ownership, strive for freedom beyond strict rules and regulations, both regarding their siting and the facility itself, and question and problematize them with their physical presence in space.

Pendants and inserts

The concept of the *insert* as a type of a capsule unit, which depends on the network in which it is placed, is directly connected with the tradition of space-frame structures, examples of which followed from Joseph Paxton's *Crystal Palace* of 1851, Alexander Graham Bell's first genuine three-dimensional space grid system from the beginning of the 20th century, to great interest and use in the 1950s and 1960s, when the main protagonists include Buckminster Fuller, Konrad Wachsmann, and André Waterkeyn, who designed the iconic *Atomium*, as the symbol of Expo 58 World's Fair in Brussels, together with André and Jean Polak. On the other hand, the heroic predecessor of megastructures, which calls for the placement of *inserts*, is Le Corbusier's famous *Plan Obus* from the 1930s, made of reinforced concrete.

Reyner Banham states that the first project resembling a megastructure was a student group project at the Architectural Association school from 1952, while he presents François Jamagne's project for Antwerp, from 1955, as one of the first examples of a megastructure with a diagonally braced space-frame supporting high-tech "capsules" which, in this case, are intended for greater flexibility for the art museum.[55] Early predecessors of Jamagne's projects, and of the concept of space-frames with inserted "capsule" units, may also include Nicolas Schöffer's *La ville spatiodynamique* (Spatiodynamic City) project, which he designed with architects Claude Parent and Ionel Schein in 1952. These early examples particularly highlight the design of the *insert* system and *a megastructural framework*—while we can only conditionally speak of genuine concepts of the capsule, in accordance with our derived definition.

Proposals for one of the most elegant, serious megastructures, but with playful infills in the form of spatial frameworks identify the activity of French "spatial urbanists," which Reyner Banham accuses of being lightweight structures devised and presented in drawings, which are impossible to be realized.[56] His criticism turned out to be justified, with the apotheosis of the space-frame above *Festival Plaza* at the Expo '70 World Fair in Osaka by Kenzo Tange, where the technical possibilities of such structures proved themselves as not-that-light, but facilitated the realization of Kisho Kurokawa's *Capsule House* and other *pendants*. Despite everything, French *urbanisme spatial* with diagram drawings by Yona Friedman and others was the one to mobilize thinking about the possible realization of mobile architecture, with extensive international influence, from Archigram to the Japanese Metabolists.[57]

Characteristic of spatial urbanism is the realization of space with the awareness of a transition from machines to the network of the postindustrial period when, in the notion of structuralism, individual units are directly influenced by the logic of connections that form a whole. While Banham took issue with spatial urbanists, as if to say that they reduced the real problems of urban planning in their projects to a distinctly visual, even stylistic, component, the term spatial urbanism was only used by a few people, and did not formally combine individual practices. Nevertheless, Larry Busbea, in his study of urban utopias in France in the 1960s and 1970s, efficiently highlights the common characteristics of many French projects, which pursued the goal of a uniform structure above or below ground, establishing the "artificial surface," and explored the topics of transportability, mobility, movement, and adaptability.[58] French projects distinguished themselves from others in their seriousness, justification with data and sociological studies, faith in technology, distrust of mass culture, and a desire to realize proposals. Following philosophical movements and opposite to structuralist, a phenomenological side, with an emphasis on individual perception and personal experience, was established in French architecture, which strove to replace the "scientific" approach of limited notions of structure and system, with a more direct and physical treatment of space.[59]

Despite the different approaches of individual protagonists of structural spatial urbanism, and phenomenological opponents of the space-frames, from the Architecture Principe, Busbea points out the duality between rationally designed steel or concrete megastructural space-frames, and adjustable, removable, changeable, and replaceable cell elements, which kept the designs in balance between the structuralist and phenomenological sides.[60] Although there is no indication of explicit designs of capsule units on either of the opposite sides, the environments which they created are particularly important for understanding the context of the seeming "megastructure international" and responses to it. Like the proposals of the Japanese Metabolists, which emphasized the separation of a dwelling from land as a prerequisite for the liberation of a modern man, proposals of spatial urbanists provided new extensive, separate from land, liberating technological environments of leisure and mobility.

At the end of the 1950s, GEAM (Groupe d'Études d'Architecture Mobile) was formed, on Friedman's initiative, built upon the ruins of CIAM which, according to Yona Friedman, did not manage to form suitable responses to the questions of mobility and mobile buildings, due to vague discussions about mobility, growth, and change, and the development and adaptability of the Smithsons and Team 10.[61] Each member had their own approach to dealing with mobility. The ones to stand out the most were Frei Otto, who became famous for his projects of suspended roof structures and expressionist environments, and Yona Friedman, who had written the manifesto on mobile architecture, *L'Architecture Mobile*, before the establishment of the group (1956), and published a program for mobile urbanism in 1959. In the latter, he stated key starting points, which result in mobility in cities:

> New constructions serving for individual shelters must:
> 1. touch a minimum surface of the ground;
> 2. be demountable and movable;
> 3. be transformable at will by individual inhabitant.[62]

Unlike his Japanese colleagues or Archigram, Yona Friedman's work shows his restraint when devising living units. With iconoclasm and technological optimism, which stemmed from his interest in information theory and cybernetics, the sociology of leisure, game theory, biology, mathematics, statistics, and demography, he wished to establish an infrastructural system of a city, where the devising of dwellings is up to the residents, through a structural and systemic approach.[63]

In addition to the nomadic projects of Archigram, such as *Blow-Out Village* from 1966 or *Free Time Node: Trailer Cage* from 1967, spiral structures of the Metabolists, waiting for random infills *à la* Le Corbusier's *Plan Obus* and Kurokawa's *Takara Beautillion* (see Figures 3.33, 3.34), paradigmatic examples of structures and capsule *inserts* include many examples of the use and derivations of the type in the 1960s. In an early and characteristic example from 1964, Wolfgang Döring proposes, as *inserts* into a steel multistory framework, rather classically devised, modular prefabricated "family" duplex cells, the designs of which hint at the possibility of fragmentation within the structure. At the beginning of the 1970s, Peter Cook acknowledged the potential for Döring and his housing projects for "making the idea of the simple prefabricated capsule a near reality."[64] Döring's living units seem to completely comply with our definition of the capsule or, in this case, the *insert*. However, attention should be paid to excessive fragmentation of individual units, which only conditionally meet the requirement

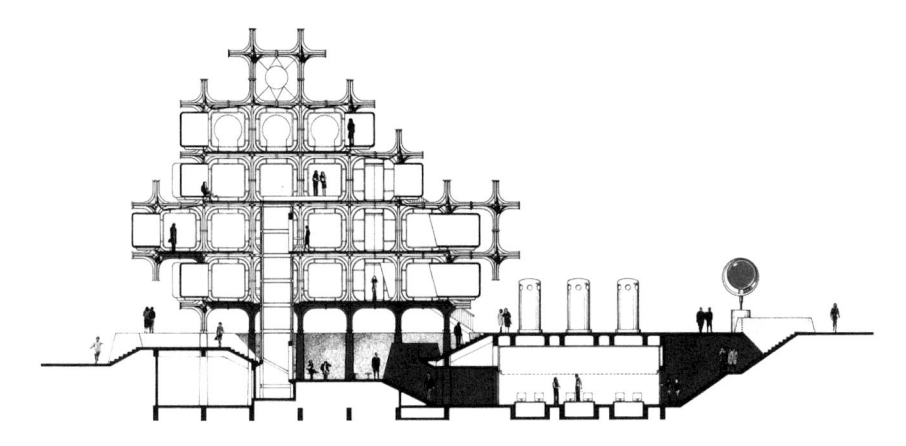

FIGURE 3.33 Kisho Kurokawa, *Takara Beautillion*, Expo '70, Osaka, 1970. Section

FIGURE 3.34 Kisho Kurokawa, *Takara Beautillion*, Expo '70, Osaka, 1970

for functional integrity, since living and service programs are traditionally organized within one volume, preventing the distinction of the *capsule* from the interior as a whole.

Equivalents to Döring's or Friedman's proposals can also be found in the territory of the former Yugoslavia. In 1988, Andrija Mutnjaković published the book, *Tercijarni grad (Tertiaty City)*, which presents a city of the postindustrial society. In the book, he presented his visionary megastructural projects and texts, which were created from the 1960s onward. With explicit references to Japanese and British contemporaries and other intellectuals, his desire was to create a flexible system with the project presented for the residential building of the Senjak settlement in Osijek, which would facilitate the fusion of the positive characteristics of individual residential construction (personal treatment and the possibility of extensions) and the positive characteristics of collective residential construction (lower construction costs and favorable urban location) in "socialist society."[65] Like in Jamagne's or Döring's projects, the system forms the basic structure of the space-frame. Apartments with a personal touch— residents may arrange the layout, form, and appearance of housing units—would help to overcome dissatisfaction with collective residential construction to date, offering a technologically feasible and rational solution in step with global trends. However, due to the planned possibility of inserting prefabricated capsule units, potentially expressed only in a model, and because the system anticipated its realization as "traditional construction," it can only be placed among *metaphorical capsular structures*.

This very distinction, which emphasizes the meaning of *functional and spatial integrity*, is crucial for the concept of the capsule in such projects to be fully confirmed. Raymond Wilson, whose articles in *Architectural Design* in the mid-1960s informed readers of the issues regarding the standardization of housing units, was aware of the fact that the response to the question about the difference between a building and a component became complicated, since prefabricated elements reached the size of parts of buildings and housing units. However, until then, no commercial system had been based on units the size of a room.[66] With technological development, the system, the basis of which was a component the size of a room, was anticipated particularly for short-term dwellings, such as hotels or motels, in the construction of which the setting-up of equal elements is the economically justifiable rule. Avant-garde and utopian contents of capsule architecture of the early 1960s were lost in economic and realization calculations.

Notes

1 The proposed taxonomy of the typology of the capsule was published in *Prostor* magazine. See Peter Šenk, "The Concept of Capsule Architecture as Experiment: Origins and Manifestations with Selected Examples from Slovenia and Croatia," *Prostor* (2.46, 2013): 350–361.
2 In the developmental perspective of the discourse on architectural types and typologies *via* Marc-Antoine Laugier, Quatremère de Quincy and Jean-Nicolas-Louis Durand, to whom nature was the reference point, through technology in modernism, the self-referential status of the typology and architectural autonomy in postmodernism, on the one hand, and utopian escapism on the other, seem to reach the most "liberating phase"—of being outside the system. When refering to the "system," we have in mind the all-encompassing universal neoliberal capitalism as not only economical, sociopolitical but also contemporary culturally dominant.
3 The term "third culture" refers to the process of the integration of literary and scientific thinking, and relates to the concept of two cultures of science and humanities, by C. P. Snow. In the 1960s, Snow proposed the emergence of the "third culture," which would transgress the duality of the literary intellectuals and scientists. Victoria Vesna, "Toward a Third Culture: Being in between," *Leonardo* (34.2, 2001): 121–125. In our use, the term also refers to the potential of the in-between of the art and science, as practiced by Marko Peljhan and others (see also n. 37).

4 Martin Powley provides a clear definition in the chapter "Technology Transfer in Architecture" of his book, *Theory and Design in the Second Machine Age*: "Technology transfer … refers to the process whereby the techniques and materials developed in one creative field, industry, or culture are adapted to serve in other creative fields, industries, or cultures." Martin Pawley, *Theory and Design in the Second Machine Age* (Oxford: Basil Blackwell, 1990), 140.

5 In addition to coordinator Vladimir Bodiansky, this project by ATBAT (Atelier des Bâtisseurs) included engineers and architects J. L. Lefebure, G. Candillis, N. Chatzidakis, C. Ganziarck, A. Josie, N. Rader, and consultants M. Marret, H. Maruvi, L. Castel, L. Pillot, J. Prouve, and A. Salomon. See Vladimir Bodiansky, "Polar Base," *Architectural Design* (January 1955): 8–9. Vladimir Bodiansky had been an aviation engineer before he joined Le Corbusier's studio. See also "Polar Shelters: Proposed Permanent Base of French Antarctic Expeditions," *Architectural Review* 716 (September 1956): 177–180; 178.

6 Marshall McLuhan, *Understanding Media: The Extensions of Man* (Corte Madera: Gingko Press, 2003), 170. First published 1964.

7 The aesthetics of science fiction linked the Finnish "flying saucer" to fascination with "canonical manifesto à la Stanley Kubrick or Kurt Vonnegut, that pushes the aesthetic and material envelope, a recurring theme in the major utopian vision of prefabricated housing in the twentieth century" on the one hand, and critical skepticism on the other: "Futuro is an exception in an otherwise golden era of elegant and understated Finnish architecture." Barry Bergdoll and Peter Christensen, *Home Delivery: Fabricating the Modern Dwelling* (New York: The Museum of Modern Art, 2008), 140–143. See also "Finnish Saucer," *Architectural Design* (October 1968).

8 Simone Jeska, *Transparent Plastics: Design and Technology* (Basel: Birkhäuser Verlag, 2008). It seems that the use of the *Futuro House* in the lighthouse program, a self-sufficient dwelling in remote conditions, realized the feedback effect in the development of the concept of the capsule. Remember that the lighthouse type served as a metaphorical prototype for Fuller's *Dymaxion House*.

9 Kiesler already highlighted the idea, which he upgraded and realized in his "endless structures," which fused the floor, walls, and ceiling into a continuous surface, in the manifesto *Space City Architecture* in 1926. See Frederick Kiesler, "Space City Architecture," in *Programs and Manifestos on 20th-Century Architecture*, ed. Ulrich Conrads (Cambridge, MA: MIT Press, 1999), 98. See also Christian Hubert, "Friedrich Kiesler: Two or Three Things We Know About Him," in *Sites and Stations: Provisional Utopias: Architecture and Utopia in the Contemporary City*, eds. Stan Allen and Kyong Park (New York: Lusitana Press, 1996).

10 dezeen Design Magazine, "Alpine Capsule by Lovegrove Studio 2," www.dezeen.com/2008/12/23/alpine-capsule-by-lovegrove-studio-2/ (2016–11).

11 Sarah Susanka is considered the pioneer of the "small house movement" also known as "tiny house movement," ever since the publication of her first book in 1998, entitled *The Not So Big House: A Blueprint for the Way We Really Live,* and continues the tradition of American countercultural projects from *Shelter* and other publications. See Lloyd Kahn, ed., *Shelter* (Bolinas, CA: Shelter Publications, 1973).

12 See micro compact home ltd., www.microcompacthome.com (2014–10). Successful and similar examples also include a range of prefabricated living cells of various dimensions, which are based on the width of a container, and facilitate road transport, by Oskar Leo Kaufman and his colleagues. See Oskar Leo Kaufman, Albert Rüf, www.olkaufmann.com/work/08-system3-new-york/ (2016–11).

13 Richard Horden, "Microarchitecture: Review of the Past and the Future Perspectives," *Detail* (12, 2004): 1426.

14 Horden, *Micro Architecture: Lightweight, Mobile and Ecological Buildings for the Future* (London: Thames & Hudson, 2008), 34.

15 See Jeska, *Transparent Plastics: Design and Technology*.

16 Larry Busbea, *Topologies: The Urban Utopia in France, 1960–1970* (Cambridge, MA: MIT Press, 2007), 58.

17 Arthur Quarmby, *Plastics and Architecture* (Washington, DC and New York: Praeger, 1974), 48.

18 The *K-67* kiosk was not intended to be a dwelling, but rather a universal element of urban equipment. Marjetica Potrč mentions that it was not likely that when they were set up the *K-67* kiosks could be a home to anyone, but today, this is no longer so unrealizable. See Marjetica Potrč, *Next stop, Kiosk (Naslednja postaja Kiosk): Moderna galerija Ljubljana, 29. 10–30 November 2003* (Ljubljana: Moderna galerija, 2003), 148; Saša Mächtig, "Kiosk sistem K-67," *Sinteza* (15, October 1969): 60–63.

19 Horden, *Micro Architecture*, 35.
20 See Liesbeth Melis, ed., *Parasite Paradise: A Manifesto for Temporary Architecture and Flexible Urbanism* (Rotterdam: NaI Publishers, 2003).
21 Sigrun Prahl, "Gimme Shelter, Short-term Solutions for a Long-term Problem: Temporary Housing for No-Income and Low-Income People," in *Transportable Environments: Theory, Context, Design and Technology*, ed. Robert Kronenburg (London and New York: E&FN Spon, 1999), 69–73.
22 Felicity Scott, "Bernard Rudofsky: Allegories of Nomadism and Dwelling," in *Anxious Modernisms: Experimentation in Postwar Architecture Culture*, eds. Sarah Williams Goldhagen and Réjean Legault (Cambridge, MA: MIT Press, 2000), 215–237.
23 Emilio Ambasz, *Italy: The New Domestic Landscape, Achievements and Problems of Italian Design* (New York: Museum of Modern Art, 1972), 137–138.
24 The unit is equipped with water and waste tanks, and an electric power system. With water being supplied and waste being removed by reservoirs, and electricity being supplied with a generator, the unit is independent of permanent distribution and sewage installations. A limited weight of the unit (about three tons) and its adjustable supports facilitate a simple erection on any kind of terrain, with no need for foundations. Ibid., 190–199.
25 Ibid., 394.
26 Courtenay Smith and Sean Topham, *Xtreme Houses* (Munich: Prestel, 2002), 118.
27 The Exbury Egg, https://exburyegg.me/ (2016-11); SPUD Group, www.spudgroup.org.uk/exbury-egg (2016-11).
28 A series of international architectural competitions on the subject of self-sufficiency should be mentioned, among attempts to open a wider discourse. Through their interdisciplinary approach, competition projects show architectural articulations of visions of dwellings and cities of the 21st century. IaaC - Institut d'Arquitectura Avançada de Catalunya, www.advancedarchitecturecontest.org/past-editions.html (2016–11).
29 Laurids Ortner, *On New Space*, www.lentos.at/images/Media/HRC_Presseunterlage_en.pdf (2016–11), first published in the catalog *Haus-Rucker-Co 1967 bis 1983*, Braunshweig (1984): 70–71. Haus-Rucker-Co was founded in 1967 by Laurids Ortner, Günter Zamp Kelp, and Klaus Pinter in Vienna.
30 Zamp Kelp, "Wind, Foam, Sense of Space," www.lentos.at/images/Media/HRC_Presseunterlage_en.pdf (2016–11), first published in *Housing is Back (Architekten beziehen)*, eds. Peter Ebner and Frauke Gerstenberg (Wien: Springer, 2006).
31 Ibid.
32 Andrea Bina, "Operating Manual for Spaceship Earth?" www.lentos.at/images/Media/HRC_Presseunterlage_en.pdf (2016–11).
33 About the *Vanilla Future* project, members of the group wrote: "Our objects are developed for a leisure society that has forgotten how to see and hear, which only reacts weakly to stimuli, because it is flooded by stimuli ... simple mental and physical experiences become conscious and intensified again, physical capabilities are activated." Ibid., Haus-Rucker-Co: Text by the artists on *Vanilla Future*. Vienna, 1968.
34 Marko Peljhan, "Insulation/Isolation Proceedings," lecture, *Documenta X* program, August 31, 1997, Zavod Projekt Atol, *Makrolab*, http://makrolab.ljudmila.org/peljhan1.html (2016–11).
35 Ibid.
36 *Makrolab* is a nonprofit project financed by state and interstate institutions, private and mobile capital, and individuals. The project is also trans-territorial. See Zavod Projekt Atol, *Makrolab*, "Makrolab Territory 2003, Isola di Campalto, Laguna di Venezia."
37 Marko Peljhan also includes Buckminster Fuller among important protagonists of the "third culture," and emphasizes that the art projects of Robert Rauschenberg, John Cage, Merce Cunningham, and others, which fused in the "third culture" in the 1960s, on the basis of concepts of historical avant-garde, of scientific and technological progress brought by World War II, and the post-war period in the USA, with the developed university system and increasing specialization of research areas are, in terms of complexity, equal to scientific and engineering projects. Narvika Bovcon, *Umetnost v svetu pametnih strojev: novomedijska umetnost Sreča Dragana, Jake Železnikarja in Marka Peljhana* (Ljubljana: Raziskovalni inštitut Akademije za likovno umetnost in oblikovanje, 2009), 220.
38 Justus Dahinden, *Urban Structures for the Future* (New York: Praeger, 1972), 21. Dahinden classified the "urban structures for the future" into Cellular Agglomerates, Clip-on and Plug-in, Bridge Structures, Containers, Marine Structures, the Diagonal in Space, and Biostructures.

39 Neither are container dwellings a novelty, for the needs of seasonal workers placed at a location, or for any other needs, for example *Portakabin*, described by Archigram, or like low-budget hotel complexes *Formula 1* and others.

40 Reyner Banham, *Megastructure: Urban Futures of the Recent Past* (London: Thames and Hudson, 1976), 105–107.

41 Malcom Purcell McLean's patent #US002853968 for the "Apparatus for shipping freight" enabled loading and manipulation of containers on the ship. The wide and economical use of containers for the transport of goods later led to the development and standardization of the containers.

42 See Jure Kotnik, *Container Architecture: This Book Contains 6441 Containers* (Barcelona: Links International, 2008); Kotnik, *New Container Architecture: Design Guide + 30 Case Studies* (Barcelona: Links Books, 2013); Hans Ibelings, "Mobile Architecture in the Twentieth Century," in *Parasite Paradise*, ed. L. Melis (Rotterdam: NAi, 2013), 148–166. The transformation of a container into a living unit was patented by Philip C. Clark in 1989 (#US 4854094 "Method for converting one or more steel shipping containers into a habitable building at a building site and the product thereof").

43 Examples include Tempohousing, with an example of a student housing *Keetwonen* in Amsterdam, *Qubic Hotgavens* student housing in Amsterdam by HVDN architects, and student housing *Spacebox* in Delft and Utrecht, Mart de Jong/De Vijf, etc.

44 Tempohousing, "Keetwonen Amsterdam Student Housing," www.tempohousing.com/projects/keetwonen.html (2016–11).

45 Tempohousing, "Housing Solutions," www.tempohousing.com/products/housing-solutions (2016–11).

46 See n. 41.

47 We named the type *connective cells* or *connectives*, which encompasses the notions of a *clip-on* and a *plug-in*, since such capsules are *connected* to the network of infrastructure of a megastructure, and they can be further subdivided on the basis of the technical manner of connection.

48 Dahinden, *Urban Structures for the Future*, 62.

49 Busbea, *Topologies*, 119.

50 *Architectural Design* (May 1971): 266.

51 Michael Rakowitz, "ParaSITE," www.michaelrakowitz.com/parasite/ (2016–11).

52 Smith and Topham, *Xtreme Houses*, 141; Rakowitz, "paraSITE".

53 Stephany Cash, "A-Z and Everything in Between," *Art in America* (April 2006): 124–131.

54 Sleepbox, http://sleepbox.com (2016–11).

55 Banham, *Megastructure*, 85; 37–38.

56 The designation "spatial urbanism" will be used as a translation of the French original "urbanisme spatial" used by Michel Ragon in his book *Où vivrons-nous demain?* in 1962 (Paris: Éditions Robert Laffont, 1963), although the "spatial" rhetoric had been used in France from at least the 1950s. See Busbea, *Topologies*; Banham, *Megastructure*, 57–64.

57 In his self-interview, Yona Friedman states that his idea of permanent support infrastructure and mobile parts, which randomly form living units in projects from the end of the 1950s, was literally borrowed by Archigram to develop their *Plug-in City* as well as his colleagues Shulze-Fielitz, Emerich, the Japanese Metabolists, and many others. Nevertheless, he did not consider these projects to be plagiarism, but he found in them a source of satisfaction brought by the success of his efforts to influence his generation. Yona Friedman, *Pro Domo* (Barcelona: Actar, 2006), 32.

58 See Busbea, *Topologies*.

59 Busbea, *Topologies*, 160–167.

60 The Architecture Principe was established in 1963 by architect Claude Parent, theoretician Paul Virilio, painter Michel Carrade, and sculptor Morice Lipsi. Virilio sought philosophical support for the phenomenological understanding of the built environment, and return to the body as the focus of the experience in the philosophy of Maurice Merleau-Ponty. See Ibid.

61 Founding members were Yona Friedman, David Georges Emmerich, Jean Pierre Pecquet (Friedman's partner in Paris), Jerzy Soltan, and Jean Trapmann, who were soon joined by Werner Ruhnau, Günther Günschel, Frei Otto, Paul Maymont, Eckhard Schulze-Fieltz, and others. In addition to "spatial urbanism" and GEAM, the international group of "visionaries" GIAP (Groupe International d'Architecture Prospective), which was established in the mid-1960s on the initiative of Michel Ragon, corroborated his thesis of the need to respond to the radical changes in society and technology with radical architecture and urban solutions. On its establishment, the manifesto GIAP was signed, in addition to Michel Ragon, by Yona Friedman, Walter Jonas, Paul Maymont, Georges Patrix, Ionel Schein, and Nicholas Schöffer. By 1970, when the group ceased its activities, it had

included many architects, engineers, critics, and experts from the fields of science, biology, medicine, psychiatry, etc. Busbea points out the diversity of the international company, in which post-communist intellectuals influenced its collective policy and its view of consumer culture in general. For a more detailed review of the establishment and activities of GEAM and GIAP, see Busbea, *Topologies*. See also Joan Ockman, ed., *Architecture Culture 1943–1968: A Documentary Anthology* (New York: Rizzoli, 1993), 273.

62 Friedman, *L'Architecture mobile: vers une cité conçue par ses habitants* (Paris: Catsreman, 1970), 62–64; Friedman, "Program for Mobile Urbanism," in Ockman, ed., *Architecture Culture 1943–1968*, 274.

63 See Sabine Lebesque and Helene Fentener van Vlissingen, eds., *Yona Friedman: Structures Serving the Unpredictable* (Rotterdam: NAi, 1999); Busbea, *Topologies*.

64 Peter Cook, *Experimental Architecture* (New York: Universe Books, 1970), 87.

65 Andrija Mutnjaković, *Tercijarni grad* (Osijek: Revija, 1988), 62–75; 68. As a starting point, Mutnjaković also mentions numerous quotes aimed at the monumentality and dictatorship of architecture.

66 Raymond Wilson, "Standardized Space or Standard Components?" *Architectural Design* (October 1965): 477.

4

MEDIUM

Typology and image

Envelope—protection and representation (exterior)

A living unit or housing, as perceived by Marshall McLuhan, is an extension of our skin and heat control mechanisms and a medium of communication. It provides comfort to the body by protecting it against climate and other undesirable external influences, including electronic impulses and information, while shaping and rearranging the patterns of human association and community.[1]

The envelope of a capsule as an external medium, which separates exterior from interior, is more precisely defined by its quality—its structure, including its physical tightness and its control mechanism, its materiality and integrity, which usually defines a capsule as a single-space element with either a frame or *monocoque* construction, and technology-related representation. The form generally depends primarily on the function, structure, and dimensions of the unit, and is perceived as a comprehensive *image*. The form may depend on the type of capsule, and the manner of its agglomeration or siting. The envelope, as an external medium, is actually the *archetype* of architecture, a paraphrase of a cave shelter from the distant past, now completed with a perfect physical control mechanism, which protects man against external influences, and more.

In the "Anthropological Preamble" to "Notes for a General Theory" related to "The Capsule and the Network" dialectics, Lieven De Cauter describes architecture in relation to McLuhan's theory as a medium which has always been an instrument of the possibility of human existence and limitations, and links it to the thought that "we are, and have been for the last 3000 years, 'voluntary prisoners of architecture.'"[2] It is thus obvious that speaking about modern "capsular civilization," the seeds of which were pointed out by De Cauter as something new, is nonsensical, a point he also makes. Metaphorically speaking, a capsule, an envelope, is actually the base and essence of architecture as functional protection of the body against external influences. As such, it has always been the conditioning instrument for the body. The envelope of a capsule, in all the addressed pioneering and contemporary examples, facilitates complete physical protection and, at the same time, is a shelter primarily for individuals. It enables individuals to be completely or selectively isolated.

Although such isolation is socially problematic, it is actually crucial. Like Kurokawa, who wants the capsule to enable each individual to withdraw from the world, flooded with information, into a contemplative environment, as the basis for the creation of diversified society, Christopher Alexander in his book, *A Pattern Language*, dedicates quite a few patterns[3] to a dwelling or shelter by breaking down the functions of architecture into individual patterns, from which it can then be reassembled more consciously. The key pattern, based on the belief that no one can be close to other people if they do not often have the opportunity to be alone, Alexander relates to sociological studies and Virginia Woolf's famous essay *A Room of One's Own*, after which the pattern described was named.[4] However, emphasizing, and withdrawing to, the complete isolation of privacy has its traps. It was, for example, totally incompatible with the collective utopia of the Situationists, who were aware of the problem of an economic system based on isolation. According to Guy Debord, the key Situationist, "Isolation underpins technology, and technology isolates in its turn; all *goods* proposed by the spectacular system, from cars to televisions, also serve as weapons for that system, as it strives to reinforce the isolation of 'the lonely crowd'".[5] According to Debord, isolation leads to alienation, which is manifested in an individual's relish of contemplation instead of in life, which results in the automation of the individual, who is no longer interested in his/her own desires, but yields completely to the market-driven false desires of the media-enforced spectacle.

According to Debord, isolation is distinctly in the service of the system, since an individual is controlled through the reception of spectacle-related messages with dominant images, which can only achieve their full power with isolation.[6] An individual, closed off in a room of his/her own, filled with media devices, is an easy target. Television, internet, or video games tempt one to use them as primary communication, as well as information sources, which are generally equipped with marketing ads and tricks, like commercials and commodified objects of desire, supporting identity manipulation possibilities. In this context, the possibility to control transmitted information, which was promoted by Kurokawa as one of the key features offered by the capsule, is also questionable. Is an isolated individual capable of consciously switching off the "contaminated" media of the (capitalist) system?

The concept of the capsule radicalized the functional relation between the privacy of the interior and the communicative character of the social space. It could be analyzed, in the history of dwellings, through various levels of mutual separation, permeability, or connection, with the realization of a completely impermeable envelope, which is also the expression the envelope acquires. The external envelope in many of the examples described, from Archigram's *Capsule Homes* and *Gasket Homes*, Kisho Kurokawa's capsules, children's move-net for Kikutake's *Sky House*, Cedric Price's capsule housing, to many others which were not all called capsules, is generally an expression of the technological process of mass production, without any expressive or meaning-related allusions. The appearance is not deceiving. Of course, it cannot be claimed that representation is left out this way. It is present, open, and unambiguous, at least at the level of the representation of architecture, its function and structure. The latter expands from the representation of complete isolation facilitated by a cellular unit without any social connections, in the manner of a hermit's dwellings through *ad hoc* aggregation, where the social space is also unplanned, random, but has no less valence to the anticipated communal space, a collective "haven" for the attachment of capsule units.

Considering the structure and manner of the aggregation of capsules and capsule compositions, the level of representation of control and power vary—from obvious total freedom bordering the anarchy of *autonomous independent* and *composite* capsule units, to more dependent freedom in megastructural compositions with *connective* units. The latter are the ones which are undoubtedly the least independent, subject to the control and regulation of the complex. Nevertheless, they still maintain their own integrity which, however, is potentially compromised when units are clipped on, but remains unchanged at the level of the unit. At this point, the key inconsistency of the representation of individuality could be highlighted, as it can be deceiving. The representation of the fragmentation of a composition of individual units, with increased level of control by the infrastructure of a megastructure, remains at the level of good wishes gobbled up by the system.

Although the idea of a capsule dwelling is a practical and metaphorical technology transfer from space engineering which is treated in modern interiors with pop, science fiction, or regional tones, the external representation layer in most pioneering examples from the early 1960s is an expression of silent technology which, however, is not expressionless. It seems that its silence speaks unwaveringly about the quality of the interior, with a Brutalist expression of its materiality and structure. Most interiors are full of equipment and devices—and with the sophisticated design of the minimum living environment—to follow the example of the space capsule. Nevertheless, the unwavering rhetoric cannot be attributed to later, more expressive projects, such as David Greene's *Living Pod*, and capsule units of certain French and Austrian protagonists, who succumb to space idolatry, streamlined design, and the "architecture as symbol" of emerging postmodernism, through pop aesthetics or irony.

The functional capsularity of the *typology of the capsule* provides shelter and facilitates withdrawal, while the functional expression of the envelope of the pioneering examples does not directly provide any allusions beyond the expression of its own structure. In this sense, we can refer to the declarative thesis about architecture, "which cannot use motives from the external world, like painting or sculpture can," since "architecture does not have any descriptive abilities."[7] This is mentioned by Aleš Vodopivec, although it was frequently turned upside down in the history of architecture. Pioneering capsules were actually the products of industrial design, which has been subject to the pressures of market economy and marketing, more than architecture. Nevertheless, designers' expressions managed to maintain the avant-garde disposition of genuine "machines for living in" transformed into "extensions of body." Therefore they could be classified among the most sincere products of the original principles of the functionalist project of the Modern Movement, which surpass these rigid orientations, with biological and technological metaphors of (mega)structures and compositions, and show the emergence of a new period which emphasizes *meaning*.

De Cauter, who is focused on the functional aspect and the structure of capsularity, links the functional mechanism of technological *capsularization* with speed, which controls contemporary daily routine, and proposed the *first law of capsularization*, which reads: "The greater the increase in physical and information speed, the greater the human need for capsules."[8] The speed of means of transport and information flow forces people to seek their own protection. On the one hand, this refers to the physical protection of the material envelope, while on the other, it refers to protection against the bombardment of omnipresent information, which protects people against "*dromospheric pollution*" described by Paul Virilio, who wonders:

> How can we resist this deluge of visual and audiovisual sequences, the sudden *motorization of appearances* that endlessly bombard our imagination? Are we still free to try and resist

the ocular (optic or optoelectronic) inundation by looking away or wearing sunglasses? Not out of modesty any more, or because of some religious taboo, but out of a concern to preserve one's integrity, one's *freedom of conscience* ... Surely it would then be appropriate to entertain a kind of *right to blindness* ...?[9]

Kisho Kurokawa's capsule provides an instant response to Virilio's question, with *cyborg architecture* as the perfect fusion of man and machine, which—selectively—protects man against all external influences, like goggles, which are an extension of a human organism. Kisho Kurokawa's cyborg architecture is a direct reference to the technological logic of capsularity, which is divided by De Cauter into "real" capsules—physical envelopes of fast mobile facilities of "sedentary nomads"—and "virtual" capsules of screens, which suck a man into a mentally and virtually enclosed space, which is not related to the actual space where a man lives.[10]

However, De Cauter does not highlight the quality of complete shutdown, which holds the key position in Kisho Kurokawa's philosophy of the capsule, and has a liberating meaning. He problematizes it as the product of blind faith in the liberating power of technology, and in the context of the emerging "capsular civilization," like the Situationists and many others before him. Both the *Capsule House* at Expo '70 and the *Nakagin Capsule Tower* provide a dwelling for an individual, which becomes the only and main expression of the architectural composition: Capsule architecture expresses an individual. The fragmentation of the compositions clearly shows the possibility of their internal changes, which depend on residents who coexist in, and co-inhabit, them. The composition is the representation of the fragmented society of individuals, whose dwelling drifted away from traditional cultural patterns, in the desire to provide minimum personal space for everyone—a space completely restrained on the outside which, by emphasizing its internal content to which an individual can randomly adapt, represents the relative insignificance of a human body, and highlights the significance of facilitating inner personal fulfillment for an individual in this space and the diversity of society.[11]

Envelope—comfort equipment and feedback simulation (interior)

The second characteristic of the concept of the capsule refers to the internal part of its envelope, and the equipment installed in it. In addition to the inner side of the envelope, comfort in a capsule is also provided by its equipment, which facilitates the regulation of the influence flow from the outside, and the creation of the desired ambiance inside, by means of an interface. Although functional autonomy is a key component of the capsule's concept, such autonomy is usually a far cry from the autarkic ideal. Instead, it remains within the scope of acceptable mechanisms of subordination to the system, the connection of which to the grid provides a capsule with the complete comfort of introverted living. Comfort is provided by the ergonomic character of furnishings on the one hand, and with constantly improving equipment in the form of electronic and information devices, which enable residents of a capsule to have controlled contact with the outside world or a simulation of its reality, on the other. In the case of the specialization of functions, a monofunctional capsule became an operative program unit of larger compositions. As in capsule living units, monofunctional capsules provide comfort with their ergonomic design, and usually calculation-based consideration of subsistence minimum, which is justified in view of the requirements for greater mobility. An interior designed in such a manner may be perceived as an explicitly conditional or restricting discipline instrument. The interior of a capsule may have a double effect, since the conditioning of the body may function parallel to the expansion of its capacities, and perhaps even its eugenic physical abilities.

Despite the fact that the concept of the capsule emerged in late *first modernity*, it may be designated as the search for a haven in the *second* or *reflexive modernity*, where an individual seeks shelter in the *space of flows*, as a utopian exit from the conditions of forced nomadism— when, according to Scott Lash, who refers to the individualization in Ulrich Beck's reflexive modernization thus: "the non-linear individual may wish to be reflective, but has neither the time nor the space to reflect."[12] Key possibilities provided by the capsule's concept in this context are the possibility of withdrawal, the possibility of having control over information flow, and the possibility to individually regulate partial or complete exclusion or conscious isolation, in space and outside it. Although the freedom offered seems perfect, Beck and Beck-Gernsheim point out that there are two sides to individualization, and that individualization does not provide undoubted freedom. In their opinion, the integration of individualized societies is potentially possible, but it does not exclude the possibility of an inwardly heterogeneous society being outwardly closed with fortified strongholds.[13]

Characteristic of modern social reality since the second half of the 20th century—particularly in the last twenty or thirty years—is individualization, which is defined and described differently by various theoreticians and researchers. Ulrich Beck speaks about individualization, and distinguishes it from individualism, individuation of depth psychology, or neoliberal egoism. In his definition, individualization is a "concept, which describes a structural, sociological transformation of social institutions and the relationship of the individual to society."[14] Individualization thus liberates people from their traditional roles and restrictions, which comprise family structures, living conditions, leisure activities, and other structures which guided the lives of individuals in the first period of modernity while, in the second, they were left to the decisions of individuals living in the conditions of a risk society. By being aware of its dark side in the conditions of globalization, however, Beck and Beck-Gernsheim do not see individualization as something negative, but particularly as a process of transformation of outdated institutions, which they call "zombie categories," categories which are dead but still alive, into new forms of social relations, which are nevertheless based on the altruistic association of individuals. However, they do not exclude the possibility that individualization and integration are mutually incompatible.[15] Do designs of capsule dwellings, from Japan to Great Britain, which clearly showed fragmentation and sometimes completely radical disintegration of the basic cell of a family, radically mirror the absence of "zombie categories" of modern society? Did they confirm Beck's theses and show their transience by denying the institution of a family, and redefining the conditions of living and the way leisure time was spent in the counter-cultural community, with open possibilities of *the life of one's own* in the 1960s?

The key feature in the design of experimental dwellings, "not enclosed or visual spaces"[16] according to McLuhan, which are related to the concept of the capsule, is the freedom of movement, without obstacles either in a mental, physical, or visual sense, and the search for the center, as discussed in Chapter 2 on counterculture. In the case of individual units, the "boundlessness" of the interior is indicated by the smooth lines of the floor, soft passages from horizontal surfaces to vertical, and organic indeterminable forms, like in a womb, the meta-phorical ideal, and the ideal in terms of design. In certain cases, design-based and installation-based simulations of the womb, and ergonomically comfortable dimensions acquired soft forms. At the same time, rounded internal forms of space presume and clearly indicate its center, which metaphorically becomes the ideal of the centered dweller—the individual. In this context, the fascination of counterculture, with Fuller's rounded and distinctly technicist geodesic dome, the center of which is turned inwards, is completely understandable.

On the other hand, media bombardment of the senses made the interior subject to the art of dislocation or expansion of the interior, and to the creation of a socialization spectacle by means of modern technology. Are we witnessing the self-organization of new communities at the physical level of a dwelling with rounded walls, and, in the case of spaces with technological devices, in stimulating experiential enclaves of urban McLuhan's "retribalization, which contribute to hive consciousness"? As we have seen, it seems that these mostly temporary, unstable, and transforming communities comply with Beck's forecast of the "new ethics," which will "establish a sense of 'we' that is like a co-operative or altruistic individualism."[17] The question that arises could be the path to the rehabilitation of capsule structures and their perception in a brighter light. Could the concept of "hive consciousness" of centered separate living cells be transferred to the context of capsule architecture in a cluster or stacked composition or *ad hoc* formations of cellular mobile living cells of modern nomads?

The key to answers lies largely beyond the capsule itself, in the question of the organization and character of a communal space although, as in the case of Kikutake's clip-on towers, as residents enthusiastically observe the lifting of a new unit, the consciousness of the community is already idealistically anticipated with the "biological" structure. Kurokawa's "spiritual haven" of capsule structures, Archigram's "plaza" and free platforms with plug-in spots, Yona Friedman's unoccupied spaces of superstructures, and NER's free platforms, are only a few examples that provide the conditions to realize the space of social interaction. The extent of genuinely public spaces which could be expected in such megastructural compositions depends on the question of their ownership and management. Potentially public places in them could soon become controlled *collective spaces of simulated public sphere.*

Prefabricated integrity (structure, function, representation)

The third characteristic of the concept of the capsule is the compactness of the composition, which may be perceived and analyzed as a unit, a spatial and program unity of the structure, which may be fragmented, but only if it functions as *one thing*, and is directly dependent on the manner of prefabrication. The unity of the composition is presented as an *image*, and a distinct quality that connects the concept of the capsule to the production of identity.

The associative path, which directed certain architectural historians, theorists, and designers to history, concluding that the capsule is similar to the *primitive hut*, is actually stimulating and relevant, as it opens the issues of the structure, function, and representation, as well as of building and dwelling in contemporary spatial reality, which has always been the subject of discussions about this archetype. Comparisons arise in the field of architectural history and theory, and in rhetorical practice. In his review of the history of architectural theory, Hanno-Walter Kruft mentions that the idea of the mobile, prefabricated individual capsule has a similar theoretical status to the primitive hut of the 18th century,[18] while Wes Jones, as one of the most eminent protagonists of modern container architecture, shows in his review the presence of the archetype and the question of the origin of architecture in modernity, in the ironic reflection of the primitive hut as an upgraded container capsule structure. Wes Jones's proposal was intended for people who collect and recycle materials, and are independent of the infrastructure of the market, like disused containers-turned-homes.

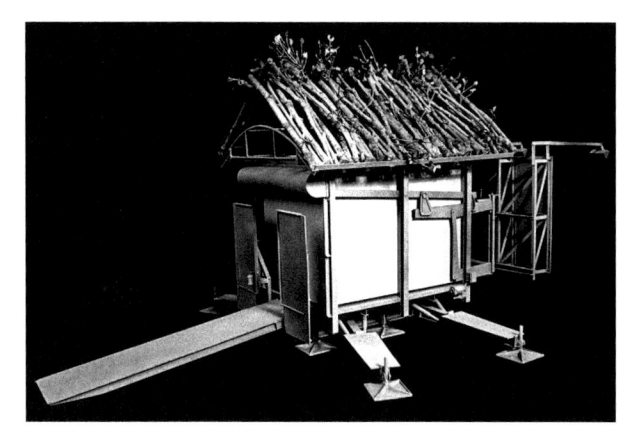

FIGURE 4.1   Wes Jones/Jones Partners, *Primitive Hut*, 1994–1998

By naming the project *Primitive Hut* (Figure 4.1), Wes Jones highlights the tension between the search for the origins of architecture in nature and an unavoidable technological archetype, which becomes the basic element of architecture, and indicates with it the possibility of independence from the system and liberation.

Although the idea of a primitive hut was present in the theory of architecture as early as Vitruvius, particularly in the sense of the origin of architecture, and the duality of functional protection and symbol which humans used to arrange their spiritual position as placement in time and space, it obtained the status of the origin of all possible forms, principles, and limits of architecture in the Enlightenment period, with Marc-Antoine Laugier.[19] The primitive hut always appeared as a paradigm of a building, as a standard by which other buildings are judged, either through rituals or myths, or through architectural contemplation. As pointed out by Joseph Rykwert, it became particularly interesting in times when it offered a return to the origins, with the intention of rethinking the existing state, and highlighting the issue of the essence of building, due to the need to restore the foundation of architecture as a discipline.[20] Playful reflections by Wes Jones, in contemporary practice, issues of type and typology in the postmodernist 1970s, modernist functionalism, and demand for material honesty all echo the need for a reference point of origin for architectural answers to time-related questions. For Laugier, it was the origin of (classical) architecture, which served as a role model and subject of imitation when designing buildings, not the *mimesis* of nature or imitation of antique patterns, but the archetype of architecture. In this sense, the capsule could not easily be attributed with such a status at first sight. Or could it?

With a hut composed of pieces of wood set upright as the archetype of pillars, pieces placed horizontally on top of them as entablature, and inclining pieces for the pitched roof and the pediment, Laugier highlights the essential elements of architecture, which also constitute the ethical dimension of architecture—architecture which follows this example is good, other building elements are destined to be caprices of an architect, and a matter of personal taste.[21] The primitive hut, as understood by Laugier, is "pure distillation of nature through unadulterated reason, prompted only by necessity," as poetically summarized by Rykwert.[22] In the ideal conclusion, when the capsule is both an antithesis of nature and technology, and their fusion—a cyborg—the similarity of the theoretical status could be interpreted, but the part referring to the imitation of the archetype, with basic elements, is only useful for the concept of the capsule metaphorically.

The basic material of the primitive hut was supposed to be wood, although Laugier's critics, like Carlo Lodoli, disagreed with that. In other geographical conditions, stone is more easily available than wood, and therefore a wooden hut could not have been a subject of imitation in stone architecture.[23] Looking beyond the issue of imitation, the structure of the primitive hut is distinctly adapted to the assumed original materiality, and has the function of basic protection, which is similar to capsule architecture, which is otherwise designed and realized with modern, including non-natural, materials. In addition to Laugier, who advocated a rational approach to architecture, and took a step forward from following the then profession of ruling architectural orders, another famous proto-functionalist, Carlo Lodoli, was the one who could be attributed with the real establishment of the ratio between function and representation, in a manner seen in modern *rhetorical functionalism*.[24] Lodoli's important position was not focused on the issue of imitation, but on understanding the properties of materials, on which architectural expression should be based. Alberto Pérez-Gómez points out that the ratio between form and matter should be metaphorical and imaginative, not only rational, as in the structural determinism of the 19th century, or reductionist elaborations of functionalism.[25] In addition to function which, at that time, meant general operation and adequate use of materials, Lodoli addresses the issue of representation with complex implications.[26] In the capsule units addressed, the explicit materiality of the envelope is emphasized as a recognizable entity, a representation which "lets materials speak," if we refer to Karsten Harries's expression.[27] In addition to the rhetorical functionality of the envelope, Lodoli's "functionalism" of the interior is literally realized in the ergonomic interior of the capsule. Lodoli is also attributed with the introduction of the term *organic architecture*, but his term refers primarily to the human body. Therefore, his works contain a distinctly ergonomic approach to the design of furniture and buildings.[28]

The story about the primitive hut indicates the origins of functionalism. Without the omnipresence of the latter in architectural theory and practice of the 20th century, capsule architecture would be difficult to imagine or comprehend. At the same time, proto-functionalism of the 18th century speaks a language similar to many architects of capsules, who wished to loosen up the reductive dogmatic *rigorous functionalism*, by emphasizing the meaning and reintroducing rhetorical function. In his essay, "Functionalism Today," Theodor Adorno also questioned strict functionalism as expressionless and non-rhetorical. Adorno believes that functionalism in architecture cannot be pure functionalism, as rigorous functionalists would like, since it hides a contradiction: "Virtually every consumer had probably felt all too painfully the impracticability of the mercilessly practical. Hence our bitter suspicion is formulated: the absolute rejection of style becomes style."[29] Moreover, something that was functional in a certain period becomes non-functional in another, since important elements lose their meaning, and thus their functionality. At the same time, "even the most pure forms of purpose are nourished by ideas—like formal transparency and graspability—which, in fact, are derived from artistic experience. No form can be said to be determined exhaustively by its purpose."[30]

A leap in the linking of the primitive hut and a capsule unit is also related to the intention of architecture. The primitive hut, as derived *post festum* from the structure of a Greek temple, to which it supposedly served as an archetype, is actually the basis of the architecture of the temple. If it was to be its modern successor, capsule architecture is the adequately radical architecture of an individualized person, which assumed the appearance of a temple, in the process of individualization from the Enlightenment on, and returned to the functionalist origins in desacralized contemporaneity, and completely relativized traditional issues of the design and art of building. A minimized capsule unit may actually be considered an archetype of modern architecture for assembling complexes from minimum parts. Remember that the issue of the size of a "building element" was emphasized as early as in the pioneering times of capsules, when prefabricated elements reached the size of one room, and stirred up speculations about capsules as the "bricks" of the city of the 21st century. A capsule unit may be treated as the basic and the smallest element of large compositions, but it cannot be attributed such universality and openness of understanding as the primitive hut.

The primitive hut was composed of building elements in their most elementary form. By analogy, the three basic elements of the hut, in a modern capsule unit, are merged in its *monocoque* or uniform envelope of a frame and infill, which makes the envelope of the capsule an indivisible basic element. Trunks and branches may only form a *small house* which, according to Nicolas Pople, was the first house in human history, and also the house which was discussed for the shortest period in architectural history, since small private houses did not become the subject of architects' interest until the 18th century.[31] The typology of capsules includes the small, if not the smallest, houses with an impermeable envelope, and physical or simulated comfort of the introverted interior, functional, spatial and visual integrity, changeability, and mobility, whereby the definition of the capsule surpasses and expands the condition of mere construction logic of the basic elements.

The elementariness of materials of the envelope of a capsule unit of steel sheet metal, plastics, or composite panels is associated again with the similarity to the elementariness of the primitive hut. In the case of the capsule, we cannot speak about natural analogy, architecture which is, by analogy, based only on nature. But from the expanded aspect of rationality, functionality, proper use of materials, and construction-related clarity, based on laws of nature or the principles of prefabrication, we cannot deny its basic elementariness in the modern technological context.

By establishing its natural authority, theories about the primitive hut speak particularly about how to build in harmony with the essence of architecture, which is to be provided by the imitation, *mimesis*, of the primitive hut, which was understood in the 18th century as the imitation of nature, and signified in architecture the imitation of its principles. Laugier's hut, as explained by Vodopivec, is an architectural prototype which substantiates architecture as an "autonomous" art. While other arts seek models for their work in nature, architecture does not know such a model, does not find it in nature beyond its own experience. Therefore, its model is only substantiated within architecture itself.[32] In addition to functionality, representation in architecture is also highlighted, which is substantiated within the autonomy of the discipline, the positions of which are also present in contemporary discourse. By establishing architecture's own language, *mimesis* drifts away from the original meaning of mere imitation, to the field of creative imitation. The imitation of an archetype shifted the issue of imitation in architecture to the field of architecture itself. Architecture is an imitating art, insofar as it imitates architecture itself, when it represents the building itself, its structure, its materiality, functionality, and its meaning. William McClung points out that the ethical dimension of architecture, compliance with nature, has remained the same—with the limitation to natural or nature-imitating materials, architectural language has been more abstract, and it imitates, conceptually, not instinctively or reflexively, the primitive act of construction—of the primitive hut.[33] Unlike strict functionalism, the ethical confirmation of architecture is imbedded in representation itself. In the case of capsules, the representation envelope may have its own tone but, in a completely modernist fashion, always in relation to content—function and structure.

The issue of function and representation is related to the process of creation/*poiesis*/and with creative imitation/*mimesis*/. As with Lodoli, who required the harmonization of function and expression, Dalibor Vesely, in Heideggerian tradition, reminds us that our perception of reality is always indirect, and the key role is played by the harmonization of representation, the unity of representation, and what representation stands for. Only such harmonization may draw us closer to the depth and fullness of reality, which would otherwise be out of our reach, and enables us to participate in it.[34]

For the concept of the capsule and the devising of its integrity, crucial changes in the reasoning of architecture and building with temporariness, mobility, and prefabrication draw the subject of architecture closer to other technical disciplines and to industrial design and, in many cases, totally fused it with them. Although the culture of building still largely resists such an approach, with today's mass production of virtually all products that used to be handmade, McLuhan's extensions of the body, from shoes, clothing, furniture, and various equipment and devices, to means of transport, proposals for many contemporary derivations, in terms of technological perfection, surpass the anticipated framework of pioneering attempts by avant-garde architects, who established a relationship between architecture, Taylorism, Fordism, and a scientific approach, in the 1920s. Prefabricated construction, which represents one-third of single-family houses in the western world,[35] is largely a continuation of traditional building patterns, which were characteristic of pre-modern prefabricated buildings, and only rarely utilizes the potential of significantly different types of construction. Most advanced cases often remain at the level of projects and prototypes.

Concern about the monotony of settlements of prefabricated houses, which culminated in Levittown in the USA in the 1950s, with a paradigmatic example of suburbanization and banal buildings, was surpassed in the same period with the active involvement of architects, with examples such as *Eichler Homes*, Charles and Ray Eames's house, projects by architects like Craig Ellwood, Pierre Koenig, and others. But the image and fear of prefabrication have been preserved until today.[36] After the period when Walter Gropius, who was, according to Sigfried Giedion, the pioneer of modern architecture most passionate about prefabrication,[37] wanted to surpass monotony with an endless number of possibilities to use exchangeable prefabricated parts, which compose various individual houses today, with digital parametric design and direct computer-controlled manufacture of mass-customized prefabricated components, fear of excessive monotony is not necessary. Risks brought by new technological possibilities lie in the exact opposite of this initial concern. Excessive openness of options drives designers to produce algorithmically generated forms that are not harmonized with the logic and processes of production. Such attempts do not supply prefabricated construction with the necessary attractiveness which would establish a connection between high-quality design and affordability. During the development of such construction, manufacturers of prefabricated dwellings were frequently focused exclusively on profitability, which helped designate prefabricated products as "cheap and functional," while individual projects, which were more ambitious, in terms of architecture and design, were only rarely realized, which designates the history of prefabrication as a "long continuum of noble failures."[38] Is more than *just* "cheap and functional" legitimately to be expected from prefabricated dwellings?

In theory and practice, prefabrication and mobility form a complementary pair, including opposing positions of their main protagonists. According to Hans Ibelings, the history of mobile architecture in the 20th century culminated with two directions. On the one strand, there are examples/projects of artists, industrial designers, and architects, including Sant'Elia, Le Corbusier, Fuller, the Japanese Metabolists, Archigram and contemporary Future Systems, and Kas Oosterhuis, who only rarely overcame the phase of a prototype, due to over-ambition or distance from reality. The other strand includes examples/projects of mobile architecture, which were actually realized, and which were fueled by distinct and immediate usefulness, more than noble ideas.[39] The second strand includes container units, exhibition pavilions, mobile sanitary units, kiosks, temporary schools, hospitals, and many other facilities produced because they are promptly needed or because there is a market for them, and which are frequently far ahead of more famous "architectural" proposals, as pointed out already by Buckminster Fuller and Reyner Banham. However, we cannot ignore the influence of visionary projects of prefabricated and mobile architecture which, as a response to changes in society, formulated and visualized questions which could perhaps be overlooked, in the delusion with technological development or autogenous conditions only established with the market.

While prefabricated construction with frames and panels greatly expanded in the post-war period, and reached mythical proportions in the Eastern bloc with the East German system of residential construction, *Plattenbau*, *monocoque* constructions were subject to efforts for designs on the scale of small living cells and mobile units. *Monocoque* constructions boomed, with the use and utilization of the characteristics of plastics in the 1950s, which gave such structures their recognizable form.

Desiring to surpass the proverbial monotony, the latter were realized with a technological tone, and were rarely, and usually intentionally, thematized or stylized, regardless of their structure. In addition to strict technological representation of the structure, panel versions, as consumer products of industrial design, often acquired a style in accordance with general taste and expectations about the look of a house. On the other hand, *monocoque* versions were more committed to their materiality, on which the structure of integrity depended. Their characteristic expression, representation within the scope of technological rhetoric, expands from the strict note of a machine to a softer note in pop manner, and to flirting with images of space engineering, and even regional tones.

Expressive comparisons of the early period of prefabricated dwellings are found in the parodic deliberation by Buster Keaton, the short movie *One Week* from 1920, and Roger Vadim's movie *Barbarella* from 1968. In *One Week*, the non-monotony of the building was achieved by accident. In the end, the house that was inappropriately erected and useless tragically collapses, as if it were a house of cards, to the misfortune of the couple who built it themselves. In the cult movie *Barbarella*, Jane Fonda, as the main heroine, is similarly helpless in her erotized pop distinctiveness in a fur-clad space capsule, pestered by technical problems. The ironic similarity with the fur-clad interior of Kurokawa's capsule two years later at Expo '70 in Osaka, is very expressive, but dubiously self-ironic. While early prefabrication was completely mechanical, structures in *Barbarella*, as pointed out by Reyner Banham, are practically a parody of unstable hardware and megalomaniacal megastructuralism, and the inauguration of software of lightweight pneumatic structures and independent flexible living capsules, like in the Archigram group in the second half of the 1960s.[40]

In contemporary production, prefabrication, hardware and software of living units are subject to operativeness. Beyond ironic, science fiction, and fictitious derivations, the concept of the capsule provides bases for many contemporary realizations of dwellings which, more or less precisely, follow the typology. Certain derivations do not refer directly to the concept of the capsule, but the latter may be attributed to them, in the form of unconscious indirect influence on the basis of our model of development.

Functional, spatial, and visual integrity of the capsule is the condition arising from the definition based on the notion of a capsule. The latter is indicated in compact, independent, and self-sufficient or even self-sustaining living units with architectural rhetoric that artificially creates a balance between a living organism and the environment. The spatial effect generated by capsule compositions is a total fragmentation of space, in relation to social dispersal, and takes place through juxtapositions: Inside–outside, uncontrolled–controlled, public–private, included–excluded, etc. The radical extrapolation of spatial relations could lead to the realization of De Cauter's cautionary *second law of capsularization*: "Exclusion leads to crime, and crime leads to exclusion," which is related to "fear" as the driving force behind the shutting off of the environment in more extensive, territorial, capsular structures.[41] Although the romantic image of a "new society" seems destined to be lost by such a forecast, the duality of temporary exclusion from spatial reality, and the possibility of personal development in isolation, are trapped in architecture—where structure, function, and representation as the *integrity* of a capsule composition, always perhaps utopian, inspires possibilities of authentic dwelling and individual liberation beyond De Cauter's theory of doom.

Temporariness (time and space)

When Manuel Castells includes, among the requirements of modern society, the requirement for flexibility and adaptability, which is realized in relation to mobility in the fields of information technology, management, production, or social relations, he points to the parallel paradigm of, for example, information technology, which is based on flexibility, the decisive virtue of which, in the company of constant changes and organizational fluidity, is its ability to be reconfigured.[42] In relation to information technology, other activities which influence space or are physically expressed in space, similarly adapt to the requirements of social reality with flexible forms of organization. Consequently, flexibility and adaptability require the perception and functioning of space as a composition of explicitly temporary components. *Autonomous* capsule units, which utilize the possibility of complete geographical freedom, are an example of a distinctly nomadic, time-dependent relation with a specific space, while *connective* units form time-dependent spatial program complexes in otherwise more durable, infrastructural and megastructural frameworks. In the examples described, the latter have anticipated permanence ratings, and are by nature temporary, replaceable, and expendable. This brings constant changes into spatial program complexes, which define a megastructure as a constantly changing system. On the other hand, temporary "nomadic" dwellings are not bound to a place, but are "uprooted" and free from constant attachment to land or a megastructural framework. This characteristic was developed to perfection from imperfect proto-capsule units into real living capsules. Their installed temporariness makes capsule units, in which flexibility is realized as *portability*, ideal structures for the requirements of modern mobile society.

Contemporary space, a space of flows, is a space of flux and hubs, which are realized in centers that differ in terms of hierarchy and meaning, specialized monocultures, and various program conglomerates. Mobility and individualism are crucial for the creation of identity, facilitate personal and economic freedom, and open possibilities for development, but are also a threat to established traditionalism, which is committed to attachment to a place.[43]

Therefore, attachment to *locus*, and the issue of the traditional notion of home and dwelling are called into question in the modern society of mobility. In the sociology of knowledge, the technological development of production, and the bureaucratic organization of social life which played the most important role in the process of modernization, depend on principles such as rationality, anonymity, and abstractness of social relations, whereas greater mobility and the functioning of an individual in various, constantly new, social contexts signifies the loss of certainty, meaning, and also of a real "home."[44]

The meaning of dwelling in modernity and the question of whether real dwelling is even possible, are topics of many architectural, theoretical, and philosophical contemplations, some of which we have already brought to light, i.e. technology-related examples, from Fuller's and Banham's technological autarky to Kurokawa's individual-oriented mobile metropolitanism, and others. In reflection of the anti-technological view, and stress on the significance of traditional values, the issue of home and dwelling in philosophy is frequently in opposition to the conditions and requirements of modernity.

The scale of a capsule highlights the duality between the heritage of existentialism faced with the nonfigurative feature of a unit, and potential, with the meaning-related openness of the structure of the Japanese Metabolists, and playful surpassing of the prescribed reality, as in the Archigram group. If the Metabolists attributed significance to the metaphorical organic feature of changing structures, the West put the aesthetics of change at the forefront, which was seen in pop experiments and existentialist criticism from the Independent Group to the ironic, intentionally irresponsible lightness of the Archigram group. In the latter, architecture became particularly the promise of an *immediate future*, more than a subject of Giedion space and time, or the placement into a specific context or sociocultural continuum. The realization of a machine for living in changed the house from a *dwelling* into a machine for the satisfaction of changing needs, in accordance with the commodified lifestyle anticipated for such dwellings. *Ad hoc* communities, which leave architecture as the permanent creation of a place in the extensive space behind it, enable individuals to constantly create new social connections and relationships with the environment.

The question that arises in the context of possibilities of dwelling in modernity is what relation such instant settlement and social formations establish in space, and what such "homelessness" means for an individual. Karsten Harries points out that utopian visions of pop art and the Archigram group lean toward the dissolution of people into collections of changing needs, which may be easily caused and manipulated with advertising, thus emphasizing the possibility for individuals to completely forget about themselves in such an environment, get lost in the moment, taking the community with them. Here, Harries turns to the requirement to recognize transience as the condition of real dwelling, which was stressed by Martin Heidegger in his famous lecture, "Building, Dwelling, Thinking."[45] At the same time, we question another stressed requirement of attachment to a place. The requirement for a building which grows roots, as told by historical examples, could lead to the *Blut und Boden* aesthetics and totalitarianism. Therefore, such a position is problematic in contemporaneity. In the anthropological sense, dwelling has always been defined between nomadism and permanent settlement, while contemporary relationships in space radicalized the seeming stability, and showed it in the opposite light as constantly changing. The thing that remains, and that could be the basis for cultural foundations in contemporaneity, is not so much physical dwellings as institutions, which must, as pointed out by Kenneth Frampton, be durable for their political needs, on which the maintenance of public space, space of public appearance, depends.[46] At the same time, we need to be aware that the very durability of institutions facilitates status quo, and prevents change.

We can agree with Harries, when he presents Heidegger's requirements as a call for individuals to be aware of their imperfection, not only in the sense of emphasized individuality and transience, but also the need for community. By tearing a place out of space, and creating time-related situations, buildings place an individual in time, not abstract time, but time shared by a community, in history. Harries advocates preservation of the architectural past, which should enable the possibility of true dwelling by creating and preserving real public space. However, his call is aimed at an integral approach to the problem, as he is aware that "playing with its fragments" cannot produce a real result.[47]

But the question of the possibility to create a community and living in *ad hoc* capsule structures, along with the realization of the forecast of new ethics of cooperative and altruistic individualism, is perhaps unnecessary.[48] Harries shows the relationship between an individual and a community, not giving primacy to either of them, with a metaphor of an ellipse with two focal points. In his opinion, modern architecture must be aware of the incomplete determination of each focal point, and the necessary tension between the two points. Building intended for dwelling must preserve and represent the tension between private and public. By reviewing the understanding of dwelling, this calls for architecture which responds to our basic incompleteness, our need for other people, for a genuine community, which must also be responsive to reason and demands the universal. According to Harries, "such architecture would present inevitably precarious interpretations of our ethos, of our place in a larger order."[49] The uncertainty and incompleteness of formulations is extremely important to Harries, as it leaves open possibilities for interpretation, to avoid any kind of totalitarianism which would stem from such formulations. Therefore, the answer to the question of dwelling to him contains many traps, and we should never leave it up to one authority. If the problem lies in the technological character of modernity which, according to Heidegger, is problematic, and does not allow authentic dwelling, the position of, for example, Emmanuel Levinas, in his essay "Heidegger, Gagarin and Us," with the Holocaust in mind, is exactly opposite. In his opinion, technology is less dangerous than the spirit of places, which divides people into locals and foreigners. By means of not unambiguous and merely liberating technology, people can break free from a place and understand people as people beyond their emplacement.[50]

In a capsule unit, the physical contact, or a relationship with the outside environment, is no longer important. However, this does not mean that the acceptance of the environment and nature is contested. But a capsule unit may also be perceived as a machine for living in conflict with nature and, at the same time, as an aspiration for withdrawal from the "unnatural" urbanized world to the idyllic environment of the "wilderness," where an individual, with the help of technology accepts, and defies, nature. The contradiction and coexistence of technology and nature in modernity is also part of the minimized Garden of Eden of a capsule. A mobile capsule does not exploit, control, and yield to land, and since it is self-sufficient, really has no need to exploit. Capsule units are explicitly lifted from land, and establish with it an a priori temporary relationship. Therefore, they cannot be called "buildings," and are excluded from the traditional architectural discourse. This discloses the capsule as a product of architecture and product design, and of industrial production, not of building in its traditional sense. In the space of flows, a capsule unit could not be denied the physical and psychological shelter for an un-centered, vulnerable, and transient individual. The possibility of the filtering of a contact with the exterior, either with direct or media content, indicates the possibility of the individual being aware of their individuality, silence in isolation, which was sought in the history of esotericism by hermits and mystics. Such a capsule unit, at least in Kurokawa's derivation, is bound to Buddhist contemplation and its inherent awareness of its transience or, better yet, "transitory-ness."

In an individualized capsule unit, control over contact with the outside is completely up to an individual, at least in concept. The utopian promise of a capsule is that it presumes a high level of individualization and critical awareness. This very position bears a high risk. If it is left to technological and media manipulations the capsule environment becomes another, even more subtle, control mechanism.

In the light of openly and vaguely defined conditions of modernity, and the possibility of dwelling in it, Hilde Heynen interprets living and modernity through a pair of mimetic moves of "to enclose oneself," which is parallel to the requirement for identity and self-realization characteristic of modernity. Therefore, modernity must always be defined and written anew, through contradictions and inconsistencies which pertain to it. Neither modernity nor dwelling is necessarily perceived as completely opposing concepts, as proposed by authors such as Heidegger or Norberg-Schulz.[51]

A capsule is an *unbuilding*, making it the subject of contemplation on the possibility of dwelling, and is understood as an open-system dwelling, where dwelling is possible if residents are aware of this and live accordingly, in it and with it.

Temporariness is the key element of consumer society, which drives the mechanism of constant consumerism of the new by not being attached to anything material and permanent. A consumer should not take firm possession of anything, be truly committed to anything, none of their needs should be fully satisfied, and no desire should be considered ultimate.[52] The temporariness of everything became a self-evident assumption for almost all material goods, while experience shows that prejudice about the durability of a dwelling is deeply rooted in society. This characteristic is crucial, enabling temporary living units to establish themselves—as their name explains—particularly as *temporary dwellings* for the needs of tourist and work environments, or in extraordinary situations, and not to have managed to establish themselves as permanent dwellings.

Mobility (movement)

By addressing the pioneering examples of capsule architecture, the notions of nomadism and mobility were restricted to the discussion of the physical possibilities of moving an architectural object, and the characteristic was also stated as its condition. Mobile facilities are completely adapted to the conditions of the contemporary space they create and constantly redefine.

The mobility of contemporary space is defined by flows, *the space of flows* described by Manuel Castells as a process, and a spatial manifestation of power and function in societies.[53] The requirement for the free movement of goods, services, and capital causes general mobilization, which also changes conditions in space. Naturally, mobility is not a new phenomenon, as it was the key factor in the formation of political and cultural geography throughout history. The main historical migration flows, which affected the formation of European space, could roughly be divided into three types: The first type, with a distinctly political motivation, which changed borders through history; the second type, which stems from economic networks of commerce and industry, and established centers of commercial networks, and the development of infrastructure and its background; and the third type, which is presented by exchanges in the field of knowledge and science.[54] Unlike previous periods, when mobility referred particularly to certain political, economic, or social structures, contemporary mobility is omnipresent, self-evident, and inevitable for everyone. "[I]mmobility is not a realistic option in a world of permanent change" in the globalized modern world, as described by Zygmunt Bauman; rejection of being, or inability to be included in the flow system means withdrawal from the economic, political, and social system, while distinctly local activity means social deprivation or degradation.[55] Total global mobility has its complementary side of isolated local static condition, which may be desired for "included elites" or involuntary for "excluded others." Today, we can hardly speak of the complete exclusion of marginalized groups or even populations from any networks. However, with this largely excluded population, particularly from the developing world, it is about its non-inclusion into the global order of decision making and the economic system of power, which generates migration flows of economic and political migrants, and opens us up to the problem of biopolitics.

Mobility and immobility are a pair, a product of socio-economic logic directly affecting spaces, which was realized in the process of suburbanization with the boom of private mobility, and transformed the model of a family living cell. Increased migration from other cultures brought about diversity and people's various preferences regarding home. The trend of suburbanization, withdrawal of the middle class to their own houses on the outskirts of cities, stimulated the development of automobile culture and mobility, while the pluralization of lifestyles completely changed the perception of the model of a "normal family," and of forms of housing.[56]

Mobile living environments open up the issues of *home* and *place*, which have been experiencing dramatic redefinitions in the inevitable space of flows of the network society. Castells's hypothesis that the space of flows blurs the important relationship between architecture and society, which leads to this very architecture through the processes of detachment from places and cultures, historical and geographical specific features,[57] points to the problem of the creation and perception of the representation of phenomena of contemporary space. Similarly, Bauman points out that writers of modern utopias did not distinguish between social and architectural order, and sought the key to organized modernity in the organization of space,[58] which is no longer the rule today. The mobility of capsules is preserved in representation, no matter how technical or silent it is. According to Castells, postmodern architectural rhetoric of certain protagonists falls to the field of the end of all established systems of meaning and new dominant ideology: The end of history, and the suppression of *place* in the space of flows.[59]

In the context of mobility, the issue of home depends on culture. Robert Kronenburg believes that the notion of home is increasingly defined by a set of personal activities, habits, and relationships, rather than with commitment to a specific geographical location and continuous living at the same location.[60] In this context, we may state De Cauter's *third law of capsularization*, which could read: "Neo-liberal individualism plus suburbanization of daily life equals capsularization."[61] Is the only possibility of living in contemporary society within a capsular environment? On the basis of the examples discussed, we may highlight that increased mobility in contemporary space generates forms of living and dwelling which differ from the traditional forms, and are not bound to place.

Although it seems that, in the space of flows, a man does not even have to physically move, as *everything* comes to him if he is connected to the network, Castells predicts the exact opposite, i.e. the development of new forms of mobile jobs, and increased physical mobility between centers of interest in space.[62] Is this (finally) prediction of a paradise for the boom of mobile living units, which adapt to changing requirements of the work organization, and their actors do not have any other options than to concede the urgency of temporary capsularization of living environments which, according to Kurokawa's prophetic words, provide the only possible living space in the space of flows? Interest in mobile capsule dwellings, from Fuller, the Smithsons, the Archigram group, the Metabolists, and many others is, today, perhaps even more than before, most relevant.

De Cauter places the proposed seventh law of capsularization in the discussion about the environment of contemporary living, as he emphasizes that we do not live in networks, but in capsules: "No network without capsules. The more networking, the more capsules. Ergo: The degree of capsularization is directly proportional to the growth of networks."[63] Is there an alternative?

Perhaps mobility and nomadism provide an answer to the question of the possibility of living outside capsular environments? Aren't the *black holes of marginality*, which Castells mentions, places of potential, places outside the system, yet part of the system, since they were created by the system, places into which individualized capsule units penetrate, places where capsule environments may create centers of double disconnection: They enable an individual to exist outside the network system and even outside the spatial system—within a capsule unit? We could also say that a combination of the effects of physical and non-physical mobility allows the *capsule* to completely disconnect, to be the *off world* of hermits, with the voluntary possibility for an individual to connect to the network with technological prosthetics.

Notes

1 Marshall McLuhan, *Understanding Media: The Extensions of Man* (Corte Madera: Gingko Press, 2003), 173. First published 1964. McLuhan treats clothing and housing together in this category.
2 Lieven De Cauter, *The Capsular Civilization: On the City in the Age of Fear* (Rotterdam: NAi, 2004), 77. Association is aimed at Rem Koolhaas and Elia Zenghelis' project *Exodus, or the Voluntary Prisoners of Architecture* from 1972.
3 The book presents a possible pattern language which has been detected in urban and architectural reality. Elements of this language are called patterns. Each of 253 presented patterns relates to a problem from the environment and describes the solution to that problem. See Christopher Alexander et al., *A Pattern Language: Towns, Buildings, Construction* (New York: Oxford University Press, 1977), 668–672.
4 Alexander, *A Pattern Language*, 668–672.
5 Guy Debord, *The Society of the Spectacle* (New York: Zone Books, 2006), Thesis 28, 22.
6 Ibid., see Thesis 172, 122.
7 Aleš Vodopivec, "Vprašanja Umetnosti Gradnje," in *Iz arhitekture*, eds. Janez Koželj and Aleš Vodopivec (Ljubljana: Krt, 1987), 48.
8 De Cauter, *The Capsular Civilization*, 79.
9 Paul Virilio, *Open Sky* (London and New York: Verso, 1998), 96.
10 De Cauter, *The Capsular Civilization*, 79.
11 In the case of the philosophical base of the capsule and Metabolism, which has been developed by Kurokawa through the "philosophy of coexistence" since the 1960s to the "philosophy of symbiosis" since the end of the 1970s, the tradition of Buddhist philosophy is about surpassing dualism, oppositions, and, by emphasizing the significance of individualism, about a desire for the non-conformist, conscious life of an individual, which is the basis for diverse and pluralist society. Kurokawa has published several books on the philosophy of symbiosis. See e.g. Kisho Kurokawa, *The Philosophy of Symbiosis* (London: Academy Editions; Berlin: Ernst & Sohn, 1994). In the case of the Archigram group, a capsule is a functionalist construct in the service of the fulfillment of the liberal ideal of "one's own life" and the production of a new lifestyle, where "new" and "different" is what makes a city (of the future) attractive.

12 Scott Lash, "Individualization in a Non-Linear Mode," in *Individualization: Institutionalized Individualism and its Social and Political Consequences*, eds. Ulrich Beck and Elisabeth Beck-Gernsheim (London, Thousand Oaks, CA, and New Delhi: Sage Publications, 2002), ix. According to Beck, the "second modernity" differs from the first—which was a period of industrialization, democratization, and modernization—in four categories of development: individualization, globalization, underemployment and unemployment, and ecological crisis. See also Beck, *Risk Society: Towards a New Modernity* (London, Newbury Park, New Delhi: Sage, 1994). If the first modernity comprised the logic of structures, the second modernity according to Castells is involved in the logic of flows.

13 Beck and Beck-Gernsheim, "Losing the Traditional: Individualization and 'Precarious Freedoms'," in *Individualization*, 1–21.

14 "Zombie Categories: Interview with Ulrich Beck," in *Individualization*, eds. Beck and Beck-Gernsheim, 202. Cf. Ulrich Beck, Anthony Giddens, and Scott Lash, *Reflexive Modernization: Politics, Tradition and Aesthetics in the Modern Social Order* (Cambridge: Polity Press, 1994); Beck, *Risk Society*; Zygmunt Bauman, *Liquid Modernity* (Cambridge, Malden: Polity, 2009).

15 Beck and Beck-Gernsheim, "Losing the Traditional," 19.

16 McLuhan, *Understanding Media*, 167–177. According to McLuhan, not enclosed spaces in a visual sense include a tent, a wigwam, and a cave.

17 Beck and Beck-Gernsheim, *Individualization*, 212.

18 Hanno-Walter Kruft, *A History of Architectural Theory from Vitruvius to the Present* (New York: Princeton Architectural Press, 1994), 435.

19 See Ranko Radović, *Antologija Kuća* (Beograd: Građevinska Knjiga, 1989), 13–20; Kruft, *A History of Architectural Theory*, 152.

20 Joseph Rykwert, *On Adam's House in Paradise: The Idea of the Primitive Hut in Architectural History* (Cambridge, London: MIT Press, 1997).

21 Marc-Antoine Laugier, *An Essay on Architecture* (Los Angeles: Hennessey & Ingalls, 1977). Cf. Rykwert, *On Adam's House in Paradise*, esp. 43–74.

22 Rykwert, *On Adam's House in Paradise*, 48.

23 Ibid., 50.

24 Since records of Lodoli's theory are not preserved, we know his work only through his students Francesco Algarotti and Andrea Memmo. However, they interpreted and presented their teacher's work differently. While Algarotti, who did not completely agree with him, presents him in a reductive manner, as a radical rationalist who highlighted the function itself, Memmo understands and presents him in a more precise and complex manner. See Rykwert, "Lodoli: On Function and Representation," *Architectural Review* 953 (July 1976): 21–26; Kruft, *A History of Architectural Theory*. Therefore, following Algarotti's tradition, he can be placed among *rigorous functionalists*, who "reject all attempts to have a building re-present its functionality," while *rhetorical functionalism* "aims at a building's self-re-presentation as a functional building." Karsten Harries, *The Ethical Function of Architecture* (Cambridge, MA: MIT Press, 2000), 121.

25 Alberto Pérez-Gómez, *Architecture and the Crisis of Modern* Science (Cambridge, MA and London: MIT Press, 1983).

26 Rykwert, "Lodoli," 22; Despite mostly rigorous interpretations of Lodoli, Alberto Pérez-Gómez points out that the notion of a function preserved the ambiguous simultaneity of abstract mathematics (numbers) and visual representation (quality) and could, therefore, be the symbol of human order; Pérez-Gómez, *Architecture and the Crisis of Modern Science*, 256.

27 Harries, *The Ethical Function of Architecture*, 121.

28 Lodoli had an ergonomically designed chair custom-made according to the principle "shoulders should shape the back, the bottom its seat," for the construction of a hospice for pilgrims to the Holy Land at the *San Francesco della Vigna* church in Venice, and he adapted the form of the gallery to human dimensions, with walls that were to lean upwards and up. Due to its narrowness, but with ergonomic design, two persons (with shoulders wider than feet), and also porters who carry luggage on their shoulders can meet. See Rykwert, "Lodoli."

29 Theodor Adorno, "Functionalism Today," in *Rethinking Architecture: A Reader in Cultural Theory*, ed. Neil Leach (London and New York: Routledge, 1997), 10.

30 Ibid.

31 Nicolas Pople, *Small Houses* (London: Laurence King, 2005), 8.

32 Vodopivec, "Vprašanja Umetnosti Gradnje," 38; The same thesis is mentioned by Frampton in relation to theories of Bötticher, Schelling, and Grassi. Kenneth Frampton, "Rappel à l'ordre, the

Case for the Tectonic," in *Theorizing, A New Agenda for Architecture: An Anthology of Architectural Theory 1965–1995*, ed. Kate Nesbitt (New York: Princeton Architectural Press, 1996), 516–528.

33 William A. McClung, *The Architecture of Paradise: Survivals of Eden and Jerusalem* (Berkeley and Los Angeles, CA and London: University of California Press, 1983).

34 Dalibor Vesely, *Architecture in the Age of Divided Representation: The Question of Creativity in the Shadow of Production* (Cambridge, MA and London: MIT Press, 2004), 13–19.

35 Barry Bergdoll and Peter Christensen, *Home Delivery: Fabricating the Modern Dwelling* (New York: Museum of Modern Art, 2008).

36 Allison Arieff and Bryan Burkhart, *Prefab* (Salt Lake City: Gibbs Smith, 2002).

37 Between 1943 and 1945, Walter Gropius and Konrad Wachsmann designed the panel system *The Packaged House System / General Panel*, where the emphasis was on the universal use of wall, floor, or ceiling panels which could be assembled with a universal connective element; this was, however, a financial failure. In his belief in the suitability of prefabricated construction, Gropius pointed out: "The coming generation will certainly blame us if we should fail to overcome those understandable though sentimental reactions against prefabrication," referring to the information that the price of an average house in the USA between 1913 and 1937 increased by 193 percent, while the price of cars dropped by 60 percent; Sigfried Giedion, *Walter Gropius* (New York: Dover Publications, 1992), 77. Unaltered republication of Sigfried Giedion, *Walter Gropius* (New York: Reinhold Publishing Corporation, 1954).

38 Arieff and Burkhart, *Prefab*, 10.

39 Hans Ibelings, "Mobile Architecture in the Twentieth Century," in *Parasite Paradise: A Manifesto for Temporary Architecture and Flexible Urbanism*, ed. Liesbeth Melis (Rotterdam: NaI, 2003), 150–151.

40 Reyner Banham, "Triumph of Software," in *Reyner Banham: Design by Choice*, ed. Penny Sparke (New York: Rizzoli, 1981), 133–136. The article was first published in *New Society* on October 31, 1968.

41 De Cauter, *The Capsular Civilization*, 80.

42 Manuel Castells, *The Rise of the Network Society*, 2nd edn. (Oxford and Malden, MA: Blackwell, 2000), 71.

43 Deborah Tall, "Dwelling: Making Peace with Space and Place," in *Housing and Dwelling: Perspectives on Modern Domestic Architecture*, ed. Barbara Miller Lane (Abingdon: Routledge, 2007), 424–431.

44 Hilde Heynen, *Architecture and Modernity: A Critique* (Cambridge, MA and London: MIT Press, 1999), 14–18. The description refers to the discussion of modernization and consciousness in the book *Homeless Mind* by Peter Berger, Brigitte Berger, and Hansfried Kellner, and emphasized similar characteristics as shown in the discussion about modernity of Ulrich Beck and others.

45 Harries, *The Ethical Function of Architecture*, 252; Martin Heidegger, "Building, Dwelling, Thinking," in *Rethinking Architecture: A Reader in Cultural Theory*, ed. Neil Leach, 100–109.

46 See Kenneth Frampton, Peter Šenk, Juan Alfonso Zapata, "Arhitektura Med Vzgajanjem Družbe in Izobraževanjem Naročnikov," interview with Kenneth Frampton, Rotterdam, January 2003, *Architect's Bulletin* 163/164 (November 2004), 2–3; Cf. Hannah Arendt, *The Human Condition* (Chicago, IL and London: University of Chicago Press, 1998).

47 Harries, *The Ethical Function of Architecture*, 264–267.

48 Cf. Beck and Beck-Gernsheim, *Individualization*, 212.

49 Harries, *The Ethical Function of Architecture*, 363–364.

50 Emmanuel Levinas, "Heidegger, Gagarin and Us," in *Difficult Freedom: Essays on Judaism*, ed. Emmanuel Levinas (Baltimore, MD: Johns Hopkins University Press, 1990), 231–234.

51 Ibid., 223.

52 Bauman, *Globalization: The Human Consequence* (Cambridge: Polity Press, 1998), 81.

53 Castells, *The Rise of the Network Society*, 409.

54 See Robert Broesi, "Euroscapes: Spatial Order in Twenty-First Century Europe," in *Euroscapes*, eds. Robert Broesi, Pieter Jannink, Wouter Veldhuis, Ivan Nio (Amsterdam: Must Publishers, 2003), 7–57.

55 Bauman, *Globalization: The Human Consequence*, 2.

56 Stephan Rammler, "'A mighty fortress …'?! On the Sociology of Flexible Dwelling," in *Living in Motion: Design and Architecture for Flexible Dwelling*, eds. Mathias Schwartz-Clauss and Alexander von Vegesack (Weil am Rhein: Vitra Design Museum, 2002), 197–218.

57 See Castells, *The Rise of the Network Society*, 448–459.

58 Bauman, *Globalization*, 17.

59 Castells, *The Rise of the Network Society*, 449. The duality of representation could be attributed to the commitment to a historic moment. Bauman distinguishes between modern "globalization" and the almost forgotten notion of "universalization." The latter belonged to the early and classical modern thought, and expressed "hope, the intention, and the determination of order-making ... in global scale," where the discussed *capsule unit* projects and megastructures from pioneering attempts could be placed, while a newer term of "globalization" refers to unintended and unplanned global effects, in the context of which the concept of the *territorial capsularity* of modern space may be addressed. See Bauman, *Globalization*, 59–65.

60 Robert Kronenburg, "Modern Architecture and the Flexible Dwelling," in *Living in Motion: Design and Architecture for Flexible Dwelling*, eds. Schwartz-Clauss and von Vegesack, 23.

61 De Cauter, *The Capsular Civilization*, 83.

62 Castells, *The Rise of the Network Society*, 426, 429.

63 De Cauter, *The Capsular Civilization*, 85.

5

CODA

In pursuit of other architecture

Reviewing the characteristic contemporary realizations of the concept and typology of the capsule, it can be summarized that the utopian connotation of the pioneering examples was replaced by productivity, efficiency, and realizability here and now. Heroic manifestos, which promised social change, were replaced by the solving of living problems of current reality. Was this perhaps the reason for the absence of the "utopian" term capsule in many contemporary examples, despite faithful derivations of the concept? However, contemporary operativeness is not always devoid of a socially critical or liberating potential.

Capsule architecture as the architecture of small houses and minimum dwellings turned out to be the ideal field for crossing and exceeding the boundaries of disciplines of art, design, and architecture, which simultaneously facilitates heterogeneity of expressions characteristic of contemporaneity and recognizability. Richard Horden with microarchitecture, Future Systems, and many other architects aim at the coexistence of architecture and industrial design. Container capsule architecture is used as a pragmatic and operative provision of dwellings and functional units in urban environments, as well as in crisis areas and experiential environments of design and art. Michael Rakowitz's and Krzysztof Wodiczko's activist mobile products function in immediate reality, exploit gaps in regulations, and flag up social problems that are pushed aside. The notion of temporariness, fueled by the smallness and mobility of capsule units, is the magic key to bypass many restrictions—temporarily, of course. But their temporariness may plant the seed of contemplation and the realization of "utopia" which, by definition, is no longer that. It functions, in a manner adapted to contemporary conditions, more convincingly than old-fashioned completely utopian schemes. This kind of approach is to affect events and open up opportunities for change with "bottom-up" operation. Such an activity is always within the system,[1] but it can exploit the system and show it its reflection. Time will tell whether that is enough to achieve real change, but it seems that this is the only possible way in the fragmented, dispersed, individualized, and ambiguous contemporaneity.

We can claim that consistency of, or at least a connection between, the structure, function, and representation, i.e. composition, program, and architectural expression of capsule units makes active participation of these units in the environment, and their rhetoric, convincing enough. Individuality, independence, rationality, smallness–related minimum ecological footprint, temporariness, adaption to an individual, etc. are the characteristics conveyed by capsule units, regardless of their materiality, shape, or appearance in general. In many examples of capsules from history, characteristics were pointed out which are also followed by contemporary derivations. Explicit, in many cases Brutalist, materiality, which loathes any kind of masking, provides contemporary examples with the existentialist tone.[2] Like Le Corbusier's *Cabanon* at the Côte d'Azur, the Smithsons' *Patio and Pavilion* or the capsules of the *Nakagin Capsule Tower*, primary cubes and rectangular solids of the *micro compact home*, the *Rucksack House*, the *Minibox*, and containers do not call for a spectacle due to their silent materiality. Like Fuller's experiments *Dymaxion*, the Smithsons' *House of the Future*, and capsules of Archigram, certain contemporary examples could be criticized for attempting spectacle in aviation or space idolatry; the *Alpine Capsule*, a bivouac, a capsule vessel, urban nomadic structures, and prototypes of the Future Systems architects are largely the product of construction logic, materiality, the adjustment to use, and to atmospheric conditions.[3] In addition to the provision of interior comfort, they are distinguished by the common characteristic of minimum contact with the ground—with a conscious protective sustainable attitude to nature and the environment in general.

With the analysis of development, historical examples of the concept and typology of the capsule, and with a selection of contemporary examples pointing out the specificity of representation with inherent ambiguity and conflicts, we wish to emphasize the issue of devising the integrity of architectural structure, function, and representation as a means of critical response to contemporary reality and the potential of *other architecture*.

In the 1980s, Fredric Jameson discussed the issue of possibilities of political or critical art in his influential work entitled "The Cultural Logic of Late Capitalism." He put this into context in the postmodern period of late capitalism. He did not perceive postmodernism as a style, but as a cultural dominant of the logic of late capitalism, "a conception which allows for the presence and coexistence of a range of very different, yet subordinate, features."[4] Like many others, Jameson is aware of the inability of functioning outside the system. With deceptive theoretical questions, his proposed approach, which he calls "the aesthetic of a new cultural form," "the aesthetic of *cognitive mapping*,"[5] and substantiates based on the experience of Kevin Lynch's work, *The Image of the City*, is aimed at the restoration of the analysis of representation on a more complex level. If Fredric Jameson's "aesthetic of cognitive mapping," which reveals the truth to art and society, and puts them in the context of social, historical, and spiritual space, is used as the basis; or if we follow Theodor Adorno's call, which relativizes the issue of function, and points out that beauty can no longer be assessed in any other manner but with the depth to which a work exhibits and exceeds contradictions, not by concealing them, but by pursuing them; we understand the search for other architecture as an attempt which meant the opportunity to surpass the state of affairs in the pioneering times of capsule designs and with modern calls for experiments and/or even utopia.[6]

However, merely emphasizing contradictions frequently does not suffice, since the system operates toward the commodification of everything, even the seemingly incompatible.[7] Such an approach, deemed by Roemer van Toorn as "Fresh Conservatism," ignores the political dimension of everyday life, and does not interfere with the order of things, but submits to it, despite subversive elements.[8] To avoid this, he proposes an orientation committed to experimentation—critical exploration and constructive actions, cracking open representation, the view of reality beyond simulation, the opening of space for conflicts, ambivalence, etc.— but also to the risk of failure.[9] Progressive projective practices, which merge many of van Toorn's approaches with interactive operation, undermine the *monologic representation*, emphasize *dialogic presentation*,[10] and by involving participants never reach the end, but remain open to interpretation.

If we point out the characteristics of certain approaches, which see, in the architecture of contemporaneity, the possibility for a proactive critical response to the current situation, their key orientations may be used to check the critical potential of the typology of the capsule:

— Contemporaneity is considered heterogeneous, full of conformisms, conflicts, and contradictions to which architecture may adopt a critical position.
— The manner of a critical response is the cracking open of representation, and potential unmasking of the institutions of spectacle with the directness of address.
— Several instruments are available which reflect disputes and disagreements with the existing situation, question it, and are expressed in architecture through structure, function, and representation.
— Artwork or architecture is open to interpretation, and stimulates an independent adoption of positions and active participation.[11]

Through the prism of these approaches, the most recurring topics crucial for the typology of the capsule[12]—technology and architectural expression, home, individual and community, attitude to land and attachment to place, idea of withdrawal and autonomy, coexistence of contradictions, and simultaneity—hint at the possibility of criticality, subversiveness, and a potential search for *other architecture* in immediate contemporaneity.

The issue of a relationship between technology and architectural expression has followed from Buckminster Fuller's research projects designated *Dymaxion*. As a criticism of the International Style, they were meant to be silent instruments, without any aesthetic purpose. Although such and such an "anti-style" position was literally assumed by many functionalists and megastructuralists, in accordance with Adorno's criticism of functionalism, it became a style. Seemingly completely technological architecture was supposed to only be about its own functionality, and experienced an ostensible apotheosis with the *Centre Georges Pompidou* in Paris, and high-tech projects which followed the new style. With Reyner Banham's essay, "A Home Is Not a House," the technology of a house shook off the traditional architectural expression, and became an expression in itself. Concurrently, it meant a disclosed break with architecture as we knew it. According to Banham, architecture is committed to its new aesthetics, which are supposed to correspond to the modernity of living (in the 20th century) and its technological reality. In such conditions, architecture could take over the guidance of the development of technology, not vice versa, like before. By emphasizing technology, architectural aspirations show the unavoidable technological character of their own structures, which were concealed and suppressed due to aesthetic unacceptability and the general idea of the representation of a building.

The Japanese Metabolists perceived the relationship between technology and architecture through the biological metaphor. Technology was not perceived as *other*, but as part of the natural process of development, and with Kisho Kurokawa also as an extension of man, enabling its fusion into a cyborg. In many cases, technological optimism was fused with iconoclasm, and was an antipode to the spectacle of consumer culture which, paradoxically, it wished to convince. Yona Friedman's abstract structures with potentially capsule inserts and a "simple, unembellished, natural, rough, and slightly sad"[13] expression of the Metabolists correspond to a lot less technological or completely non-technological aesthetics of predecessors and contemporaries—the New Brutalism. The described examples are not about embellished representation, but about the *presentation* of reality "as found."

Capsule units are largely an expression of the technological process of mass production without any meaning-related allusions, and could be classified as one of the most sincere products of functionalism. However, in some cases, the ironically critical moment of representation is still recognized. For example, David Greene's *Living Pod*, as a hybrid between a lunar module and a primary shelter in the shape of a womb, where every explorer of psychedelic states would undoubtedly like to wake up or simulate them without using intoxicating substances. Or as an explicit otherness, even outside the dimension of the earth, as a flying saucer—Matti Suuronen's *Futuro House*. Or Coop Himmelblau's and Haus-Rucker-Co's pneumatic structures as literal clip-ons in the form of light bulbs. These projects, as well as many others, bear witness to the connection with technology, and express the awareness of homelessness. Beyond the traditional architectural expression, they resort to technological, science fiction, and ambivalent natural analogies.

In addition to the blind faith in its liberating nature, the expressive rhetoric of the technology by megastructuralists and their successors shows the duality of the moral of general taste, which closes its eyes to technology, while at the same time requiring more comfort provided by it. In the vision of a bright, technology-supported future, tension and ambivalence are expressed in the early works of Arata Isozaki: In places where the new emerges, there are also ruins. In a Metabolist tone, it highlights the transience of everything in cyclical episodes. Explicitly, however, the new is based on the ruins of the old. Such a criticism from the field of architecture and spatial planning could, without a second thought, be transferred to the context of human activity in general.

The idea to redefine home, individual, and community in the context of the concept of the capsule has been pursued at least since Fuller's proto-capsule formations, which should express individuality, facilitate contemplation and innovative dwelling and are, in their purpose and expression, merely distinctly anti-monumental "service equipment." A similar redefinition of home is also proposed by Teige, in his definition of "subsistence minimum." He sees, in an individual cell, a revolutionary method to undermine traditional values of home, homeland, family, and "slavery to home" and, consequently, the conditions for the emergence of a new psychological type of man. In American counterculture, and with British, Japanese, and other European contemporaries, the reformation of the traditional concepts of room, home, family, and community changed, and stimulated the search for an appropriate expression.

The fragmentation of the structure of individual living units, groups, *ad hoc* organized clusters of dwellings, and completely independent mobile units, which are not bound to the system, is a mimetic expression of fragmented individualist society. This is reflected in basic living cells for the most intimate personal needs, and in transformed places of the former hearth of a community, in a communal and, at least in theory, public space of a city. It is significant that, on the inside, individual capsule units are very ergonomic. In addition to liberating mobility, their space is also restricted by economic pressure. They are equipped with electronic devices. As the most intimate space, they are, in many cases, also extremely comfortable, and function as a paraphrase, a *mimesis*, of a womb, as a refuge in extreme situations. An individual is left to the duality between the biological archetype of a dwelling, and the alienation of the information city, which highlights the issue of dwelling in modernity. It was radicalized by the issue of community in capsular environments, and shows a complete commodification of relationships in contemporary space.

Hannah Arendt, who found support for the definition of private and public in the ancient Greek definition of *polis* and *oikos*, designated the vague field between the two as "social,"[14] Lieven De Cauter and Michiel Dehaene tried to find, in the Greek *polis* in Foucault's text, answers to open questions about *other places—heterotopia*. Hippodamus's division of land into sacred, public, and private space[15] shows the basis of the interim area, where other places are organized transversely to *oiko*s and *agora*, between *acropolis* and *necropolis*: Theaters, a stadium, the *Palestra*, a hippodrome, etc., which correspond to Hippodamus's "third sphere" or "third space." These are neither household/economical (private) spaces nor political (public) spaces, but sacred ones, which are most appropriately deemed the "cultural sphere" in today's secularized world, including spaces for religion, arts, sports, and leisure.[16] In the state of generally politicized and economized space, capsular environments are most clearly described, with hybrid intrusions such as the "economization of heterotopia," with examples of museum, libraries, theaters, and churches, the "heterotopianization of the *oikos*" of thematized gated communities, and of the "heterotopianization of the political sphere," when the political becomes a spectacle,[17] and with a paradigm of a theme park, which squeezed into each pore of public spaces, from transport hubs, gentrified city centers to hybrid structures of the third order, thematic shopping malls, contemporary non(public)-squares.

While heterotopic spaces are described through the functioning of real spaces, which show reality as an illusion, or are perfected, even more rational and organized than normal, De Cauter derives the transformation of the concept of heterotopia as an exception in space, from Foucault's second principle of heterotopology, into its rule

> which must maintain the illusion of normality in chaos, the idea of livability in an unlivable environment, the idea of the everyday in a vacuum, a center in the omnipresent periphery of the network, a "place to be" in the "space of flows."[18]

In the case of the capsule which, by Kurokawa's definition, represents a living space when a man cannot live elsewhere, the relationship with heterotopia seems completely open, since an individualized capsule arises from the private sphere, and does not have the heterotopic characteristic of "communal" or collective. However, in a radical derivation, the typology of the capsule may be described as a hybrid space of the "politicization of the *oikos*" or a torn out, mobile fractal of a sacred, internalized space of private economized heterotopia, due to the otherwise controlled media environment of the interior of a private living unit. The process of hybridization or dedifferentiation between the spheres is marked by De Cauter and Dehaene as problematic, and they call for the preservation or reestablishment of their relative autonomy in order to preserve a relatively healthy political body.[19] Isn't it seemingly paradoxical that the typology of the capsule is the instrument for preventing the intrusion of the public/political into the private sphere, by filtering unwanted information and external influences? Through the concept of heterotopic otherness, the typology of the capsule reproduces otherness toward *other* otherness.

———————

A multilayered attitude of architecture to land and non-attachment to a place discloses Machine Age man's attitude to the environment. While nature meant the domain of colonization and exploitation during the First Machine Age, responses including capsular endeavors in the transition into the Second Machine Age and in contemporaneity are generally more sustainable. Fuller's world architecture is utopian, philanthropic, universal, and devised to defy difficult natural conditions with as little contact with the ground as possible. The examples discussed through the detachment of a dwelling from land question the traditional myth of their connection. Although the Smithsons' *House of the Future* is embedded in the ground, its repetitive generic nature indicates the possibility of it being placed anywhere. It is designed for adverse climate, making it introvert. In contrast with the environment, the house was a response to a place, which is not necessarily traditionalist or in harmony with the environment. It was more important to achieve the feeling of protection and facilitate the fullness of life and, with the isolation of a piece of land, also creativity and personal fulfillment.

Reyner Banham explicitly emphasized the necessity of a psychological and aesthetic break as the condition for liberation from the attachment to land. In addition to the psychological and aesthetic purpose, the liberation from land had a completely political connotation with certain contemporaries. At first sight, utopian schemes of Kikutake's collective artificial land with clip-on private "capsule" units are only futuristic visions of a liberated society, and may even be feasible. At the same time, they are also an expression of problems of private land manipulations of post-war Japanese reality, which prevented urban development. Capsule architecture on artificial islands, some of which are also buoyant, seeks its haven outside economic frameworks. A reaction to the inability to build on the ground is presented in extraterritorial artificial land. In many Metabolists' projects, the liberation from repressive mechanisms connected with the ownership of land was related to other political ideals, such as democracy, equality, and freedom of movement. Like mobile houses or caravans, Ekuan's capsules, Archigram's *Living Pod* and *Cushicle*, and other examples of the typology of the capsule which are liberated from contact with land, work toward anti-planning, anti-bureaucracy, or even anarchy. Also contemporary examples, such as parasites of the *Miele Space Station*, mobile structures of the Atelier van Lieshout, Michael Rakowitz's portable envelopes for the homeless, and other examples set up within the scope of the *Parasite Paradise* exhibition on the lawn of the residential settlement of Leidsche Rijn in Utrecht, are the ultimate shelter from completely planned used space appropriated by land technocracy.

Although uprootedness and nomadism, as shown by Bernard Rudofsky with examples of vernacular architecture, are not modern phenomena, the advocacy of temporary and mobile architecture gives rise to a question of cultural continuity and the permanence of institutions which should provide it. Are not the questioning and resistance against institutional and institutionalized values the targets of nomadic lifestyles, which may also be supported by capsules? In capsule nomadism, we may emphasize the simultaneity of resistance against the spatial and sociopolitical state of affairs, and a search for possible alternatives which, however, hide more traps of the disintegration of the system and complete anarchy; or the opposite, of cybernetic complete control, than many playful protagonists of capsule architecture wished to admit. Unlike the social and reform goals of the concept of the capsule in the 1960s, the concept, in most cases, in contemporaneity is operational, politically correct, and part of the story of sustainable development—structures of Richard Horden's *microarchitecture*, which "touch the earth lightly," either in natural or urban environments, are a representative example of such an approach. Despite Marko Peljhan's *Makrolab* being based on many similar assumptions, this is the example which also shows the operative political potential of the typology of the capsule and *other architecture* through non-attachment to a place by functioning within the system and, at the same time, offering its critique through enabled scientific/artistic activities.

A metaphor from the life of St. Jerome, which was used by Alison Smithson who emphasized the duality between man's withdrawal to nature, subordination to its laws, relief of the responsibility for its functioning, and of the functioning of a serviced study in isolation in a civilized world which, like isolation in nature, facilitates creative activity that depends on isolation, appears with many authors, and in different forms, in the review of the genealogy of the concept of the capsule. Like Alison Smithson, Kisho Kurokawa perceives isolation of an individual as a prerequisite for the development of one's own potential and self-realization. As the *Patio and Pavilion* was exhibited, Henderson, Paolozzi, and the Smithsons wrote that the architect's task was to provide context for the individual's self-realization. While, after the First Machine Age, the case of complete subordination to the laws of nature seemed completely unrealistic, the case of a house-machine, which was transformed into a body extension and which, in addition to protection and space for withdrawal, also provides relative autonomy—independence from the outside world—was realized in the typology of the capsule.

The idea of withdrawal from the "unhealthy urban world" to the lap of nature was nurtured by Buckminster Fuller throughout. He realized it most expressively with the transparent geodesic dome the "Garden of Eden," to observe weather phenomena and the liberated dwelling of a man in nature in a protective envelope, which opens the view toward the sky. A similar characteristic of proto-capsule architecture, which is totally enclosed, introverted, and directs the view toward the sky, may be encountered in the Smithsons' *House of the Future*. Appropriately for modern times, by means of advanced technology which facilitates carefree material life in a chosen environment, proto-capsule structures could be understood as an aspiration of an individual who withdraws to solitude in a hermit-like style, and can also dedicate himself to spiritual life—symbolically on the vertical axis. Capsules differ from the aforementioned proto-capsule examples particularly in that they are even more sealed and introverted. The realistic and symbolic connection with the environment of this potentially contemplative environment is provided by electronic devices.

However, introversion and isolation cannot be accepted as unambiguous. If an individual's withdrawal to an introverted controlled space is still subject to free will and under the individual's control, the "liberation of man" with technological prosthetics is always in a relationship with the "control system." The topics of withdrawal and autonomy open up the issue of a relationship between the completely private space of an individual and a communal space. In contemporary urban context, this issue is reflected in the siting of parasites and additional spaces, such as the *Rucksack House*, and *Minibox* or *Snail Shell*, in space itself, with Andrea Zittel's *A-Z Escape Vehicle* or Arch Group's *sleepbox*, in the natural environment with Future Systems structures, LEAPfactory's *LEAPs1*, *Ecocapsule*, and Richard Horden's many capsule structures. The architectural expression of the structures of withdrawal and autonomy are diverse, but are usually merely an expanded tone of the technological structure and use. St. Jerome's equipped room can be moved from the civilized world to "wild" nature, which it accepts but also defies. In awareness of their relationship, the responsibility for their coordinated functioning lies with the engineer/architect/designer. At the same time, due to chaotic and unbearable conditions in the urban environment of contemporaneity, Kurokawa's prediction that the capsule is a device or a habitat for men when they can no longer live elsewhere is being realized. Such a perception of the typology of the capsule presumes the assurance of autonomy which, however, is no longer subject to free choice, but a way out in an emergency, and the only chance of survival.

Through representation of their own conflicts, the addressed topics of technology and architectural expression, home, individual, and community, attitude to land, and attachment to a place, the idea of withdrawal and autonomy facilitate the establishment of an open dialogue of contradictions of contemporaneity. Potentially, they also disclose issues and relationships of building factors, attitude to the public, and the dependence of building on the economic situation. The more topics that disclose reality, as they are opened by a project, the stronger is their critical stance or potential subversiveness.

The coexistence of contradictions was recognized as characteristic of openly perceived contemporaneity, while in projects, this facilitates an expression which opens up possibilities of interpretation and its incompleteness. The openness, which was nurtured by members of the Independent Group by rejecting the "either-or" dualism and adopting the "both-and" stance, and which may be related to erasing the boundaries of modern visual culture, the fusion of high culture with pop, and to the world of everyday culture flooded with consumer products, undoubtedly affected the playfulness of Archigram. In projects, their surpassing of the dualism between utopia and everyday life fused into an attractive, but non-reflected conglomerate, which could be attributed to a subversive political tone, despite the denial of the latter, and lack of knowledge about the protagonists' background. In addition to the socially visionary duality, Reyner Banham also emphasizes the coexistence of the disciplines of architecture and industrial design, joined by art, which share the creative field of the concept of the typology of the capsule with the ambition of the third culture. The fact that certain proto-capsule structures were politically acceptable for the most distant political or mindset options is completely in accordance with ambivalent modernity. The geodesic dome surpassed geopolitical boundaries, the boundaries between disciplines, and was, at the same time, acceptable for military needs, mainstream culture, trade fair arrangements, as well as for drop-out dwellings in countercultural communes and avant-garde projects of socially engaged architects worldwide.

In addition to utopian projections, the coexistence of high technology and tradition, in the form of a connective spirit—non-visual rules and individual material elements—is also present in capsule architecture of Japanese protagonists. Many of their structures are an expanded *mimesis* of the teahouse, or are at least based on the measurement system of *tatami* floor mats. Should this mean "the teahouse is lost in modernity, long live the teahouse as the paraphrase of space for private withdrawal?" In accordance with Buddhist philosophy, which facilitates the surpassing of the "either-or" dualism with the concept of the coexistence of oppositions, Kisho Kurokawa wished to establish a third space in architecture, which would enable conflicts to coexist in harmony with each other and preserve diversity. In a similar fashion, the latest parasitic and other capsule structures promote the coexistence of opposites.

While capsule dwellings for the homeless solve the problem of overnight accommodation, they also exploit incomplete definitions in legislation, and by providing the homeless with lodging and their presence in public space disclose suppressed and negated characteristics of contemporary society. In the tradition of parasites from 50 years ago, financially difficult to realize options of living in a city, utilizing space, and establishing development stimulations of the city, and the rigidity of institutions which assess the suitability of such proposals, are expressed with projects like the *Rucksack House* or the *Minibox* unit. Marko Peljhan's *Makrolab* project is also an example of coexistence and the surpassing of the traditionally opposite disciplines of art and science. *Makrolab* can be treated as a structure of multilayer subversive criticism, the functioning of which is enabled by the realized typology of the capsule. The explicit living unit, with all the necessary equipment which aims at autarky, has the same technological expression. In the context of remote locations, where it was sited, its otherness was highlighted, both in its content and expression. Its context is the non-material global world of flows, not the formal context of location. It is sited on land but does not make the land subordinate with its self-sufficiency system. The *Makrolab* living unit was a temporary home for modern migrants, specialists in various fields, for whom permanent location does not enable functioning. In isolation, an individual, committed to his mission, can realize his own potential, as predicted by the Smithsons, Kurokawa, and others. At the same time, *Makrolab* is a social experiment of the coexistence of various individuals in isolation.

———————————

To better understand the simultaneity of the functioning, let's take a look at a comparison of two contemporary capsule units: Marko Peljhan's *Makrolab* from the field of art, and Richard Horden's *m-ch*, with a distinctly operative engagement. Both *Makrolab* and *m-ch* open up all the highlighted topics of the capsule's concept, and of the critical response to modern reality: Through technology and the architectural expression of otherness, and attitude to land and non-attachment to a place, they question the spatial context. By redefining home, and the role of an individual and of community, they trigger various social, personal, and cultural issues. Both units are intended for temporary dwelling, which means that they strive to establish a notion of a temporary home and its realization. In *Makrolab*, the issue of minimum production units of society, units which replaced the basic cell of a family with (project) interest communities of individuals, is related to the living unit. In the *m-ch* unit, on the other hand, the highlighted issue is that of the provision of individuality, while social space is formed by combining individual units in various platforms. *Makrolab* uses the idea of withdrawal and autonomy to point to the (only) option of functioning beyond the conditioning of the system, and shows, with the coexistence of opposites of disciplines, and simultaneous isolation and full connection with the outside world, the potential of third cultures, which do not reject diversity, but attempt to use it for its ability to unmask by functioning within the system. Unlike *Makrolab*, the everyday, potentially self-sufficient, *m-ch* unit in the realized case of a student campus depends more on the system. However, aspirations for individuality, withdrawal, and autonomy are expressed in independent setups. The unit addresses the topic of the coexistence of opposites with issues of technology, and the principles of traditional construction, the permanence of home and mobility, architecture and design, and poetic siting "between earth and sky."[20] Unlike *Makrolab*, which functions in the field of art, and explicitly expresses the desire to question the system on its verge, the *m-ch* unit is potentially subversive in a softer manner, with it functioning completely within the system and affects, through the aesthetics of the object of desire, the perception of different options of dwelling in contemporaneity.

Does this mean surrender, the commodification of potential subversion, the use of special features placed within the system to strengthen that very system? Is it merely about the product of fresh conservatism, despite functioning in the field of various topics of the typology? Standpoints and interpretations may differ, but the thing that counts, and has subversive potential, is the promotion of the awareness of otherness, temporariness, sustainable contact with land, options of non-prescribed and temporary creation of spatial relations and the social space of interactions, minimum dependence on supply, and last but not least, of different options of dwelling expressed with the need to withdraw to complete individuality, as an expression of the awareness of reality, and the basis for new, potentially non-commodified, sociality.

In relation to the topics discussed and the diversity of critical responses to the situations in individual projects in the field of the typology of the capsule, it could be argued that the subversive potential of otherness of a project is greater the more its structure, function, and representation, attuned to its architectural integrity, are multilayered. Despite the inevitable commodification of individual subversive elements in a project, the multilayeredness provides for opportunities. Taking into account the inability of the system to utilize all, even contradictory, subversive elements for its purpose, there is the possibility that those very non-commodified elements would facilitate the promotion of the synergistic subversive effect of the whole comprised of individual parts.

In pursuit of the genealogy of capsule units many, also contradictory, starting points were mentioned and the conclusion is that the development of the typology of the capsule was by no means linear, and requires an open dialectical approach. In many practices, the required anti-functionalism, as resistance against the decrees of the Congrès Internationaux d'Architecture Moderne (CIAM), and the continuation of its tradition, which was realized with the "pop-ergonomic" functionalism of the British, and with the "biological" functionalist derivation with regional tones of its Japanese protagonists, even with the requirements, and beyond the theoretical bases of subsistence minimum, found itself under the common denominator of the non-reflected unconditional faith in the technologically supported better future. The technocratic complete control of the organization of city structures was replaced by the principle of self-regulation, which was reflected in technological and biological metaphorical, and pop and anthropological Structuralist proposals.

What the early proposals from capsule units had in common was to ensure the structure of a minimum, prefabricated, mobile, fully equipped dwelling for a modern man or a monofunctional unit, which may be clipped onto the host building, network, infrastructure, or megastructural framework. With the idea of complete independence, faith in the liberating power of technology, and open opportunities provided by the latter, proposals for capsule units were well improved from Fuller's early autarkic experiments, which led to designs of completely autonomous, mobile, flexible, adaptable, and non-monumental living units, which can exist without the help of a megastructure or another supply system. The self-regulation of composite and clip-on units may be attributed to the planned possibility to create a community, while the latter is completely open and left to coincidence, and potentially leads to anarchy, in the case of independent cells. Space can, from now on, be filled by individual living units with individuals who do not need the physical interaction due to media equipment in capsules or even deem it redundant. On the other hand, the free functioning of individual mobile living units in space facilitates deliberation on liberated non-permanent, uncontrolled, and non-representative *ad hoc* forms of communal spaces. The latter may occur with the desired interaction of individual residents of capsules, and could, following the example of heterotopia, be a time-dependent alternative to traditional permanent spatial arrangements of urban spaces.

However, since such spaces can change their character in time, again following the example of heterotopia, can we expect such a potential change of communal space to bring about the extreme version of De Cauter's warning?[21]

In the context of "doom prophecy" used by Lieven De Cauter to draw attention to the multilayered and varying spatial manifestations, which appear in all areas of contemporary life and space, and to highlight the problem of their joint functioning, which can lead to "capsular civilization," "space in a post-civil society," "militarization of public space," "ghettoization," etc., the typology of the capsule, as a phenomenon of capsularity per se, can be understood and accepted as an anti-urban, or even anti-democratic, phenomenon.

However, due to the origin of the capsule's typology in sincere technological optimism, utopian faith in social transformation of the Metabolists, technological pop lightness of the immediate future of Archigram, the heritage of existentialism, Brutalism, and *architecture autre*, Cedric Price's utilitarian application, which was transformed into *high-tech*, critical instrumentality and expansion of awareness of Haus-Rucker-Co and Coop Himmelblau, with the reference of drop-out counterculture, and in the fundamental desire for liberation, individuality, self-sufficiency, and technical perfection via Buckminster Fuller, it provides, in the default general state of contemporary space defined with notions of a generic city, the space of flows, etc., the potential for contemplation of the otherness of dwellings, different understanding of contemporary delimited and controlled structures, and the consideration of different options for their functioning.

Explicit otherness of the concept of the capsule in architecture can be understood as explicitly different from the natural or urban environment, where an architectural object is sited. Otherness is manifested in both expression and content. The fusion of art, life, and politics, and of liberated form, self-building, and socially unacceptable lifestyle were the orientations of counterculture in the USA. Informality, architecture as a direct consequence of life, and the Smithsons' expression "without rhetoric," on the other hand, promised a break with the traditional, and the perception of architecture as explicit, Brutalist otherness. The aspiration for asceticism, authenticity of the use of materials, and for the truth, for the non-representation of May, Stam, and the early Modernists in the 1920s, whose echo can be found in the New Brutalism of the 1950s, strove to realize this ascetic ideal of a minimum dwelling and authenticity with subsistence minimum. The presentation of rough reality as found, which unmasks the anticipated and predictable system of spectacle with the unembellished expression of explicit otherness, is realized in architecture in the relentless rough materiality, which was succeeded by many capsule structures.

Although Reyner Banham gave up the possibility of other architecture at the end of the 1950s, British experimentalists accepted certain aforementioned patterns in the 1960s, and metabolized them into commodified and more conformist pop aesthetics, without realization, which did give Banham hope for *architecture autre*. Otherness is always divided in the duality of the technological expression and popular culture, and technology and nature, and exceeds the binary. Like pioneers of capsule architecture before them, the latest successors devise capsule structures which can be understood through the prism of otherness. Otherness is expressed in the potential presentation of the everyday, and the cleansed, non-commodified minimum technological expression which, in search of otherness, following the early period of the pioneers of capsules, frequently escapes into the sphere of playfulness. Ski lodges and shelters in nature, from the GK Design, Suuronen, Richard Horden, spherical hanging houses, Future Systems capsule units to mountain bivouacs have always expressed a tension between nature and the temporary structure placed in it. The forms of these units provide a functional shelter, and are usually the consequence of the requirement for successful defiance of conditions in nature, and the fulfillment of transport conditions. At the same time, they emphasize the issue of human activities in nature, which is today only conditionally pristine. Instead of subtle minimalism or chameleon mimicry, the aforementioned temporary structures largely highlight the contrast with the environment, while intentionally they do not match it. When perceiving a technological architectural object as unnatural, this can be understood as an ethically more suitable position, which also meets the needs of man in this environment, with a minimum ecological footprint, and problematizes the need of its placement with its presence.

The capsule does not open outwards. All openings are tightly closed. The appearance frequently leans on the original reference of the space capsule. The technical shell of a projectile in a commodified grounded space is converted into the technical shell of a container realized in a more or less sophisticated manner. The latter often insists on Brutalist ethical commandments of the exposed visible construction, and the use and evaluation of materials in view of their own characteristics. From specific names like capsule, *move-net*, cocoon, monad or parasite, *gasket*, *pod* to container, as the most generic similar products, the representation of the typology of the capsule, with its own distinctly utilitarian rhetoric, is spread between indeterminacy and recognizability. The historical memory of the expression of the technological process of mass production, prefabrication, and open and unambiguous representation is indirectly transferred to contemporaneity, through the capsule. It applies to many of the examples discussed that representation does not deviate from the reality of the function and structure of an architectural object, and is actually its *presentation*, which could be compared with the notion of an image which marks, as with Banham, more than its appearance alone. An image, which must facilitate direct understandability, is the architectural condition. In the interdisciplinary environment, the complexity of the task—to combine the structure, function, and representation into an imageable whole—highlights the key role of an architect.

In this sense, this other architecture can be regarded as an architecture of resistance—resistance against the predictability of the traditional comprehension of architecture; resistance against the conformity supporting the status quo between institutions and the living environments; resistance against the cynical fear of imagining alternative possibilities in architecture and its visions of a better future; and resistance against the solely commodified and partial comprehension of architecture.

The concept of the capsule as a building element of architecture, as well as a spatial element, can therefore be regarded with generative potential for an architecture of personal space for the individualized person, as well as a potential territory in which architecture can express its collective critical and educative roles.

In the recognition and distinct communicativeness of the recognized, the notion of a capsule has an important role of imageability. At the same time, the awareness of its characteristics and mechanisms potentially stimulates the possibility of a multilayered response. The typology of the capsule is one of those phenomena of modern architecture which openly emphasized conditions for the architectural articulation of always relevant, but not always fashionable, issues of technology and architectural expression, home, individual and community, dwelling, attitude to land and attachment to place, the idea of withdrawal and autonomy, the coexistence of opposites, narrative, ethical stance, and transcendence. With its direct manifestation, comprehensive image, and complex representation, it addresses participants in space, and presents the social relevance of design, architecture, and urbanism.

Calls for a democratic public, communal space are, both in expert communities and among the general public, relatively well-established, while the requirement for a private, i.e. necessary personal space of the individual is rarely expressed. The concept and typology of the capsule show the relevance of the attempt to establish such other architecture, for which initiatives were found in various modern and contemporary discourses. Nevertheless, it seems that, in recent contemporary architecture, these practices are mostly lost.

The purpose of this book is also a call for a "dialectical rehabilitation" of the capsule as a typology which is, despite conceivably problematic links to the spatial context as a potentially controlled and controllable instrument for conditioning or even eugenic transformation of the body, also an attempt at providing a contemplative environment, allowing for the individual's (self)-reflection, a completion of the call for "a room of one's own" for everyone. As a consequence, it encourages (critical) reflection on architectural instruments, for a potentially utopian but also responsible and heterogeneous society.

With its structure, function, representation, complex *image*, and metaphorical message, a capsule, a comfortable shelter for a contemporary nomad, is constantly engaged in a dialogue between pragmatism and utopia. It potentially serves as an instrument for unmasking ideology and various types of institutional values which, in a contemporary space within an integral society of spectacle and control, are carried out without excluding the mainstream visual culture, but rather within it: With the cracking open of representation through spatially visual dialogues and conflicts.

In the desire for a brighter future, the depth of imagination, with the awareness of potential dark derivations, might be expressed through the utopian *not yet*, only in pragmatically more acceptable *other*.

Notes

1 When referring to the "system," we have in mind the all-encompassing universal neoliberal capitalism as not only economical and sociopolitical but also contemporary and culturally dominant.

2 The iconoclastic position of many protagonists of proto-capsule and capsule architecture (Fuller, the Smithsons, Price, Kurokawa, etc.) in search of authenticity and direct address, consciously or unconsciously rejected the primacy of the visual, and by emphasizing materiality and haptics, highlighted the physical and participative moment of architecture, which may be related to the "denigration of vision," particularly in the 20th century. Cf. e.g. Martin Jay, *Downcast Eyes: The Denigration of Vision in Twentieth-Century French Thought* (Berkeley and Los Angeles, CA: University of California Press, 1994).

3 Prototypes of Future Systems are *monocoque* or semi-*monocoque* constructions, which stabilize the constructiveness of the envelope with their form, and adapt to use with aerodynamics. Richard Horden's *Ski House* is adapted to the placement on uneven ground, requiring function in alpine conditions and transport; N55's *Micro Dwelling* is welded from sheet metal of regular shapes, which form a stable polyhedral tight structure and which may stand, hang, or float; while the *Miele Space Station* is composed of recycled sides of washing machines which, by being assembled, form a stable polygonal rim.

4 Fredric Jameson, *Postmodernism, Or, the Cultural Logic of Late Capitalism* (Durham: Duke University Press, 1991), 4.

5 Ibid., 51.

6 See Jameson, *Postmodernism*; Theodor Adorno, "Functionalism Today," in *Rethinking Architecture: A Reader in Cultural Theory*, ed. Neil Leach (London: Routledge, 1997), 19; Cf. Aleš Erjavec, *Estetika in Kritična Teorija* (Ljubljana: Znanstveno in Publicistično Srediče, 1995); Aleš Erjavec, *Ljubezen Na Zadnji Pogled* (Ljubljana: Založba ZRC SAZU, 2004); Peter Cook, *Experimental Architecture* (New York: Universe Books, 1970); Roemer van Toorn, "Fresh Conservatism," *Quaderns* 215 (1998); www.roemervantoorn.nl/Resources/Fresh%20Conservatism.pdf (2017–1); Roemer van Toorn, *Architecture against Architecture: Radical Criticism within the Society of the Spectacle* (Graz: Film + Arc 2 catalogue, 1993); Hilde Heynen, "The Need for Utopian Thinking in Architecture," *Hunch, the Berlage Institute report* 6/7 (Summer 2003): 241–243.

7 For the dilemma about the criticism of social reality in global capitalism see Petra Čeferin, "Delineating Project Architecture," in *Project Architecture: Creative Practice in the Time of Global Capitalism*, eds. Jeff Bickert, Petra Čeferin, and Cvetka Požar (Ljubljana: Arhitekturni muzej, 2010), 17–31.

8 "Fresh Conservatism is a situation where a certain degree of conflict (subversion and radicalism) serves as stimulant and identity, thus forming an essential element in a fragmented society where the results of conflicts in power and interests are swept under the carpet," van Toorn, "Fresh Conservatism," 2–3.

9 "The architect must make his own manipulation and that of the client and context visible in the work by incorporating references to the accepted codings. The work is recognizably artificial, a construct, an ideological instrument in the permanent discussion about contrasts in social reality." van Toorn, *Architecture against Architecture*, 5; van Toorn, "Fresh Conservatism." Similarly, Hilde Heynen also advocates the expansion of representation through the concept of *mimesis* toward the truth, which should be used by architecture to present a program of requirements, the physical context, the typological order, individual design idioms, or historical connotations, and facilitate an insight into reality in an open, incomplete manner, which opens and highlights issues included in it, in an understanding of modernity, with all its conflicts and contradictions. See Heynen, *Architecture and Modernity: A Critique* (Cambridge, MA and London: MIT Press, 1999), 192–218.

10 Presentation is perceived as the performance of a dialogue. Van Toorn relates to Scott Lash's lecture "Difference or Sociality" at the conference "The Theory of the Image," Van Eyck Academy, Maastricht, 1995. See van Toorn, *Architecture against Architecture*.

11 We are aware of the fact that the selection may be deemed incomplete and reductive. However, our hope is that it is operative enough for our projection section, where we wish to show the relevance of the concept and typology of the capsule in pursuit of other architecture.

12 The list of topics could be randomly supplemented, but most characteristics are mentioned here, on the basis of which we wish to show the possibilities and manner of the critical and subversive potential of the concept and typology of the capsule in pursuit of other architecture.

13 References in this concluding chapter that were previous cited earlier in the book are not recited here.

14 Hannah Arendt, *The Human Condition* (Chicago, IL: University of Chicago Press, 1998); Cf. Peter Šenk and Zala Volčič, "Late Capitalism—Defensor Fidei: On Private and Public in Late-Capitalism," *Architect's Bulletin* 141–142 (November 1998): 99–103.

15 Aristotle, "Politics," in *The Complete Works of Aristotle: The Revised Oxford Translation/ edited by Jonathan Barnes, vol. 2* (Princeton, NJ: Princeton University Press, 1995, 2012), 2011–2014 (1267 b 22–1268 b 27).

16 Lieven De Cauter and Michiel Dehaene, "The Space of Play: Towards a General Theory of Heterotopia," in *Heterotopia and the City: Public Space in a Post-Civil Society*, eds. Michiel Dehaene and Lieven De Cauter (Abingdon: Routledge, 2008), 87–102.

17 Ibid.; De Cauter and Dehaene, "Hippodamus's Third Space: Towards a General Theory of Heterotopia," in *Comment Vivre Ensemble: Prototypes of Idiorrhythmical Conglomerates and Shared Spaces*, eds. Paola Pellegrini and Paola Viganò (Rome: Officina, 2006), 129–140. The blurring of spheres resonates the de-differentiation stated by the notion of camp/camp-like conditions by Giorgio Agamben and relates to the understanding of the conditions of the emerging post-civil society.

18 De Cauter, *The Capsular Civilization: On the City in the Age of Fear* (Rotterdam: NAi Publishers, 2004), 70.

19 De Cauter and Dehaene, "Hippodamus's Third Space," 139. Cf. Arendt, *Human Condition*, esp. sub-chapter "The Location of Human Activities," 73–78.

20 Horden relates his approach of *light architecture* in the 1996 lecture to Eero Saarinen's maxim "Architecture consists largely of placing something between earth and sky, which is in many ways relevant for his more contemporary projects as well." Richard Horden, *Light Architecture* (Michigan, MI: University of Michigan, 1996).

21 De Cauter, *The Capsular Civilization*.

SELECT BIBLIOGRAPHY

Abel, Chris. *Architecture and Identity: Responses to Cultural and Technological Change*, 2nd edn. Oxford: Architectural Press, 2000.

Alexander, Christopher, Ishikawa, Sara, Silverstein, Murray, Jacobson, Max, Fiksdahl-King, Ingrid, and Angel, Shlomo. *A Pattern Language: Towns, Buildings, Construction*. New York: Oxford University Press, 1977.

Allen, Stan and Park, Kyong, eds. *Sites and Stations: Provisional Utopias: Architecture and Utopia in the Contemporary City*. New York: Lusitania Press, 1996.

Ambasz, Emilio. *Italy: The New Domestic Landscape, Achievements and Problems of Italian Design*. New York: Museum of Modern Art, 1972.

Androtti, Libero and Costa, Xavier, eds. *Theory of Dérive and Other Situationist Writings on the City*. Barcelona: Actar, 1996.

Arendt, Hannah. *The Human Condition*. Chicago, IL: University of Chicago Press, 1998.

Arieff, Allison and Burkhart, Bryan. *Prefab*. Salt Lake City, UT: Gibbs Smith, 2002.

Augé, Marc. *Non-Places: Introduction to an Anthropology of Supemodernity*. London: Verso, 1995.

Bahamón, Alejandro and Asensio, Cerver Francisco, eds. *Mini House*. New York: Harper Design International, 2003.

Baldwin, James Tennant. *Bucky Works: Buckminster Fuller's Ideas for Today*. New York: John Wiley & Sons, 1996.

Banham, Reyner. *The New Brutalism: Ethic or Aesthetic?* Stuttgart: Karl Krämer Verlag Stuttgart, 1966.

Banham, Reyner. *Megastructure: Urban Futures of the Recent Past*. London: Thames & Hudson, 1976.

Banham, Reyner. *Theory and Design in the First Machine Age*. Cambridge, MA: MIT Press, 1980.

Banham, Reyner and Sparke, Penny, eds. *Reyner Banham: Design by Choice*. New York: Rizzoli, 1981.

Bauman, Zygmunt. *Globalization: The Human Consequence*. Cambridge: Polity, 1998.

Bauman, Zygmunt. *Liquid Modernity*. Cambridge: Polity, 2009.

Beck, Ulrich. *Risk Society: Towards a New Modernity*. London, Newbury Park, CA, and New Delhi: Sage, 1994.

Beck, Ulrich and Beck-Gernsheim, Elisabeth. *Individualization: Institutionalized Individualism and its Social and Political Consequences*. London: Sage, 2002.

Beck, Ulrich, Giddens, Anthony, and Lash, Scott. *Reflexive Modernization: Politics, Tradition and Aesthetics in the Modern Social Order*. Cambridge: Polity, 1994.

Bergdoll, Barry and Christensen, Peter. *Home Delivery: Fabricating the Modern Dwelling*. New York: Museum of Modern Art, 2008.

Bernik, Stane. *Pogledi na novejšo slovensko arhitekturo in oblikovanje*. Ljubljana: Park, 1992.

Bickert, Jeff, Čeferin, Petra, and Požar, Cvetka, eds. *Project Architecture: Creative Practice in the Time of Global Capitalism*. Ljubljana: Arhitekturni muzej, 2010.

Borries, Friedrich von. *Klimakapseln: Überlebens-bedingungen in der Katastrophe*. Berlin: Suhrkamp, 2010.

Bovcon, Narvika. *Umetnost v svetu pametnih strojev: novomedijska umetnost Sreča Dragana, Jake Železnikarja in Marka Peljhana*. Ljubljana: Raziskovalni inštitut Akademije za likovno umetnost in oblikovanje, 2009.

Boyd, Robin. *New Directions in Japanese Architecture*. London: Studio Vista, 1968.

Braham, William and Hale, Jonathan A. *Rethinking Technology: A Reader in Architectural Theory*. Abingdon: Routledge, 2007.

Brayer, Marie-Ange, Migayrou, Frédéric, and Nanjo, Fumio. *Archilab's Urban Experiments: Radical Architecture, Art and the City*. London: Thames & Hudson, 2004.

Bürger, Peter. *Theory of the Avant-Garde*. Minneapolis, MN: University of Minnesota Press, 1984.

Busbea, Larry. *Topologies: The Urban Utopia in France, 1960–1970*. Cambridge, MA and London: MIT Press, 2007.

Castells, Manuel. *The Rise of the Network Society*, 2nd edn. Oxford: Blackwell, 2000^2 $(1996)^1$.

Cavell, Richard. *McLuhan in Space: A Cultural Geography*. Toronto, ON: University of Toronto, 2002.

Conrads, Ulrich, ed. *Programs and Manifestoes on 20th-Century Architecture*. Cambridge, MA: MIT Press, 1999.

Cook, Peter. *Architecture: Action and Plan*. London: Studio Vista, 1969 (1967).

Cook, Peter. *Experimental Architecture*. New York: Universe Books, 1970.

Cook, Peter, ed. *Archigram*. New York: Princeton Architectural Press, 1999.

Crompton, Dennis, ed. *A Guide to Archigram 1961–1974*. London: Academy Editions, 1994.

Crompton, Dennis, ed. *Concerning Archigram*. London: Archigram Archives, 2002.

Crowley, David and Pawitt, Jane. *Cold War Modern: Design 1945–1970*. London: V&A Publishing, 2008.

Dahinden, Justus. *Urban Structures for the Future*. New York: Praeger, 1972.

De Cauter, Lieven. *The Capsular Civilization: On the City in the Age of Fear*. Rotterdam: NAi, 2004.

Debord, Guy. *The Society of the Spectacle*. New York: Zone Books, 2006.

Dehaene, Michiel and De Cauter, Lieven, eds. *Heterotopia and the City: Public Space in a Postcivil Society*. Abingdon: Routledge, 2008.

Duran, Sergi Costa, ed. *Prefab Houses*. Köln: Evergreen, 2009.

Erjavec, Aleš. *Estetika in kritična teorija*. Ljubljana: Znanstveno in publicistično središče, 1995.

Ford, Simon. *The Situationist International: A User's Guide*. London: Black Dog, 2005.

Foucault, Michel. *Življenje in prakse svobode: Izbrani spisi*. ed. Jelica Šumič-Riha, trans. Jelka Kernev Štrajn, Mojca Mihelič, Vojislav Likar, Katarina Rotar, Samo Tomšič, Ana Žerjav. Ljubljana: Založba ZRC SAZU, 2007.

Frampton, Kenneth. *Modern Architecture: A Critical History*. London: Thames & Hudson, 2002^3 $(1980)^1$.

Friedman, Yona. *Pro Domo*. Barcelona: Actar, 2006.

Garner, Philippe. *Sixties Design*. Cologne: Taschen, 2003.

Giedion, Sigfried. *Walter Gropius*. New York: Dover, 1992. Unaltered re-publication of Giedion, Sigfried. *Walter Gropius: Work and Teamwork*. New York: Reinhold, 1954.

Gili Galfetti, Gustau. *Model Apartments: Experimental Domestic Cells*. Barcelona: Editorial Gustavo Gili, 1997.

Gordon, Alastair. *Spaced Out: Radical Environments of the Psychedelic Sixties*. New York: Rizzoli International, 2008.

Gorman, Michael John. *Buckminster Fuller: Designing for Mobility*. Milan: Skira Editore, 2005.

Harries, Karsten. *The Ethical Function of Architecture*. Cambridge, MA and London: MIT Press, 2000.

Harrison, Charles and Wood, Paul, eds. *Art in Theory 1900–1990: An Anthology of Changing Ideas*. Oxford: Blackwell, 1996.

Haussmann, Robert and Schulte, Karin, eds. *Wieviel Raum braucht der Mensch? Wohnen für das Existenzminimum*. Munich: Aries, 1996.

Hays, Michael Kenneth. *Oppositions Reader: Selected Readings from a Journal for Ideas and Criticism in Architecture, 1973–1984*. New York: Princeton Architectural, 1998.

Heidegger, Martin. *Predavanja in sestavki*. Trans. Tine Hribar, Andrina Tonkli-Komel, Aleš Košar, Ivan Urbančič. Ljubljana: Slovenska matica, 2003.

Hetherington, Kevin. *Expressions of Identity: Space, Performance, Politics*. London, Thousand Oaks, CA, and New Delhi: Sage, 1998.

Heuvel, Dirk van den and Risselada, Max, eds. *Alison and Peter Smithson – From House of the Future to a House of Today*. Rotterdam: 010 Publishers, 2004.

Heynen, Hilde. *Architecture and Modernity: A Critique*. Cambridge, MA and London: MIT Press, 1999.

Horden, Richard. *Micro Architecture: Lightweight, Mobile and Ecological Buildings for the Future*. London: Thames & Hudson, 2008.

Ibelings, Hans. *Supermodernism: Architecture in the Age of Globalization*. Rotterdam: NAi, 1998.

Jackson, Leslie. *The Sixties: Decade of Design Revolution*. London: Phaidon Press, 1998.

Jameson, Fredric. *Postmodernism, or, the Cultural Logic of Late Capitalism*. Durham, NC: Duke University Press, 1991.

Jay, Martin. *Downcast Eyes: The Denigration of Vision in Twentieth-Century French Thought*. Berkeley, CA: University of California Press, 1994.

Jeska, Simone. *Transparent Plastics: Design and Technology*. Basel: Birkhäuser, 2008.

Kahn, Lloyd, ed. *Shelter*. Bolinas: Shelter, 1973.

Kawazoe, Noboru. *Contemporary Japanese Architecture*. Tokyo: Kokusai Bunka Shinkokai, 1968.

Kawazoe, Noboru, Kikutake, Kiyonori, Kurokawa, Noriaki, Otaka, Masato, and Maki, Fumihiko. *Metabolism 1960: The Proposals for New Urbanism*. Tokyo: Bijutu Syuppan Sha, 1960.

Kepes, Gyorgy, ed. *The Man-Made Object*. New York: George Braziller, 1966.

Kikutake, Kiyonori and Vitta, Maurizio. *Kiyonori Kikutake: From Tradition to Utopia*. Milan: l'Arca Edizioni, 1997.

Koolhaas, Rem and Obrist, Hans-Ulrich, eds. *Project Japan: Metabolism Talks*. Cologne: Taschen, 2011.

Koolhaas, Rem, Sassen, Saskia, Abel, Chris, and Augé, Marc. *Mestomorfoze*. Ljubljana: Založba ★cf.: Sorosov center za sodobne umetnosti, 1999.

Košir, Fedja. *K arhitekturi: razvoj arhitekturne teorije, prvi del*. Ljubljana: Fakulteta za arhitekturo, 2006.

Kotnik, Jure. *Container Architecture: This Book Contains 6441 Containers*. Barcelona: Links International, 2008.

Koželj, Janez and Vodopivec, Aleš. *Iz arhitekture*. Ljubljana: Krt, 1987.

Krausse, Joachim and Lichtenstein, Claude, eds. *Your Private Sky: R. Buckminster Fuller: The Art of Design Science*. Baden: Lars Müller, 1999.

Krausse, Joachim and Lichtenstein, Claude, eds. *Your Private Sky: Discourse, R. Buckminster Fuller*. Baden: Lars Müller, 2001.

Kronenburg, Robert, ed. *Portable Architecture*. Oxford: Architectural Press, 1996.

Kronenburg, Robert, ed. *Transportable Environments: Theory, Context, Design and Technology*. London: E&FN Spon, 1999.

Kronenburg, Robert, ed. *Transportable Environments 2*. London: Spon Press, 2003.

Kruft, Hanno-Walter. *A History of Architectural Theory from Vitruvius to the Present*. New York: Princeton Architectural Press, 1994.

Kurokawa, Kisho. *Metabolism in Architecture*. London: Studio Vista, 1977.

Kurokawa, Kisho. *New Wave Japanese Architecture*. London: Academy Editions, 1993.

Kurokawa, Kisho. *The Philosophy of Symbiosis*. London: Academy Editions, 1994.

Le Corbusier. *Towards a New Architecture*. New York: Dover Publications, 1986. Re-publication of the work originally published by John Rodker (London, 1931).

Leach, Neil, ed. *Rethinking Architecture: A Reader in Cultural Theory*. London: Routledge, 1997.

Lebesque, Sabine and Fentener van Vlissingen, Helene, eds. *Yona Friedman: Structures Serving the Unpredictable*. Rotterdam: NAi, 1999.

Lin, Zhongjie. *Kenzo Tange and the Metabolist Movement: Urban Utopias of Modern Japan*. Abingdon: Routledge, 2010.

Lüchinger, Arnulf. *Structuralism in Architecture and Urban Planning*. Stuttgart: Karl Krämer, 1981.

McClung, William Alexander. *The Architecture of Paradise: Survivals of Eden and Jerusalem*. Berkeley, CA: University of California Press, 1983.

McHale, John. *R. Buckminster Fuller*. New York: George Braziller, 1962.

McLuhan, Marshall. *Understanding Media: The Extensions of Man*. Corte Madera: Gingko Press, 2003[2] (1964)[1].

McLuhan, Marshall and Powers, Bruce. *The Global Village: Transformations in World Life and Media in the 21st Century*. New York: Oxford University Press, 1989.

Mallgrave, Harry Francis. *Modern Architectural Theory: A Historical Survey, 1673–1968*. Cambridge: Cambridge University Press, 2005.

Massey, Anne. *The Independent Group: Modernism and Mass Culture in Britain, 1945–59*. Manchester: Manchester University Press, 1995.

Mathews, Stanley. *From Agit-Prop to Free Space: The Architecture of Cedric Price*. London: Black Dog, 2007.

Meier, Richard Louis. *Science and Economic Development: New Patterns of Living*. Cambridge, MA: MIT Press, 1964[3] (1956)[1].

Melis, Liesbeth, ed. *Parasite Paradise: A Manifesto for Temporary Architecture and Flexible Urbanism*. Rotterdam: NAi, 2003.

Mestomorfoze. Ljubljana: Založba ★cf.: Sorosov center za sodobne umetnosti, 1999.

Miller Lane, Barbara. *Housing and Dwelling: Perspectives on Modern Domestic Architecture*. Abingdon: Routledge, 2007.

Mumford, Eric. *The CIAM Discourse on Urbanism, 1928–1960*. Cambridge, MA and London: MIT Press, 2000.

Ockman, Joan, ed. *Architecture Culture 1943–1968: A Documentary Anthology*. New York: Rizzoli, 1993.

Pawley, Martin. *Theory and Design in the Second Machine Age*. Oxford: Basil Blackwell, 1990.

Pérez-Gómez, Alberto. *Architecture and the Crisis of Modern Science*. Cambridge, MA and London: MIT Press, 1983.

Pople, Nicolas. *Small Houses*. London: Laurence King, 2005.

Price, Cedric. *Cedric Price: Works II, Architectural Association*. London: Architectural Association, 1984.

Quarmby, Arthur. *Plastics and Architecture*. Washington, DC: Praeger, 1974.

Risselada, Max and Heuvel, Dirk van den. *Team 10: In Search of a Utopia of the Present*. Rotterdam: NAi, 2005.

Ritter, Roland and Knaller-Vlay, Bernd, eds. *Other Spaces: The Affair of the Heterotopia = die Affäre der Heterotopie*. Graz: Haus der Architektur, 1998.

Rykwert, Joseph. *On Adam's House in Paradise: The Idea of the Primitive Hut in Architectural History*. Cambridge, MA and London: MIT Press, 1997.

Sadler, Simon. *The Situationist City*. Cambridge, MA and London: MIT Press, 1999.

Sadler, Simon. *Archigram: Architecture without Architecture*. Cambridge, MA and London: MIT Press, 2005.

Schaik, Martin van and Máčel, Otakar, eds. *Exit Utopia: Architectural Provocations 1956–76*. Munich: Prestel, 2005.

Schwartz-Clauss, Mathias and Vegesack, Alexander von, eds. *Living in Motion: Design and Architecture for Flexible Dwelling*. Weil am Rhein: Vitra Design Museum, 2002.

Scott, Felicity Dale. *Architecture or Techno-Utopia: Politics after Modernism*. Cambridge, MA and London: MIT Press, 2007.

Slavid, Ruth. *Micro: Very Small Buildings*. London: Laurence King, 2009.

Smith, Courtenay and Topham, Sean. *Xtreme Houses*. Munich: Prestel, 2002.

Stewart, David B. *The Making of a Modern Japanese Architecture: 1868 to the Present*. Tokyo and New York: Kodansha International, 1987.

Tafuri, Manfredo and Dal Co, Francesco. *Modern Architecture Vol. 2*. Milan: Electa Editrice, 1976.

Teige, Karel. *The Minimum Dwelling*. Cambridge, MA and London: MIT Press, 2002.

Vesely, Dalibor. *Architecture in the Age of Divided Representation: The Question of Creativity in the Shadow of Production*. Cambridge, MA and London: MIT Press, 2004.

Vidler, Anthony. *Histories of Immediate Present: Inventing Architectural Modernism*. Cambridge, MA and London: MIT Press, 2008.

Whiteley, Nigel. *Reyner Banham: Historian of the Immediate Future*. Cambridge, MA and London: MIT Press, 2002.

Williams Goldhagen, Sarah and Legault, Réjean, eds. *Anxious Modernisms: Experimentation in Postwar Architecture Culture*. Montreal, QC: Canadian Centre for Architecture, and Cambridge, MA and London: MIT Press, 2000.

Selected Periodicals

Architectural Design, Architectural Review, Arhitektov bilten, Art in America, Assemblage, Bauen+Wohnen, Detail, Domus, Filozofski vestnik, Grey Room, Hiše, Hunch, Japan Architect (JA), Journal of the American Institute of Planners, Journal of Architecture Planning(AIJ), Journal of Asian Architecture and Building Engineering, Kenchiku Bunka, Kokusai-kentiku, L'architecture d'aujourd'hui, Likovne besede, Mechanix Illustrated, Oris, Places: A Quarterly Journal of Environmental Design, Prostor, SD – Space Design, Sinteza, Time, Zbornik za umetnostno zgodovino.

INDEX

9781138280342

9781138280342